Saving Einstein

Also by Stuart McLaren

Norfolk Fair and Suffolk Fair. An Index to the County Magazines

(Plumtree), 2000

St Augustine's Church Norwich, Norfolk

(The Churches Conservation Trust), 2004

Somewhere in Flanders. A Norfolk Padre in the Great War

(Larks Press), 2005

They Are Not Dead. A Norwich Parish in the First World War

(Larks Press), 2014

Front cover: Shotgun at the ready at the Roughton camp. Left to right: Locker-Lampson, Einstein, Margery Howard.

Back cover: The dashing Commander Locker-Lampson DSO CMG RNVR MP. Lloyd's Magazine, May 1918.

Saving Einstein

When Norfolk Hid a Genius

The Double Life of Oliver Locker-Lampson

Stuart McLaren

Poppyland Publishing

This edition 2021 published by Poppyland Publishing, Lowestoft, NR32 3BB.

www.poppyland.co.uk

ISBN 978 1 909796 90 4

Designed and typeset in 10.5 on 13.5 pt Gilgamesh Pro.

Picture credits:

Anderson, E. 153
Archant front cover, 11
Author's collection back cover*, 9*, 27, 36*, 37, 39*, 40, 42*, 45*, 46, 47, 51*, 52*, 56, 59*, 62*, 68*, 69*, 70*, 82, 105, 109*, 110, 113, 118†, 119†, 121‡, 127‡, 126*, 144*, 152, 158, 159*, 162, 167-169*, 170, 172*, 182*, 183, 189, 195, 204*, 202*, 207
Brück & Sohn Kunstverlag Meißen ((CC0 1.0) public domain) 96
ETH-Bibliothek Zürich, Bildarchiv ((CC0 1.0) public domain) 14
German Federal Archives (CC BY-SA 3.0) 145
Keystone Press / Alamy 88
Library of Congress 101
Museum Boerhaave 156
Museum für Kunst und Gewerbe, Hamburg ((CC0 1.0) public domain) 95
Royal Museums Greenwich 33
University of Toronto, Robarts Library ((CC0 1.0) public domain) 35
unknown 86 (CC BY-SA 4.0), 183

* courtesy of Stephen Locker-Lampson
† courtesy of Robert Thurston
‡ courtesy of Philip Colman

Contents

Acknowledgements

THE author is grateful to the following for their help: the Albert Einstein Archive, Hebrew University of Jerusalem; Eddie Anderson; Archant (formerly Eastern Counties Newspapers) Picture Library; Association of Jewish Refugees; Birmingham City Local Studies Library; Board of Deputies of British Jews; British Newspaper Archive; Brown University Library, Rhode Island; Cambridge Local Studies Library, Cambridgeshire Libraries Service; Professor Alan Camina; Churchill Archives, Churchill College, Cambridge University; Cherwell Archive, Nuffield College Library, Oxford University; Philip Colman; Cromer Library, Norfolk Libraries Service; Cromer Museum, Norfolk Museums Service; Clive Dunn; House of Lords Records Office; Huntingdon Library, Cambridgeshire Libraries Service; Library of Congress, Washington, DC; Liddle Collection, Leeds University Library; Anthony Locker-Lampson; Jonathan Locker-Lampson; Stephen Locker-Lampson; National Archives, Kew; National Library of Israel; Norfolk Constabulary; Norfolk Record Office; Norfolk Studies Collection, Norfolk Libraries Service; Andrew Robinson; Paul Robinson; Steve Snelling; Robert Thurston; Patricia Walker.

Speaking Relatively

HIS story become a family legend, recollected with the same degree of fascinated incredulity as if he had said he had once seen the Loch Ness Monster. It was this. When he was a boy he had met Albert Einstein walking the heath and lanes of Roughton, his childhood home in north Norfolk. Born in 1924, Frank Emery shared a surname with a famous family of Sheringham boat-builders. A coincidence, as his father, Oscar, the village policemen at the time of Einstein's stay, came from a long line of Kent 'hammer men' and had begun his own working life aged 14 at Vickers, the huge armaments manufacturer in Erith where his father also worked as a gunsmith. There can be little doubt which ancestry Einstein would have preferred for the local bobby's son—boats and sailing he loved, weapons and war he detested.

Mobilised from the Territorials into the Royal Field Artillery on the outbreak of war in August 1914, Oscar Emery had immediately been seconded back to Vickers to help carry on its crucial war work. Demobbed in 1921 after three years in the newly formed RAF, Oscar moved to Norfolk where he joined the County Constabulary. For some reason, perhaps to do with his personality, which was easy-going and sociable, his police career failed to advance. By the time he was posted to Roughton in 1931 he had been stationed at five beats and was still only a constable, despite having twice been commended for zeal and attention to duty. The job came with a small house and a wage of 90 shillings (£4.50) a week, providing his family with a modest measure of security during the hard years of the Depression. Roughton would prove to be the last and longest-lasting posting of his police service. In an isolated rural community with little in the way of crime beyond the odd bit of poaching, PC Emery's duties were not onerous and life generally moved along at a slow and predictable rate. A policeman was not always a welcome neighbour in a close-knit community where everyone knew each other's business. Outsiders were viewed with suspicion and the police were commonly regarded as little more than the uniformed enforcers of the local landowners and employers, who also tended to be the justices of the peace. A village policeman at that time was expected to remain aloof from the social side of the community he served. Oscar, however, after his peregrinations around the county, seems to have been keen to be accepted as part of the village; perhaps a little too keen, earning himself a reputation as the 'laughing policemen' due to his fondness for playing practical jokes, socialising in the public bar of the village's only pub and enthusiastically joining in the fun at local fetes and dances—activities his superiors in the police force made clear their disapproval of. Among the Emerys' closest friends in the village were Mr and Mrs Philip Colman of Hill Farm, which straddled Thorpe Market Road to the east of the village. Here their three young children would be entertained by Farmer Colman's simple conjuring tricks with a matchbox, until one September when he conjured up his greatest illusion—a strange, wild-haired man camped in his top field who talked to goats and scraped away at a fiddle as he wandered across the heath, guarded day and night by a gamekeeper, a poacher and a posse of young women armed with rifles and shotguns under the command of an alarmingly short-tempered ex-naval officer. The name of the stranger would have meant little to most of the villagers other than it sounded German, in itself sufficient cause for suspicion less than fifteen years after the end of a terrible war in which many local men had lost their lives and their own homes had been threatened by Zeppelin bombs and naval bombardment.

As the years passed and the Second World War came and went fewer and fewer people in Roughton remembered that Einstein had once lived among them, however briefly, and the story entered the realm of scarcely believed local folklore like Black Shuck—the phantom hound said to haunt this part of the county. For years, whenever I took the train from Norwich to the north Norfolk coast, I would look out for a small station just before Cromer called Roughton Road and think of Uncle Frank's story, imagining his father as a kind of *Pirates of Penzance* policeman 'tarantara-ing' around the country lanes hereabouts, a discreet distance behind an eccentric professor who had developed a theory that if you travelled fast enough in a rocket ship you could come back younger than the twin you had left behind. I couldn't imagine what reason such a world-renowned scientist could possibly have had for being here. Could it be true? It seemed improbable. Nevertheless, I promised myself that one day I would discover the truth of Uncle Frank's story.

Many years later, browsing in a Norwich bookshop, I picked up a thick, paperback copy of a recently reprinted biography of Einstein. Flicking through the illustrations, compressing the great man's life from shy schoolboy to craggy-faced old man in a few seconds, my attention was caught by one that showed him, typically tousle-haired, dressed in an old sweater and baggy trousers, standing in a field and smiling at the camera as he patted the mane of a small, sleepy-looking horse. With him was a group of unfamiliar characters. Two young women dressed in polo shirts, jodhpurs and riding boots stood either side of him: one with dark curly hair, hatless, holding a rifle nonchalantly under her right arm; the other fair-haired, sporting a beret at a jaunty angle, a shotgun pivoted under her left arm. An older man, tall, slim and similarly dressed for riding, sat astride the horse, which was much too small for his long legs—like an adult on a seaside donkey. Another man stood stiffly to attention to one side, his shotgun at shoulder arms. Smartly dressed in the traditional outfit of a gamekeeper—tweed jacket, moleskin trousers, leather leggings and a trilby hat sporting a feather—he had, I noticed, a slightly bemused look on his face. The photograph, taken on Roughton Heath in Norfolk, showed, so the caption said, "Einstein 'in hiding' in fear of his life". The quotation marks around in hiding suggested an element of pantomime about the tableaux. Despite the guns, nobody looked particularly in fear of his or her life.

Einstein on Roughton Heath, September 1933. Left to right: Margery Howard, Einstein, Tom Wilson, Locker-Lampson, Barbara Goodall, Herbert Eastoe.

So, Frank's story was true! From that moment on I was gripped. I had to discover the whole story. The world's most famous scientist, the man who had single-handedly altered the way we view space and time, in hiding in a hut on a Norfolk heath, guarded by a motley crew of 1930s' types straight out of central casting. Surely, this was the stuff of fiction not reality. So many questions needed answering. Why had Einstein come here? How long had he stayed? What had he done while he was there? Whom had he met? Who were the other people in the photograph and what connected them? Most of the books I consulted took me little further in my quest. Frustratingly, most of Einstein's many biographers either made no mention of the episode or skipped over it in a couple of sentences. Comparing accounts I noticed that some of those who touched on it confused or conflated it with incidents from visits he had made to Britain earlier the same year. Only three books provided anything more substantial. One was the very biography I had flicked through in a Norwich bookshop. Many of its details of Einstein's visit to Norfolk were based on interviews its author, Ronald W. Clark, had had with people who were now dead, as was the author himself. [1] Another was the autobiography of the Modernist sculptor Jacob Epstein, who had visited the Roughton camp to sculpt a bust of his near name-sake.[2] To these I later added a highly colourful account of a visit to the camp by Einstein's stepson-in-law, Dmitri Marianoff.[3]

These accounts answered some of my questions but posed many more. The long-legged man incongruously seated astride the small horse was the impressively named Commander Oliver Locker-Lampson but who were the others?—The gamekeeper? The two young women with guns?—On these matters the books were silent. Suspecting the local press would have been interested in the visit to Norfolk of so newsworthy a person, I searched through the microfilmed pages of the two main county newspapers of that period at the Norfolk Studies Centre in Norwich. Sure enough, in both the weekly *Norfolk Chronicle* and the *Eastern Daily Press* (*EDP*) there were lengthy reports, mainly dating from the beginning of Einstein's surprise appearance in Norfolk in September 1933 when his flight to England had been reported in almost all the British national and provincial newspapers. Both papers had first-hand accounts, apparently written by staff reporters who had interviewed Einstein and his host as the events unfolded; reports that had perhaps not been read since they were first published and contained intriguing details not mentioned in the national press and apparently also missed by Einstein's many biographers, including Clark, who had written a letter to the *EDP* in 1969 while writing his biography, appealing for information from any Norfolk people who had come into contact with Einstein in the late summer of 1933 but seems to have had no response.[4] Among the contemporary local reports was one in the *EDP* that printed a second photograph of Einstein at the 'secret camp'; capturing him in a relaxed moment, reading a book, seated in bright sunshine in a low armchair outside a log cabin. A dark-haired young woman, recognisable from the small horse photograph, stands behind him looking over his left shoulder at something in the book. Both are smiling as though sharing a joke. Locker-Lampson, meanwhile, sits cross-legged on the ground beside them, looking up at Einstein, a shotgun laid nonchalantly across his lap. The ever-vigilant gamekeeper, still sporting his dapper trilby, stands posed like a sentry in the background, his shotgun resting on his shoulder. Beyond him can be glimpsed the gorse and bracken of Roughton Heath.

On visiting the photograph archive of Eastern Counties Newspapers (now known as Archant), I was shown another photo taken at the Roughton camp (see p. 9). It had clearly been taken only moments before or after the small

Shotguns at the ready at the Roughton camp. Left to right: Locker-Lampson, Einstein, Margery Howard, Herbert Eastoe.

horse one in Clark's biography. In this a third man, dressed in a dark coat and trousers and wearing a flat cap, appears to have joined the group gathered around Einstein. On closer examination of the similar photo in Clark's biography, I realised he had been there all along. I had simply not noticed him as he was so positioned there that only a small portion of his left leg was visible behind Einstein. Who was he? On the back of the third-man photo someone had printed the name and address of the gentleman who had sent it to the newspaper several years earlier, prompted by a controversy then raging in the Norfolk press about the design of a proposed village sign for Roughton and whether or not it should feature a reference to Einstein's visit.

A week or two later I found myself walking up a garden path in the north Norwich suburb of Catton with its rows of neat retirement bungalows and immaculately tended flower beds. In his eighties, Philip Colman was still remarkably spry and overflowing with eagerness to tell me in his high, sing-song accent the story of his long life farming in Norfolk. Although he admitted he had not seen Einstein himself, he was well aware of his visit as the secret camp was located in the top field of his father's farm where it bordered Roughton Heath. Only once had he tried to see for himself what was going on and been chased away by the Commander brandishing a shotgun. Locker-Lampson, he said, "was a rich man's pig of a son but quite likeable in an eccentric way". He got to know him quite well later on before the war when he did odd jobs for him, such as driving him about the narrow country lanes at high speed in his father's Morris Cowley with its brake on one wheel; the local gamekeeper literally riding shotgun in the front as the Commander bellowed from the rear: "Drive on! Drive on! We will be late." From Philip I learned the gamekeeper's name, Herbert Eastoe, and something of his hard working life. I also learned the identity of the third man, partly hidden in one of the small horse photos, Tom Wilson, who worked for Locker-Lampson at his grand summer residence in Cromer, part of which had been converted into an exclusive hotel after the First World War. Like many local men, he was a veteran of the Commander's extraordinary Royal Naval Air Service Armoured Car squadrons, which had served on both the Western and Eastern Fronts during the war. I also learned the names of the two young women—Locker-Lampson's private secretaries and loyal acolytes. The dark-haired one was Margery Howard; the fair-haired, Barbara Goodall, who a few years later would become his second wife and mother of his two sons. According to Philip, another secretary, an older woman, also regularly visited the camp—the much put-upon Miss Billing, who was frequently reduced to tears by the Commander's brusque manner. There was also Mona, a live-in cook at the camp hired from an agency in London during Einstein's stay. Collectively, according to Philip, they were known in the village as 'Locker's harem'. Philip also told me about the role in the story taken by Albert 'Lal' Thurston, a well-known local character with a reputation as a poacher. I later learned more from Lal's son Robert, whom I met at his home in Overstrand. Only that June before Einstein's arrival Lal had been fined £1 plus costs and bound over to keep the peace after being convicted of assaulting a mole-catcher over an argument about the ownership of a brace of rabbits.[5] Lal the poacher, oddly enough, was the son-in-law of Herbert Eastoe the gamekeeper, which is how he got the job—paid in beer—of helping guard the camp, especially at night when men of his calling were wont to ply their trade. I even learned the name of the small, sleepy-looking horse, Tom, whose job when not helping to guard geniuses was to pull a cart loaded with milk churns to Gunton Station each morning. Tom also drew a barrel of fresh water up to the camp each day for cooking and washing, as there was no mains water or well there.

From Norfolk my research spread out across the world, first to New Zealand where Locker-Lampson's younger son Stephen had settled in the 1960s, and later to South Dakota, where a distant cousin of his, Mrs Patricia Walker, was researching the American Lampson side of the family and proved to be unfailingly helpful and encouraging. Listings of a book on the internet about diving on treasure wrecks off the coast of Australia by Stephen Locker-Lampson tempted me to email his publisher. I was astounded when Steve himself (he preferred Steve to Stephen) replied a couple of days later. This led to a voluminous exchange of emails over several years about his remarkable father and fascinating family history before we finally met at Rowfant House, the Locker-Lampson family's former main home in West Sussex. Here I also had the pleasure of meeting Steve's older brother Jonathan—Jack—and Jack's son Tony, who kindly drove me about during my visit, including, memorably, to the Anglo-Saxon church of St Nicholas's in Worth, where Oliver Locker-Lampson's ashes were interred in the grave of his first wife Bianca close by the tombs of his parents and maternal grandparents. Sadly, Steve's death in 2012 cut short our friendship. I am grateful for his generosity and that of other members of the Locker-Lampson family in sharing with me copies of family papers and photographs without which this book would have been immeasurably the poorer. This book is dedicated jointly to the memory of late Steve Locker-Lampson and to my late uncle, Frank Emery, whose childhood memory of seeing Einstein in Roughton started me on my quest to uncover the plot to save Einstein.

Notes

1 *Clark, Einstein, pp.465–7.*

2 *Epstein, Let There Be Sculpture, pp.78–9.*

3 *Marianoff, Einstein, pp.160–3.*

4 *Eastern Daily Press, 16 April 1969.*

5 *Ibid., 27 June 1933.*

Einstein shortly after achieving world-wide fame, Berlin, 1920.

Let Einstein Be!

THE image most people have of Einstein is of an old man: his brow creased with wrinkles, his eyes sunken and weary, his hair a halo of unkempt white locks. In recent years numerous biographies and films drawing on the ongoing publication of his private papers have revised this image, shifting attention away from his final years in post-war America, where he was looked upon as either a secular saint or a dangerous subversive, to the emotional turmoil and intense intellectual struggle of his early manhood in pre-First World War Europe. Between these two there is a third, less well-known Einstein: grown a little stout and grey, beset by the world's problems, his greatest achievements in physics long past. In the 1930s he found himself increasingly out of kilter with the direction a younger generation of physicists were taking the universe he had radically redefined, virtually single-handedly, in the early years of the 20th century. The Europe he had grown up in had been torn to shreds by the Great War and a dark force of murderous racial intolerance, state-sponsored criminality and militaristic aggression was now on the rise in the land of his birth. This is the Einstein who visited Norfolk in 1933.

Albert Einstein was born in Ulm in southern Germany on 14 March 1879, the only son of Hermann and Pauline, a cultured, middle-class Jewish couple whose ancestors had lived in this fertile region between the Danube and the Swabian Mountains for generations. By an odd coincidence Ulm, possibly because of its association with merchants with a reputation for financial acumen, was known as the 'city of mathematicians'. The infant 'Albertl', as his family lovingly called him, had little chance however to absorb its mathematical ambience as when little more than 14 months old, his father closed his failing electrical engineering business there and moved about 93 miles (150 km) south-east to the heavily industrialised city of Munich. Here, with his brother Jakob, Hermann set up another electrical manufacturing works but this too would not prove to be the success he had hoped. For Einstein, these do not seem to have been especially happy years. Temper tantrums, hesitancy of speech and a dislike of playing with other children made his parents fear he might be mentally abnormal, which in a sense he was. Today such behaviour might have been diagnosed as resulting from the frustration felt by an exceptionally intelligent child without sufficient mental stimulation, perhaps even as symptoms of autism spectrum disorder, but in the 1880s paediatric medicine offered no reliable explanation. Between the ages of 5 and 6, two events allowed him, perhaps for the first time, to bring his creative imagination to bear on something worthy of his prodigious intelligence—he was given a small compass to play with when ill in bed one day and he began to receive violin lessons. Pondering the unseen forces underlying magnetism and the structure of musical harmony seem to have given him the keys that unlocked his incredibly versatile creative imagination.

It was in Munich Einstein first attended formal education with other boys his age. Here, despite his unusually keen and inquiring mind, he did not shine, being temperamentally unable to conform to the rigid and unimaginative pedagogic system in practice in most German schools at this period. He later said his formative years here decided him on two courses of action—to become a scientist and to leave Germany at the earliest opportunity. Surprisingly, in view of the anti-Semitism that was then on the increase in Germany, stirred up by economic depression and the rise of ultra-nationalism, he later said it was not racial bigotry that first alienated him from the country of his birth. In fact, he claimed never to have experienced any in his youth and, as he later said, he did not feel himself especially Jewish until the Nazis reminded him of the fact. It was the unbending nature of Germany's social organisation, where seemingly every aspect of life was conducted along militaristic lines with little space for creativity or individuality, which bored and irritated him. He did not thrive in such an environment and did not achieve anything like his enormous potential while at school there, where his recalcitrance and rebelliousness was looked upon as an oddity at best and at worse a bad example to his fellow students. In 1894 the Einstein family moved once again, this time to Italy, leaving the miserably unhappy teenage Albert behind in Munich to finish his secondary education. As soon as he was able he left Germany and briefly joined his parents and younger sister Maria—always known as Maja—in Milan before attending the Swiss Polytechnic in Zurich for the next six years. Here, under a more imaginative and progressive educational regime, his extraordinary intellectual abilities began to blossom. It was here too he met and fell in love with a fellow physics student, Mileva Marić, a reserved and serious Serbian three years his senior. During this period he gave up his German nationality and remained stateless while waiting for his application for Swiss citizenship to be granted, something he was not to achieve until 1901 due to his lack of the necessary financial resources.

The following five years were among the busiest of his life. He was now in his early twenties and acutely aware most scientists and mathematicians did their best creative work before their forties. Time was running out and he still didn't have a secure job, let alone the academic post he craved. In 1902 he obtained a position in the Swiss civil service, checking the scientific validity of applications submitted to the Patent Office in Bern. The prized post in academia had, for the time being, to remain a distant hope. In recent years it has been discovered that a daughter, Liserl, had been born to Albert and Mileva in the same year Einstein began his job in Bern. Unmarried and financially insecure, the couple may have given her up for adoption, possibly to foster parents in Serbia; however, all trace of her seems to have been lost and her fate remains a mystery to this day. In January 1903 Einstein finally considered himself financially secure enough to be able to marry Mileva, although this was very much against his now widowed mother Pauline's wishes. In 1904 their second child, Hans Albert, was born.

Honour and recognition within the sphere of advanced physics finally came to Einstein while he was still at the Swiss Patent Office with the publication in 1905 of a remarkable series of papers that introduced his Special Theory of Relativity. This startlingly original and ground-breaking work eventually secured him his first full-time academic post, and over the next fourteen years he moved step by step up the academic ladder: first at Prague, then still part of the Austro-Hungarian Empire, then back to Switzerland and the University of Zurich, before returning to Germany in 1914 to take up a position at the Kaiser Wilhelm Institute of Physics at the University of Berlin. Ironically, as Europe teetered on the brink of war he was back in the land of his birth, the land he had rejected twenty years earlier because of his detestation of its militarism. These years saw the birth of a third child, Eduard, known within the family as Tete (Teddy), a bright but physically frail boy who would later be diagnosed with schizophrenia. It was during this period Albert and Mileva's marriage began to fall apart. During the war Mileva and the two boys lived in Switzerland, while Einstein continued his scientific work in Berlin, always refusing to do any work directly contributing to the German war effort, unlike his friend and colleague Fritz Haber, who worked on the weaponisation of chlorine gas. Feeling loveless and lonely Einstein renewed a relationship with his cousin Elsa Löwenthal, a divorcee with two young daughters, Ilse and Margot. He was now working intensely on his next great leap forward—the General Theory of Relativity. It was during this period that he first became actively involved in the cause of pacifism, especially the movement to set-up an international organisation to resolve disputes between nations peaceably. After the collapse of the German Reich in November 1918, Einstein re-acquired German nationality. The following year he and Mileva were divorced and he married Elsa. It was a time of great change. The old world order had been transformed almost beyond recognition and within a year his own very private world was to change too, propelling him from academic obscurity to worldwide celebrity as he was hailed as one of the greatest scientific thinkers of this and any other age.

Like many of the great theoreticians Einstein had indeed produced his most creative and original work before his forties. However, while this had won him the respect of a small circle of physicists, few outside this rarefied community had any notion just how revolutionary his theories were. In 1907 he had argued that light waves had mass and were therefore subject to the effect of gravity; at the time an unproved and controversial theory that went counter to the Newtonian model of the universe that had dominated science for two hundred years. He realised the gravitational force experienced on Earth was too weak for the effect of gravity on light to be measured accurately with the technology then available. He calculated, however, that light from distant stars passing close to a massive gravitational field such as another star—the Sun, for example—would shift as their light bent towards the epicentre of the star's massive gravitational pull. The displacement of the distant stars' position in the sky could then be gauged against their position when their light was not being bent by the Sun's gravitational field. The period during a total eclipse, when the sky darkens and stars appear clustered around the blackened disk of the Moon covering the Sun, would be the ideal moment to test his theory. Unfortunately, the outbreak of war in August 1914 prevented a German expedition from travelling to Russia to observe a total eclipse there, and five years were to pass before another opportunity presented itself—this time in the southern hemisphere.

On 7 November 1919 Einstein woke to find himself hailed as the greatest scientific phenomenon of the age. Dramatic proof of his controversial theories about light and gravity immediately caught the public's imagination, eager for fresh, visionary revelations after the horror and grief of the war years. Before this date many scientists had not been prepared to accept his theories. If proved, the laws of physics, based on a predictable, clockwork-like universe, would need to be radically redrawn. Now his predictions had finally been verified by the eagerly awaited publication of the findings of two groups of astronomers. Two expeditions had been mounted to observe a total eclipse of the Sun on 29 May 1919. One group, led by Andrew Crommelin of the Royal Greenwich Observatory, had travelled to Sobral in Brazil; the other, led by the Astronomer Royal Frank Dyson and Arthur Eddington of Cambridge University, had travelled to Príncipe Island in the Gulf of Guinea in West Africa. After numerous logistical difficulties and rain and cloud that obscured sight of the stars for most of the transit of the Moon, the two teams were able to record statistical observations of the deviated light from stars in the constellation of Taurus, which were then compared. Eddington later penned a poem celebrating the findings:

> Oh leave the Wise our measures to collate.
> One thing at least is certain, LIGHT has WEIGHT
> One thing is certain, and the rest debate—
> Light-rays, when near the Sun, DO NOT GO STRAIGHT.[1]

On 6 November at a joint meeting in London of the Royal Society and the Royal Astronomical Society the findings were made public and hotly debated, though significantly, when considering the later rejection of his theories by the Nazis as mere 'Jewish science', there were still some such as Rutherford who refused to accept Relativity theory had any relevancy for physics other than perhaps for astronomy. Einstein is said to have been unimpressed by the expeditions' findings. As far as he was concerned, if they had not matched his predictions then either the observations were faulty or God Himself had made a mistake. Privately, he was delighted.

Fame came to Einstein at the age of 40 and never left him. He once wrote to a friend: "With fame I become more and more stupid, which is of course a very common phenomenon."[2] Were this true he would by the end of his life have become one of the most stupid men of all time, for he certainly became one of the most famous. It was something he was never easy with, finding it all rather baffling, sometimes even frightening. He didn't see how what he ate for breakfast or whether or not he liked wearing socks could possibly be of interest to anyone, neither did he have any time for reporters and would-be biographers intent on discovering the 'real' Einstein. His own 'autobiographical' writings, first collected under the title *Mein Weltbild* (*The World as I See It*), contain virtually no personal details, being almost entirely devoted to the development of his ideas in politics, science and philosophy. The nearest anyone came in his lifetime to the status of official biographer was probably Rudolf Kayser, husband of his stepdaughter Ilse. Having reluctantly agreed to contribute a preface to Kayser's book, he showed how little he thought of it, writing that while true to the facts of his life the book was flawed because it omitted the oddities of personality and the experience of living in an irrational world that gave shape to a person's character. This was somewhat ironic as these were just the sort of things he usually professed to regard as either too trivial or private for publication. Unpleasant as he found it, he had to face the fact that his life had changed forever, as the world's press placed before a baffled but fascinated public the over-thrower of Newton and the new master of the universe. In 1926 the British writer J. C. Squire wittily summarised the public's bafflement, answering Alexander Pope's 18th-century epigram:

> Nature and Nature's laws lay hid in night:
> God said, 'Let Newton be!' and all was light.

with:

> It did not last: the Devil shouting 'Ho!
> Let Einstein be!' restored the status quo.

His name quickly became a byword for genius and wherever he went crowds flocked to catch a glimpse of this German–Italian–Swiss—no one could decide which nationality he was—phenomenon of the age. Civic authorities from Los Angeles to Tokyo hung up the bunting and struck up the band as he stepped, a bemused, slightly crumpled and shyly smiling figure from motor car, train or ship. Writers, artists, movie stars, royalty and politicians clamoured to meet him, to be seen in his company and spoken of as his friend and confidant. One of the most famous, Charlie Chaplin, once remarked to him at a film premiere: "They're cheering us both, you because nobody understands you, and me because everybody understands me."

Over the next fourteen years Einstein travelled the globe lecturing to packed audiences. Many of those who managed to get into the lecture hall would not have had the slightest idea what he was talking about, not simply because of the advanced maths and physics but also because he habitually delivered his scientific lectures in German. While resenting the impact such celebrity had on his private life, he recognised that his status provided him with a platform on which he could speak about the non-scientific issues he felt most strongly about—world peace, social justice, political freedom and racial tolerance. Witnessing the rise of Nazism in Germany in the 1920s and early 1930s, with its rampant militarism and racist ideology directed with especial venom towards his fellow Jews, Einstein did not hesitate to use his position as an internationally respected figure to speak for the oppressed, even though he knew the consequences for himself would be dire. In the years that followed 1919, honours were heaped upon him, including the 1921 Nobel Prize for Physics, as he became a kind of one-man, globe-trotting genius show. In each country he was questioned not simply as a scientist but as an opinion-former on political and social matters, particularly on pacifism and the setting up of a safe Jewish homeland. These were causes to which he was prepared to devote a large proportion of his time and energy, though each in turn caused him a great deal of trouble.

By the early 1930s the period of his greatest scientific achievements was long behind him. For the rest of his life Einstein continued to work on what he hoped would be his crowning achievement, the Unified Field Theory; an attempt, ultimately unsuccessful, to discover a formula that would unify the forces of electromagnetism and gravity, the glue he believed bound the universe together. In the world of physics, while he still held a place of special honour, he was by now in conflict with a younger generation of physicists for whom quantum theory and the uncertainty principle showed that everything in the universe was subject to chance and not capable of being measured rationally, as events were altered by the very act of their observation. For Einstein this was anathema, for, as he was fond of saying, he simply could not believe in a universe in which God played at dice. For him there was nothing that could not be measured or predicted given the right set of equations. Meanwhile, events in Europe were moving him inexorably towards the end of his present way of life, when even his faith in one of his most cherished beliefs, pacifism, would have to be re-evaluated. Matters came to a head in 1933, a year that would prove to be pivotal for him and indeed for the whole world. It was the year in which he would renounce his German citizenship for the second and final time, make public his change of mind about the wisdom of absolute pacifism with its rejection of all armed defence and leave Europe forever. The malign force motivating all was the same—the rise to power of Hitler and the Nazi Party in Germany. Einstein as an advocate of pacifism and tolerance of personal belief became a figure of hate for the extreme nationalists and racists coalescing around Hitler. Being a Jew would have been sufficient in itself to incur their hatred but being also a renowned and revered intellectual who wasn't afraid to criticise them put him at the top of their list of enemies. By the autumn of 1933 not just Germany but the whole of continental Europe had become too dangerous for him, driving him across the Atlantic to the USA where he would remain for the rest of his life.

The year began for Albert and Elsa mid-ocean on board the passenger liner *Oakland* as it steamed towards the Panama Canal. They would be seeing a lot of the Atlantic that year, crossing it three times. At this time they were heading for California, where Einstein had a three-month engagement at the California Institute of Technology (Caltech) in Pasadena. His arrival there was not universally welcomed. In November 1932 a hostile pressure group calling itself the Woman Patriot Corporation (WPC) began petitioning the FBI and the US immigration service to prevent his planned entry into the country. He was, they declared, "a radical, an alien red and not even a real scientist," who was intent on fermenting socialism, anarchism and bloody revolution. The FBI files on Einstein, now available under US Freedom of Information legislation, make for uncomfortable reading. The president of the WPC, the appropriately named Mrs Harriet Frothingham, foamed at the mouth with hatred of the man she depicted as intent on the overthrow by violent means of the US Government. In her fifteen-page deposition to the US Visa chief, Anderson Dana Hodgdon, she condemned him as having "more anarcho-communist affiliations than Stalin". As for his science, he was "merely the advocate of a 'cosmic religion' of relativity, intent on the destruction of Christian values". He was also accused of belonging to a pacifist organisation with an allegedly left-leaning leadership, the War Resisters' International, which she claimed was a front for Soviet-funded agents. Furthermore, she had heard "he apparently cannot talk English".[3] As his ship docked in the Port of Los Angeles Einstein must have felt he had jumped out of the frying pan into the fire. His response, however, was typically good-humoured. He had, he said, never experienced such a rejection from the fair sex or, if he had, not by so many all at once. Back in Germany a far more dangerous enemy than Mrs Frothingham was now stalking the Earth. On 30 January 1933 Hitler was appointed Reich Chancellor. He immediately set about dismantling the democratic system that had elected him. On 27 February a fire gutted the

German parliament building, the Reichstag. Even though the man arrested on suspicion of setting the fire was judged to be mentally deranged, the public outrage gave Hitler the opportunity to impose draconian measures curbing political liberty, allowing for the suppression of demonstrations of political opposition and the persecution of those whom the Nazis saw as Germany's internal enemies, including Jews, Slavs, gypsies, communists, socialists, homosexuals, trade unionists and liberals.

The possibility he might not be able to return to his home and professorship in Berlin suddenly became a reality, not simply because of the physical danger to himself and his family, but because he did not wish to be associated with a country in which innocent people were routinely being attacked in the streets, imprisoned without trial and tortured in prison cells. Interviewed by a reporter from the *New York World Telegram* in Los Angeles on 10 March, he stated that as long as he had a choice in the matter he would choose to live in a country in which "civil liberty, tolerance and equality before the law prevailed". Shortly after he made this statement an earthquake struck LA, killing more than a hundred. The reporter who had interviewed him at Caltech contributed to the stock of Einstein myths by describing how she saw him walking calming across the campus, oblivious to the shock waves beneath his feet. The worst effects of the earthquake, while devastating, were in fact confined to the Long Beach area and she later admitted she was actually driving her car on Sunset Boulevard when she felt the shock but the image of the imperturbable, other-worldly genius was too good not to use. Einstein's statement, however, reverberated around the world. Although he had deliberately avoided specifically mentioning the situation in Germany, his 'Earthquake' speech was noted there with outrage by the Nazis, who immediately accused him of "cultural intellectualism, intellectual treason and pacifist excesses", branding him an "atrocity-monger and traitor".

The following day Albert and Elsa boarded a train for New York, where they were to meet the *Belgenland*, the ship that was to take them back to Europe and an increasingly uncertain future. On 14 March, Einstein's 54th birthday, the couple stopped overnight in Chicago and attended a dinner there in his honour, a civic function at which, ironically, the German Consul had been invited to congratulate his fellow countryman. Privately, he warned Einstein not to go home. The following day Albert and Elsa arrived in New York, having received a telegram *en route* informing them their Berlin apartment had been ransacked by the Prussian secret police, forerunners of the Gestapo. In New York Einstein repeated his LA 'Earthquake' manifesto to the assembled press. This inevitably provoked further outrage in the Nazi-controlled press in Germany. One of his most forceful critics was Alfred Rosenberg, a prominent Nazi theorist and editor of the Nazi Party's official newspaper, *Völkischer Beobachter* (*The*

People's Observer), who was also at that time the Nazis' unofficial foreign affairs spokesman. In addition, propaganda minister Josef Goebbels now informed Germany's Jews they could blame Einstein for their present troubles because he had set a bad example that only confirmed people's poor opinion of them. Thus, in the space of only a few months, he had been transformed in the German press from a renowned and honoured German citizen to a reviled traitor and liar.

As their ship prepared to leave New York, Einstein and Elsa received more shocking news: their beloved summer villa at Caputh, a gift of the Berlin City authorities, had been broken into by members of the Nazi Party's thuggish paramilitary Brown Shirts—the *Sturmabteilung*. The *New York Times* reported they had searched his house, ostensibly to find weapons rumoured to have been concealed there by communist terrorists. All they found was a bread knife. The fact that jack-booted Nazis had stomped all over their house and rifled their personal possessions while the local police stood by without raising a finger to stop them was an outrage that deeply shocked them. On hearing the news, Einstein issued a statement deploring the fact that in Germany today the powers of the police had been handed over to a uniformed mob. In the short time left to him in America he visited Princeton University, which he was due to attend later that year to take up a temporary appointment at the Institute of Advanced Study. While there he spent a few hours looking for suitable accommodation. It was a process he was to find himself spending more and more time on over the next six months, as he found himself effectively homeless and stateless.

On Sunday 26 March 1933 the *Belgenland* arrived at Southampton Water. Though he could hardly have imagined it at the time, this was to be the first of four occasions that year when he would enter British territorial waters. Einstein's fame, coupled with the controversy then raging over his recent anti-Nazi statements, made his arrival, even though he was merely *en route*, newsworthy enough to be reported in numerous British papers. According to Saturday's shipping news, the *Belgenland* was due to arrive at Southampton on Sunday at 5 p.m. While the ship lay at anchor, disembarking mail and passengers, those going on to Antwerp remained in their cabins, partook of an early dinner or took a turn on the deck to look at the lights of the harbour. At 6 p.m., listeners all over the country tuned in to the BBC Home Service as it began a religious programme with readings from the Old Testament that told the story of the Prophet of Bethel, who having foretold the destruction of the altar in a holocaust of fire and ash was forbidden by Jehovah to return home: "So he went another way, and returned not by the way that he came … ."[4] Less than 48 hours later the *Belgenland* docked in Antwerp. Here, like the ancient prophet, Albert Einstein too went another way, destined never to return to the land of his birth.

Notes

1 *Overbye, Einstein in Love, p.357.*

2 *Calaprice, The Quotable Einstein, p.6.*

3 *FBI files on Albert Einstein, section 1, file no. 61-7099; accessed online: https://vault.fbi.gov/Albert%20Einstein*

4 *Authorised (King James) version, I Kings 13:10.*

The Arch Intriguer

AS the *Belgenland* bore Einstein ever closer to Europe and an uncertain future, a British member of parliament sensing an opportunity entered his Westminster office and dictated a letter; a letter that would involve the world's most celebrated scientist in one of the most bizarre episodes of his life, begin an unlikely friendship and lead to the largest public demonstration against Nazism seen in Britain up to that date. The MP, Commander Oliver Locker-Lampson, had already played a not insignificant role in some of the greatest events of the age, including the Great War and the Russian Revolution. He had entered parliament as a Conservative Unionist in January 1910 aged 29, one of the youngest MPs in the House. Brash, bright and energetic, he was tipped for high office but for one reason or another by 1933 his political career had stalled and was now firmly stuck in a rut. Aged 52, he still cut a striking figure on the back benches. A self-proclaimed champion of the underdog and upholder of what he regarded as an essentially British sense of fair play, he looked every inch the clean-cut *Boy's Own* hero. Tall and straight-backed, his well-cut lounge suits hung elegantly on his still athletic physique. Beneath a fine head of greying hair lay a clean-shaven, finely chiselled face; his nose long and aquiline, his chin jutting and determined, his eyes hawk-like and keen, betraying a predatory intellect.

On the face of it he was someone who should have gone far. His social credentials were impeccable. An old Etonian and graduate of Trinity College, Cambridge, he possessed an unusual, not to say unique, war record as the commander of a fleet of armoured cars that had served on the Western and Eastern Fronts between 1915 and 1917 under the flag of the Royal Naval Air Service (RNAS). He had emerged from the war relatively unscathed with a long row of medals from the grateful Allied governments of Belgium, Romania and Imperial Russia, as well as the Distinguished Service Order (DSO) and Companion of the Order of St Michael and St George (CMG) from the British Government, the latter an honour normally only given to high-ranking civil servants and diplomats not reserve naval officers. During the war hardly a week seemed to pass without the exploits of Locker-Lampson and his armoured car men on some far-flung battle front appearing in the provincial and national newspapers in Britain and around the British Empire, including in his North Huntingdonshire constituency and Norfolk, his adopted home county. Throughout his parliamentary career, which lasted unbroken for thirty-five years, his name was regularly before the public connected with some political cause or other: 'Imperial Preference' (reform of import trade tariffs in favour of the Empire's Dominions), the promotion of working-class Conservative candidates to parliament, defending the Union and opposing Home Rule in Ireland and exposing the notorious insider share-dealing and 'cash for honours' scandals that blighted the reputation of Liberal governments before and after the war. Throughout the 1920s and early 1930s, he relentlessly attacked the Soviet Union's perceived malicious influence on Britain's social, economic and political life, speaking in parliament and at public meetings all over the country under slogans such as 'Rout the Reds' and 'Hands off Britain'. During the General Strike in 1926, with the help of his nephew Edward Delmar-Morgan, he organised the printing of the *British Gazette*, a government-sponsored anti-strike newspaper edited by Winston Churchill.[1] He also supported Churchill's reactionary defence of the status quo of White rule in the British Empire, particularly in India. Moving increasingly towards the far right of politics in the late 1920s, he set up and led a uniformed political faction known successively as the League of Loyalty, the Sentinels of Empire and, finally, the Blue Shirts. Then, in the early 1930s, in a huge *volte face*, he began to campaign with equal energy to raise public awareness of the threat posed by the rise of fascistic nationalism in Britain and on the Continent; advocating increased public spending on rearmament, particularly of the air force, and criticising his own party leaders' policy of appeasement of the dictators, promoting at the same time regulated immigration into the British Empire of Jewish refugees from the Third Reich and Eastern Europe, especially into the British Mandate of Palestine.

Despite social connections among the highest levels of society as well as not inconsiderable personal wealth, good looks, panache and a wide-range of skills and experience, Locker-Lampson's early promise and a 'good war' were not followed by post-war success. 'The Political Careerist', an essay by his brother Godfrey, might well have been written with Oliver's stalled political career in mind: "It is safer for a politician 'on the make' to follow a party than an individual."[2] A piece of advice Oliver never failed to ignore, hitching his wagon to a succession of political stars. Throughout the 1920s and 1930s he was repeatedly overlooked for government posts by successive prime ministers despite the advocacy of influential mentors, including Winston Churchill, F. E. Smith (Lord Birkenhead) and Austen Chamberlain, whose Parliamentary Private Secretary (PPS) he was for a few years after the war. Prime Minister Andrew Bonar Law lost faith in him after he failed in a covert Conservative Central Office-financed plot to seize control of the *Daily Express*, out-manoeuvred by Max Aitken, the future Lord Beaverbrook. Stanley Baldwin harboured suspicions he was mixed up in some sort of financial impropriety, despite reassurances from Churchill that the rumours were unfounded. Neville Chamberlain shared Baldwin's low opinion of him and secretly warned his older half-brother Austen he was

Locker-Lampson, the arch intriguer, ploughing his own furrow. Postcard. Huntingdonshire, General Election, 1918.

"very badly served by Oliver", who was an "arch intriguer" and did "underhand things in his name without his authority".[3] Disastrously, a streak of arrogance also made him unpopular with many of his fellow back-benchers. The Tory MP Cuthbert Headlam was probably only exaggerating slightly when he confided to his diary that he was "a terrible fellow whom no one likes".[4] Despite being one of Churchill's most loyal supporters, even his son Randolph thought him essentially a "political henchman" and not to be trusted.[5]

Part of the problem was that he was seen as being too fond of controversy, too prone to speak his mind and tread his own path, to fit comfortably into a system based on patronage, 'clubability' and deference—even his telegraphic address was 'Combative'. Austen Chamberlain pinpointed another of his weaknesses, confiding to his diary: "I wish I could get him to take a larger part in the work of the House, but he has too many irons in the fire."[6] In addition to his various political hobbyhorses, he was a director of several companies, including the Norwich-based motor traders Duff, Morgan and Vermont, which he had co-founded in 1905—the Vermont element standing in for Locker-Lampson as his mother refused to allow the family name to be associated with 'trade'. The other partners were Colonel Granville Duff, a one-armed, one-eyed Boer War veteran, and Jack Delmar-Morgan, Locker-Lampson's brother-in-law, a brilliant mechanical engineer and inventor who designed and build many of the innovative features used by his armoured car division in the First World War.[7] He also harboured ambitions to become a press baron, having tried but failed to gain control of first the *Daily Express*, then the *Pall Mall Gazette*, the *Times Literary*

Supplement and a number of other journals between 1912 and 1914. After the war he acquired controlling ownership of two Conservative Unionist-supporting newspapers in his constituency, the *Huntingdonshire Post* and the *Peterborough Standard*, and continued to own them until 1930, long after he had quit the constituency. He also took over the 'conductorship' of a monthly, Conservative-leaning literary journal, the *Empire Review*, which became the launching pad for Brendan Bracken's political career when Locker-Lampson introduced him to Churchill's inner circle. Meanwhile, he continued to contribute articles on domestic and world affairs to the Harmsworth and Beaverbrook presses, and was not above using his friendship with the big political beasts of the era to get articles commissioned.

Locker-Lampson was the archetypal loose cannon, simply too protean and unpredictable to fit neatly within the party machine. His masters in Conservative Central Office didn't know what to do with him and after a while gave up and did nothing to exploit his undoubted energy and talent. Today he is a largely forgotten figure, scratching out a posthumous existence in the footnotes of other men's biographies, where he is often characterised as no more than a "lightweight crony" and a faintly ridiculous, failed opportunist.[8] Yet if the scattered fragments of his eclectic career are pieced together a more complex figure emerges, a man who at almost every turn deliberately took the road less travelled: a barrister who distained to follow a comfortable but dull career in the law; a war-time reserve naval officer in the fledgling RNAS who commanded not ships or sea planes but armoured cars; a long-serving MP mistrusted by his own party's leaders and ostracised by many of his fellow back-benchers; a radical right-winger with decidedly fascistic tendencies who ended up opposing fascism in the 1930s as vigorously as he had opposed communism in the 1920s. That *volte face* began in the spring of 1933 when he embarked on what would prove to be the most intriguing campaign of his long political career—the plot to save Einstein.

Notes

1 *Gilbert, Winston S. Churchill, pp.158 & 166.*

2 *Godfrey Locker-Lampson, The Country Gentleman, p.26.*

3 *Self, The Austen Chamberlain Diary Letters, 19 March 1924.*

4 *Ball, Parliament and Politics in the Age of Baldwin and MacDonald, 25 June 1926.*

5 *Boyle, Poor, Dear Brendan, p.110.*

6 *Ibid.3, p.292.*

7 *Barratt, History of Duff Morgan; D. J. Barratt, letter, 'Shedding Light on Locker-Lampson', Eastern Daily Press, 6 April 1998, and corr. between the author and Mr Barratt.*

8 *Campbell, F. E. Smith, p.6.*

Ancestral Voices

BEFORE exploring Oliver Locker-Lampson's dramatic and unexpected intervention in the life of Albert Einstein, it may be helpful to trace how his extraordinary family history helped shape him and made Norfolk the natural focus of his plot to save him.

Remembering him in her memoirs more than fifty years after he had helped her escape the Holocaust, Austrian Jewish refugee Anna Lambert recalled that his name was "Lord Locker-Lampson", to which her editor added the forename Godfrey.[1] It was a common mistake. Non-existent ranks and titles seem to have been drawn to his name like iron filings to a magnet. It is also fairly common to find him confused with his older brother, Godfrey, who was also a Conservative MP but not a lord, and even with his cousin Miles Wedderburn Lampson, British Ambassador in Egypt during the Second World War, who indeed did become a lord. While Locker-Lampson's pedigree was not noble it was certainly notable. To a remarkable extent his lineage may be traced not in *Burke's Peerage* but in the *Dictionary of National Biography* (*DNB*), that monumental compendium of the lives of the nation's great and good first published in the 1880s, the decade of his birth. Here, as a youth, he might have read concise biographies of his grandfathers, two great grandfathers, two great great grandfathers and an impressive number of remoter ancestors back to the early 17th century. In later editions entries on his father, the poet Frederick Locker, and uncle, the author and publisher Arthur Locker, would also be included. From his earliest years it would have seemed perfectly reasonable for him to assume his family had played a not inconsiderable part in the history of England and the British Empire and that he was surely next in line to strut upon that stage, always assuming Godfrey was as dull and unadventurous as he always thought him to be.

Oliver Stillingfleet Locker, the name he was christened with, made his dramatic entrance onto the world's stage as a first-born twin—even at birth he was competitive—at his parents' London home in Chesham Street, Belgravia, on 25 September 1880. His parents were cultured, wealthy, well-connected members of the Victorian upper class, below the aristocracy in rank but comfortably above the necessity to earn a living. His father, Frederick Locker, was a successful and admired poet and an avid book collector; his collection of rare first editions and literary manuscripts was rated one of finest in private hands in Europe. The paternal Locker side of the family had been comfortably ensconced in the middling ranks of the English establishment for two centuries—in the law, the Church, the army, the civil service and, most notably, the Royal Navy. By contrast, the maternal Lampson side of the family had sprung in only a couple of generations from New England obscurity to immense wealth and baronial eminence. His mother, Hannah Jane, was the only daughter and favourite child of Sir Curtis Miranda Lampson, an American-born, self-made millionaire who had fallen out in turn with each of his three sons. Her mother, Lady Jane Sibley Lampson, numbered two American Civil War generals among her cousins—one grey, one blue. After Sir Curtis's death in 1885 Frederick Locker changed his family name by deed poll to Locker-Lampson as a condition of his father-in-law's will. Sir Curtis had originally specified Lampson-Locker but the poet in Frederick rebelled against this on the ground of euphony—it just didn't sound right to his sensitive ears.

The family name Locker, variously spelt Locke, Lockier and Lockyere, occurs in early English documents from at least the 13th century, possibly meaning a locksmith or someone who looks after livestock in an enclosure or 'loke', which is also a Norfolk dialect word for a narrow lane or alley. The curious symmetry between the possible meaning of his paternal family surname and his guarding of Einstein in a fenced-off paddock near the top of a Norfolk loke is almost preternatural in its synchronicity. The earliest of Locker-Lampson's paternal ancestors anything is known about was one John Locker (1624–1698). About whom practically nothing is known other than he dwelled or traded in the now lost Silver Street near Cripplegate in the City of London. Shakespeare lodged there for several years from 1604 in the home of a Huguenot family. Silver Street, as its name suggests, was at the centre of the City's silversmith trade and was also known for its money-lenders, a profession associated with Jews because of the medieval Church's ban on Christians lending money at interest. A character in one of Ben Jonson's plays calls it "the Region of Money, a good seat for an Usurer". While Oliver Locker-Lampson always denied he had any Jewish ancestry when his enemies said this was the reason why he helped Einstein and other Jews, there are hints he may have had Jewish roots. Locker is a fairly common Jewish family name and in his autobiography, Oliver's father, Frederick, noted somewhat obliquely that the family was said to be of "foreign extraction". Hinting perhaps at such an ancestry, he quoted with something more than simple mischief a racially offensive remark made by his friend the Poet Laureate Alfred Lord Tennyson that he looked like "a famished and avaricious Jew".[2] John Locker's son Stephen Locker (1651–1725) is described in the *DNB* as "a scrivener in the Old Jewry", a type of public notary who worked in the commercial heart of the City of London. He clearly did well in his profession, for his only surviving son, another John Locker (1693–1760), was educated at Merton College, Oxford and went on the Grand Tour of Europe, that essential finishing school for the English gentleman. He was subsequently called to the Bar and in 1719 was appointed to the prestigious post of Clerk of the Leathersellers' Company—a wealthy and powerful London craft guild. His real love, however, seems not to have been law but literature and languages. Dr Johnson described him as "a gentleman eminent for curiosity and literature", recalling how he once presented him with a collection of word definitions for his dictionary.[3] He is said to have befriended an Orthodox priest he found starving on the streets of London, giving him shelter in return for lessons in modern Greek. A family tradition of helping refugees may be said to have started here.

John Locker's marriage to Elizabeth Stillingfleet, an Anglican clergyman's daughter, explains Locker-Lampson's unusual middle name and provides his family's earliest known association with Norfolk. The Stillingfleets produced three generations of notable Anglican clerics in the 17th and 18th centuries. Elizabeth's grandfather, the theologian Edward Stillingfleet (1635–1699), who was at one time chaplain to Charles II and was later enthroned as the bishop of Worcester, is said to have disputed the meaning of the Trinity with the English philosopher John Locke—quite possibly another distant Locker relation. Elizabeth's father, Dr Edward Stillingfleet (1660–1708), was also a clergyman and a physician—a Fellow of the Royal Society and Gresham Professor of Physics at Cambridge—who practised medicine in King's Lynn and held the livings of Wood Norton and Swanton in West Norfolk. Elizabeth's brother, Benjamin Stillingfleet (1702–1771), who was born in Wood Norton and educated at Norwich Grammar School and Trinity College, Cambridge, was also in holy orders but held no living, being much too busy engaged in a variety of the arts and sciences, including writing librettos for operas and oratorios and translating learned treatises on mathematics and the natural sciences, including the curiously titled *Discourse on the Irritability of Some Flowers*. An authority on the classification of grasses, he was a friend of the pioneering Norfolk naturalist Robert Marsham. Early in his career he was employed as a tutor to his cousin William Windham of Felbrigg Hall, not far from the village of Roughton where Locker-Lampson would one day play host to Einstein. A love poem to a local beauty that Stillingfleet scratched into a glass pane at the Hall can still be seen there.[4] Despite his many notable accomplishments, Benjamin Stillingfleet is chiefly remembered today, if at all, for his association with the phrase 'blue-stocking', thought to be derived from his habit of wearing bluish-grey worsted socks with his otherwise uniformly black clerical garb while in the company of a coterie of intellectual ladies.

The Norfolk connection continued through one of John Locker's younger sons, William Locker (1731–1800). Augustine Birrell, Oliver Locker-Lampson's brother-in-law and his father's biographer, noted perceptively: "Through the

Locker lineage on the paternal side there ran a curious double streak of the Senior Service and the Virtuoso, of the Quarter-deck and Christie's."[5] The naval side of that streak seems to have begun with William. Sent to sea at 15, in a long career he rose from midshipman to commodore before retiring from active sea service to become Lieutenant-Governor of Greenwich Naval Hospital. Although a respected naval officer in his own right, his chief claim to fame is as the 'Sea Daddy' of Horatio Nelson.[6] In 1777 Captain Locker's ship the *Lowestoft* was the first on which the newly commissioned Lieutenant Nelson saw active service. Nelson served under Locker in the West Indies during the American War of Independence, distinguishing himself by boarding a commandeered American schooner in a rough swell after the ship's more senior lieutenants excused themselves this perilous honour. It was also through Captain Locker that Nelson took command of his first ship, the captured schooner, which Locker renamed the *Little Lucy* after one of his daughters. Locker's mentorship laid the foundations of the Nelson touch: the care for and comradeship with the band of brothers he fought with coupled with direct and decisive action when engaging the enemy. It was a style of command Oliver Locker-Lampson would seek to emulate in the First World War with some success, having the ability and confidence to make decisions quickly and the organisational skills to promptly put his decisions into action. His men, like Nelson's, were fiercely loyal and proud of their association with his elite force, and he took great care to see they were well cared for.

Nelson and Locker became lifelong friends and exchanged many letters. Those from Nelson remained treasured family heirlooms for over a century until sold by Godfrey along with their father's entire library in the 1900s, a betrayal of the family's heritage Oliver never forgave. In a letter written in 1799 to Locker, Nelson, now a Rear-Admiral of the Fleet, recalled his former Sea Daddy's advice:

> I have been your scholar; it is you who taught me to board a Frenchman … it was you who always told me, 'Lay a Frenchman close, and you will beat him', and my only merit in my profession is being a good scholar; our friendship will never end but with my life.[7]

Nelson's duties under Captain Locker were not always so heroic. On one occasion Locker ordered him to organise a press gang, an unpleasant duty he sweetened by arranging for him to have his portrait painted while ashore. John Rigaud's portrait of the 19-year-old Nelson is the epitome of the fresh and youthful hero before the scars of battle had taken their toll. Twenty years later, in October 1797, now partially blind in one eye and shortly after he had lost most of his right arm at the Battle of Tenerife, Nelson sat for another portrait, this time by Lemuel Abbott. The sittings where held at Commodore Locker's home in Greenwich Hospital where, by family tradition, his youngest daughter Elizabeth is said to have stood on a chair to help Nelson on with his heavy, gold-

Nelson in action under the watchful eye of Locker-Lampson's great grandfather, Captain William Locker of the Lowestoft, 1777. Painting by Richard Westall.

laced and be-medalled tunic. According to Locker family lore, Nelson, who is said to have retained his native Norfolk accent, told her: "If you be a good gal, if you be a roight good gal, next toime I'm agoin' to grow my arm again and save you the bother of helping me into this here cumbersome coat."[8] Although she was certainly diminutive enough to have needed a chair, as a child of 5 or 6 she is said to have been so small she could walk under tables without stooping, it seems improbable a 21-year-old unmarried gentlewoman would have been allowed to undertake so delicate a task. Nelson's right sleeves had in fact been slashed to allow his servant to manoeuvre his still raw stump into his close-fitting coats with the least discomfort. On Locker's death in 1800 Nelson wrote to Locker's second son John: "The greatest consolation to us, his friends who remain, is that he has left a character for humour and honesty which none can surpass, and very, very few attain."[9]

William Locker's youngest son, Edward Hawke Locker (1777–1849), was also associated with the Royal Navy throughout his career and it is through him the Locker-Lampson line of the family is descended. Named after his father's former naval commander during the Seven Years' War, Admiral Lord Edward Hawke, victor of the Battle of Quiberon Bay, he was born at Greenwich Naval Hospital in 1777 and began his career in the Naval Pay Office before being appointed Civil Secretary to Admiral Sir Edward Pellew during his command of the East Indies fleet. Continuing the family tradition of encounters with celebrities, he made an ascent with the French balloonist André-Jacques Garnerin in 1802, travelling from Lord's Cricket Ground to Chingford in fifteen minutes. He met the Duke of Wellington in Spain in 1812 during the Peninsular War and Napoleon Bonaparte when in exile on Elba in 1814. Edward Hawke Locker's share of prize money from captured enemy shipping brought him considerable wealth, which enabled him to obtain the office of Civil Commissioner of the Royal Naval Hospital at Greenwich, following in his father's footsteps there. A skilled artist in his own right, he established Greenwich's collection of naval portraits, the foundation of the National Maritime Museum's art collection. He also achieved a modest degree of literary fame as a publisher and writer of travel books, particularly about Spain. Two of Edward Hawke Locker's four sons, Frederick and Arthur, also achieved literary success. Arthur Locker (1828–1893) travelled extensively in India and Australia, where he lived for several years caught up in the Gold Rush of the 1850s. When he eventually returned to England he became editor of the *Graphic*, a popular illustrated weekly newspaper. He also published several novels and schoolboy yarns based on his adventures. His son Arthur Algernon Locker was also a newspaper editor and it is not difficult to see how the examples of his uncle and cousin may have influenced Oliver Locker-Lampson's largely unsuccessful ambition to become one too.

Oliver's father, Frederick Locker (1821–1895), was, like his brothers, born at Greenwich Hospital. A sickly child, there were fears he might be mentally 'feeble' as he had early learning difficulties and was rejected as unteachable by seven schools in six years. His working life began unpromisingly in 1837 when he became a clerk in a ship broker's office near the Thames. Five years later he obtained a civil service post at the Admiralty, where he was employed to write summaries of reports submitted by naval officers. Roaming London in his leisure hours he acquired a passion for collecting old books, manuscripts, engravings and *objets d'art*, on which he would spend a large proportion of his modest salary.

Something of a dilettante with a gift for friendship and literary ambitions, he was temperamentally unsuited for the life of a humble clerk and found himself strongly drawn instead to the fashionable salons of the capital's literary and artistic elite. Fastidious in his habits—he wore kid gloves at work to prevent his hands becoming stained with ink—he was also something of a valetudinarian, prone to chills and melancholy moods. On his father's death in 1849 he inherited sufficient capital to allow him to escape the world of ship's requisition orders and half-pay officers' petitions, and the following year married Lady Charlotte Bruce, daughter of the 7th Earl of Elgin, the man who removed to Britain much of the classical marble relief from the Parthenon in Athens. Lady Charlotte was something of a catch for a semi-retired Admiralty clerk on extended sick leave. Intelligent and charming, her social status helped Frederick gain entrée to the highest echelons of society. One of her sisters, Lady Augusta, was a lady-in-waiting to Queen Victoria and married to Arthur Stanley, Dean of Westminster. It was Dean Stanley who first introduced Frederick to the new Poet Laureate, Alfred Tennyson. They became life-long friends. In 1857 Frederick published the first edition of *London Lyrics*, a collection of comic and witty light verse. Today his poetry is out of print and almost completely forgotten, though during his lifetime it was popular and admired, and was reprinted in numerous editions. After Tennyson's death in 1892 he was even briefly considered as a successor to the office of Poet Laureate along with Swinburne, Ruskin and William Morris.[10] With Frederick's increased prosperity and leisure time he became an ever more avid collector of rare books and manuscripts, developing a new type of bibliophilic study known as the 'cabinet collection'. Exquisitely chosen, his collection focused on English literature, including rare early editions of Shakespeare and his contemporaries. Literary success, astute connoisseurship and a talent for friendship helped to place him within the inner circle of Victorian high culture. He knew, was friends with and corresponded with almost all the literary giants of the age.

Cartoon of Frederick Locker by Frederick Waddy.

Frederick Locker and Lady Charlotte had one child, Eleanor, born in 1854, a Pre-Raphaelite-like beauty who was photographed by Julia Margaret Cameron. In 1872 Lady Charlotte died suddenly. Two years later the 53-year-old Frederick married Hannah Jane Lampson, a rich heiress twenty-five years his junior and only eight years older than his daughter. Her father, Sir Curtis Miranda Lampson (1806–1885), seems to have had all the attributes of the born entrepreneur—cunning, resourcefulness, daring and luck. After moving to Canada from Vermont in the early 1820s he made his first fortune working for the Hudson's Bay Company, trading furs before moving to England where he acted as John Jacob Astor's London agent. In 1848 he became a naturalised British subject and in 1856 was appointed the principal director of the Atlantic Telegraph Company, which had been set up to lay the first transatlantic telegraph cable between Ireland and North America. For the next ten years Lampson, the company's vice-chairman, continued to expertly steer the project through its many technical, engineering and financial problems. When the project was finally completed successfully in 1866 he reaped huge rewards, both in terms of the return on his investment and in prestige. That year Queen Victoria made him a baronet, reputedly the first US-born, naturalised subject to be so ennobled.

Drawing of Jane Locker-Lampson by Edward Clifford.

In 1878 Frederick's family was joined by marriage with Tennyson's when Eleanor married his younger son Lionel. The couple had been childhood friends, were deeply in love and seemed destined for each other. Their relationship, however, was seldom stable and after the birth of three sons in five years, their marriage began to fall apart. Lionel began to have affairs and Eleanor in retaliation openly flirted with other men. On a trip to India in 1886 Lionel became unwell with malaria and died on board ship returning to England. Stories of Eleanor's ship-board flirtations while Lionel lay on his sick bed began to circulate. Back in England and still in the strict formal mourning period she began an affair with a married friend of her late husband, Richmond Ritchie, a nephew of Thackeray's.[11] After this fizzled out she began a romantic relationship with the poet James Kenneth Stephen, who was later declared insane and has the dubious distinction of being a Jack the Ripper suspect along with his pupil the Duke of Clarence.[12] She subsequently married the Liberal politician and author Augustine Birrell, who later became Secretary of State for Ireland. Her life ended tragically in 1915 when an inoperable brain tumour brought insanity then death.

Because of the lateness of his second marriage Frederick Locker was a relatively elderly man by 19th-century standards by the time the children of his second marriage were old enough to remember him. The older children, Godfrey and Dorothy and the twins Oliver and Maud were known collectively as the 'Rowfant Quartos', after their father's remarkable library of rare books housed in the family home. The author and illustrator Kate Greenaway, one of Frederick's protégées, seems to have been used by the family as an unpaid childminder. Nicknamed 'Limner Kate' in Frederick Locker's poem 'The Twins', she paid tribute to her mentor and her fondness for his young family by depicting them on the frontispiece to her book *Little Ann*. The children also provided models for many of her book's impossibly sweet, clean, well-behaved little children, and she designed charming *ex libris* bookplates for each member of the family. Frederick was characteristically less sentimental when describing his children:

> I think Godfrey is, perhaps, the least stupid, and I cannot bring myself to believe that Dorothy will ever be vicious. Oliver will, I expect, always find some people to think him attractive, whilst I feel quite certain that Maud will never be really plain.[13]

Their mother, Hannah Jane—known within the family as Janie—was a devout, evangelical Christian who strove constantly to exert a strong moral influence on her children. Her religiosity sometimes bordered on the eccentric. As a child she preached to workmen in the brick works near Rowfant House, her

Rowfant House, Surrey.

father's main home in Sussex, and as a young wife organised prayer meetings for the navvies working on the railway near the family's summer residence in Cromer. A strict Sabbatarian, letters and parcels delivered to the house on a Sunday, however urgently anticipated, could not be opened until Monday morning. On Sundays the children were forbidden to go outside other than to church or play any sort of game unless it had a clearly religious purpose such as a board game called 'Missionary Lotto'. A mischievous streak in Frederick—known within the family as Fred—caused him to invent alternative versions of games such as 'Missionary Billiards' in which each ball was named after an Apostle and the cue was christened "Jehu—for he driveth furiously".[14] Frederick Locker, while conventionally Christian, was uninterested in religion and bored by his wife's over-scrupulous attention to the pieties. The author and traveller Wilfrid Scawen Blunt, who lived near Rowfant, recalled how Fred would often call on him after Church on Sunday and end up remaining the whole evening "in stealth from Sabbath bonds strange to his heart. Childlike he prized these truant bursts of fun."[15] Given Janie's worries over her husband's casual attitude to his own salvation, it is ironic Fred's gentle, stoical acceptance of his own frail mortality, which he wrote about unaffectedly in his memoirs *My Confidences*, would be cited by the American philosopher William James as an example of "on the whole a religious state of mind, although I dare say that to many of you it may seem too listless and half-hearted to merit so good a name."[16]

Somewhat surprisingly, given their differences in age, temperament and spiritual outlook, they seem to have been a happy and devoted couple. While Janie was a doting if over-protective wife and mother, Fred was an indulgent father and husband. He arranged the publication of some of Janie's children's stories, including *What the Blackbird Said. A Story in Four Chirps*, in which she mildly mocked the innate conservatism of the English landed gentry: "You see this old Rook was very patriotic, and of course a great Tory to boot. He disliked change of every sort and kind. … Yes, 'Old England for ever!' was still the watchword of the rooks."[17] Janie was not unaware of her husband's indulgence. What exactly the Blackbird said was later explained to Oliver by his mother who showed him an inscription written by his father in her copy of the book: "Jane is exceedingly spoilt by Fred; that is, of course, what the Blackbird said." Having been something of a sickly child Janie had grown up suspecting all sorts of fatal contagions lurked in the cold, damp English countryside. Her children were often confined indoors behind firmly closed windows in stuffy, over-heated rooms and only allowed out smothered in heavy clothing. Her obsession with hygiene developed into an eccentricity. Her belief that low-value copper coins were infected with the germs of the lower classes brought Oliver a schoolboy perk, as she considered only golden sovereigns or silver coins handled by the gentry were clean enough for him to have as pocket money. She also had a morbid dread rabid dogs and murderous tramps lurked around every bend in the road. For his own protection she therefore allowed the young Oliver to carry a loaded revolver. The danger of entrusting a lethal weapon to a headstrong twelve-year-old was apparently the lesser peril to her mind. Oliver was particularly proud he managed to keep his gun at Eton without it being confiscated. The habit of carrying a loaded weapon with him in public stayed with him for the rest of his life, to the alarm of his fellow railway compartment travellers whenever he flung his large naval revolver onto the seat beside him.

Among the properties Janie inherited in her own right on her father's death in 1885—the recently enacted Married Women's Property Act saw to that—were a large, rambling, partly Elizabethan manor house near Crawley in Sussex known as Rowfant House and a hunting lodge and deer park at Cromer on the north Norfolk coast, which she refashioned with red-brick, baronial pretensions and renamed New Haven Court after her father's birthplace in Vermont. After their mother's death in 1915 Oliver's older brother Godfrey inherited Rowfant while he inherited New Haven Court, later running part of it as the Royal Cromer Hotel, attracting a select clientele of VIP guests, including international tennis stars, artistic, literary and political luminaries and a cavalcade of European royalty, including Princess Marie Louise of Schleswig-Holstein; the exiled king and queen of Greece, George II and Elisabeth of Romania; the King of Greece's young cousin Prince Philip, the future Duke of Edinburgh; and minor members

Locker-Lampson bags another royal. Prince Philip with Oliver and Barbara at a Cromer gymkhana, 1934.

of the Russian and Georgian royal families. Remembering the house fifty years later, Oliver Locker-Lampson recalled "although the house was new and raw without, within in became, under my father's magic ministrations, a pavilion of charm".[18] Nevertheless, the house does not seem to have been at all popular with its guests. Its reputation for draughts was commemorated in verse by Fred himself:

> This is the house by Cromer town!
> Its bricks are red, though it looks so brown.
> It faces the sea on a windswept hill,
> In winter it's empty; in summer it's chill;
> Indeed, it is one of earth's windiest spots,
> As we know from the smashing of chimney pots.
> In August I ask for an extra quilt;
> This is the house that Jane built.[19]

Postcard of New Haven Court, Cromer.

Thackeray's daughter Anny Ritchie was unimpressed, describing the house as "horribly Spartan".[20] Charles Tennyson, one of Eleanor's sons, wrote bitterly of summer holidays spent there as a child: "The house was without architectural charm, and the site bleak, sandy, and apparently capable of producing little but an unending host of earwigs."[21] Badly damaged by fire in 1963, the estate was sold for building land and the house demolished. Nothing now remains except its gate-keeper's lodge, its name in a cul-de-sac of neat retirement bungalows and flats, and a large, rusting gate leading to one of Cromer's old smugglers' lanes from the site of the house's former covered tennis courts where stars of Wimbledon once played.

By the time Fred and Janie had built New Haven Court, the north Norfolk coast had become a fashionable resort for the middle and upper classes. The arrival of the Great Eastern Railway in 1877 made the area easily accessible for the first time from London and the Home Counties. During the early 1880s a series of articles appeared in the *Daily Telegraph* under the title 'Poppyland', extolling the delights of the Norfolk coast and the old-world charm of its simple country folk, crumbling cliffs and mournful, romantic ruins. The articles, the work of journalist and poet Clement Scott, helped to popularise the area, especially after they were collected into a best-selling book. At New Haven Court the Locker-Lampsons entertained numerous artistic and literary visitors. Tennyson visited with his wife and elder son Hallam, who later recalled his father's impressions of Norfolk:

> At Cromer the Locker-Lampsons were our hosts, taking us on excursions to Gunton, Felbrigg, and Hempstead, and one day we sailed on Wroxham Broad, a large inland lake, surrounded by woods and fringed with willow-herb and bulrushes.[22]

In nearby Overstrand the former Liberal MP Cyril Flower, ennobled as Lord Battersea, resided at The Pleasaunce, a vast 'cottage' designed by Sir Edwin Lutyens. His wife, a Rothschild by birth, became a close friend of the Locker-Lampsons, and was among Oliver's earliest Jewish friends. In her *Reminiscences* Lady Battersea noted the essentially loving nature of Fred and Janie, despite their contrasting characters:

> Frederick Locker-Lampson was a dear friend and guest at our country house. His wife Jane … was in some ways the very opposite of her husband, but she provided him with the happiest of homes … her name was immortalised in her own visitors' book, for a friend inscribed the following two lines, which she good naturedly accepted as they were meant: As Delilah was to Samson, So is Jane to Locker-Lampson.[23]

According to Major Herbert Dent, a retired Army doctor and frequent guest at New Haven Court, the couplet, which Lady Battersea had slightly misquoted, was penned by General Hamley, a military historian and Conservative MP for Birkenhead. Far from accepting the verse "good naturedly", Janie had in fact asked for it to be pasted over. Oscar Wilde was another guest and is said to have played golf with his lover, Lord Alfred Douglas, on Cromer Links. Major Dent recalled seeing Wilde, by then a rather pallid, obese figure, at New Haven Court in September 1892.[24] At this time Wilde was renting a cottage on the nearby

Felbrigg Hall estate while writing *A Woman of No Importance.*[25] Oliver Locker-Lampson would later make the acquaintance of Wilde's son, Vyvyan Holland, through their mutual friends Lord and Lady Birkenhead.

Fred filled his Norfolk home with books and bric-a-brac. A particular favourite was the Baltic amber occasionally found on the East Coast, especially those pieces with imprisoned insects. Not liking fresh air over much, Fred usually bought these from local dealers in Cromer and Norwich rather than hunt for them himself along the strand, and was sometimes duped into buying suspiciously treacly-looking specimens containing rather too many perfect insects. As a boy Oliver was much more interested in doing the beach-combing for himself. Despite the restrictions on his movements placed on him by his mother, he often managed to escape and explore the countryside, armed with his treasured revolver. A glimpse of his boyhood in Cromer is found in the preface he wrote for Alfred Savin's *History of Cromer.* Savin, a well-known local amateur naturalist and curio dealer, seems to have been something of a hero to the young Oliver, and it is tempting to see here a foreshadowing of the genuine admiration he had for Einstein. He found in Savin's company an oasis of wonder in a desert of starched Victorian gentility; an avenue to adventure out of the over-cosseted atmosphere that enveloped him at home. His description of Savin, whom he continued to visit well into the 1930s, is written with rare affection:

'Always keep ahold of nurse, for fear of finding something worse.' Locker-Lampson and nanny (right) with the other 'Rowfant Quartos'. Left to right: older siblings Godfrey and Dorothy and twin Maud, New Haven Court, c.1885.

> As a boy I remembered Mr Savin bending over boxes of amber in the shop with the curved front in Church Street; and I recollect long walks along the shuddering shore in the days when the fossil bed lay exposed at low tide, and we could return laden with pre-historic bones. ... Even as I write this, in our far fog Babylon, my mind flashes back to Cromer and I am skipping up the steps to Mr Savin's room on the second floor; where behold this remarkable man, standing in the centre of a room, literally walled with shelves and drawers and exhibition cases. There is a rattle of keys as Mr Savin opens a treasured desk, screws a magnificent glass into his eye to inspect the latest find, bringing it to the window for examination; or I picture him seated in his arm-chair—the only one I have ever seen with a window-pane let into the side—through which the green light of the Colza lamp pours its mellow rays at night.[26]

In his unfinished memoirs written near the end of his life Locker-Lampson recalled the summer holidays of his childhood spent in Cromer with evident glee. The whole family travelled by train from Sussex, where the family had its own railway station in the grounds of Rowfant House, in their own private compartment, hired, Fred said, in order to spare their fellow passengers the hullabaloo of four rioting children:

> As a family we travelled down yearly to Cromer *en masse*, a welter of trunks, luncheon baskets, pails and nurses, and to avoid overflowing a saloon would be attached to the train, wherein we might bivouac undisturbed. I have since thought of the pain four boisterous children must have caused a sensitive poet on these routs; and for peace he would establish each of us at a window, and promise sixpence to the one who saw Cromer lighthouse heave into view.[27]

More than forty years later the view to the lighthouse would be one Locker-Lampson would share with Einstein, who would go on to talk of lighthouses as places of potential refuge for young scholars in the last public speech he made before leaving Europe forever.

Notes

1 *Lambert, Du Kannst Vor Nichts Davonlaufen, p.158*

2 *Frederick Locker-Lampson, My Confidences, pp.4 and 12.*

3 *Johnson, 'Life of Addison', Lives of the Poets (1779–81).*

4 *Ketton-Cremer, Norfolk Portraits.*

5 *Birrell, Frederick Locker-Lampson, p.15.*

6 *Sharman, Nelson's Hero.*

7 *Rawson, Nelson's Letters, pp.223–4.*

8 *Steve Locker-Lampson, Nothing to Offer But Blood.*

9 *Ibid.7, p.300.*

10 *Hutchinson, The Private Diaries of Rt. Hon. Sir Algernon West.*

11 *Garnett, Anny, pp.245–55.*

12 *McDonald, The Prince, His Tutor and the Ripper.*

13 *Ibid.5, p.72.*

14 *Ibid.8, p.28.*

15 *Godfrey Locker-Lampson, The Rowfant Library.*

16 *James, The Varieties of Religious Experience, pp.39–40.*

17 *Hannah Jane Locker-Lampson, What the Blackbird Said.*

18 *Ibid.8, p.10.*

19 *Jones, Poppyland in Pictures, pp.45–6.*

20 *Ibid.11, p.232.*

21 *Charles Tennyson, Stars and Markets, p.46.*

22 *Hallam Tennyson, Alfred Lord Tennyson, p.326.*

23 *Battersea, Reminiscences, pp.221–2.*

24 *Dent, 'Reminiscences of a Cromer Doctor'.*

25 *Ellmann, Oscar Wilde, p.356.*

26 *Savin, History of Cromer.*

27 *Ibid.8, p.14.*

One of the Cruder Bounders

OLIVER Locker-Lampson's childhood idyll ended at the age of 9 when like most boys of his social class he was packed off to boarding school. Founded in 1645, Cheam considered itself superior to all comparably sized private schools by virtue of its age alone and was reckoned one of the most expensive in the country. His brother Godfrey had gone there five years earlier. It was, in Oliver's own words "an unsavoury school with a super-sadist as a headmaster". This was the Rev. R. S. Tabor, described by former pupils Charles Hardinge, later Viceroy of India, as "one of the greatest snobs I ever met" and by Clive Bigham, a contemporary of Godfrey's, as "an unctuous, rotund, old gentleman, not unaddicted to the aristocracy".[1] While boys of titled parents were given cake and an avuncular pat on the head on admission, the offspring of less obviously patrician families were cold-shouldered. The daily routine consisted of the traditional boarding school medley of cold baths, bad food and ritualised sadism. On his first day Locker-Lampson minor was closely questioned by some older boys:

> 'What's your name?' I had been warned that it was un-manly to give my Christian name. 'Locker-Lampson' I said therefore and they looked at one another with puckered brows. 'Gosh, what a mouthful!'[2]

Having, in addition, a mere poet for a father did not impress. Four years later he went to Eton where he eventually flourished, becoming a member of the school's elite society Pop. While at Eton he discovered a talent for lifting weights and learning languages, winning both the school's shot-putting cup and the Prince Consort's Prize for German Composition, achievements he never failed to include in his *Who's Who* entry until the end of his life. In 1899 he went up to Trinity College, Cambridge, where he read History and Modern Languages. Here he was a contemporary with many of the coming century's up-and-coming literary and scientific elite, including Arthur Eddington, the astronomer who would help prove Einstein's General Theory of Relativity in 1919. Locker-Lampson himself achieved an honourable footnote in the University's literary

Locker-Lampson: Eton's champion weightlifter.

annals as co-editor of the undergraduate magazine *The Granta*, persuading old literary friends of his father to contribute pieces. An anonymous satirical profile in the magazine, possibly penned by himself, described him as "a being superb in all the stateliness of manly beauty; his eagle eye, his classical features, his flowing raven locks proclaimed one far removed from the vulgar herd".[3] While at Cambridge he found a talent for acting and became president of the Amateur Dramatic Club (ADC). During these extra mural activities he cultivated friendships with men who would become significant movers and shakers of the British Empire, including Edwin Montagu, his co-editor at *Granta*, who became Secretary of State for India in 1917, and the soldier, writer and diplomat Mark Sykes, his best friend at the ADC, who went on to broker the Sykes–Picot Agreement, which divided up much of the former Ottoman Empire's territory between Britain and France after the First World War.[4]

On graduating in 1903 Locker-Lampson caused his widowed mother considerable anxiety by running off to join the circus and a travelling theatrical troop. However, the reality of life as a big top strong man and jobbing actor soon disillusioned him of the glamour and excitement he had hoped to find. He next turned his attention, not without a wistful backward glance, to the law, that cockpit of many a frustrated thespian, training as a pupil at the Inner Temple. In 1907 he was called to the Bar and in 1909 briefly worked at the Court of Admiralty under Lord Justice Bigham, father of his brother's contemporary at Cheam, who would later chair the Board of Trade inquiry into the sinking of the *Titanic*.[5] Still searching for his metier, he next turned to politics and in November 1907 hit the jackpot when he was selected on a pro-Tariff Reform ticket as the prospective parliamentary candidate for the Conservative and Unionist Party in the North Huntingdonshire constituency of Ramsey; a place he secured by sheer force of personality, for he was unknown to the local Tory grandees and without either personal wealth or influential backers. A future editor of the *Daily Telegraph*, Colin Coote, recalling his youth in Huntingdonshire when he had helped the Liberal Party during in 1910 elections, thought Locker-Lampson one of the best parliamentary candidates he ever saw, to whom the epithet "unflappable" fitted perfectly.[6] Touring the constituency, drumming up support for his candidacy in the January 1910 General Election, Locker-Lampson had to swim for it when "over-estimating the width of a bridge", as he put it in his memoirs, his car overturned in a flooded Fenland ditch; going on to

'Over-estimating the width of a bridge'. Locker-Lampson's scrape with death in the 1910 General Election campaign.

the deliver his speech that evening in borrowed trousers that were far too-short for his long legs, a red knitted scarf and carpet slippers. Dorothy L. Sayers, the precociously intelligent 15-year-old daughter of the Rector of Bluntisham-cum-Earith, who had put Locker-Lampson up for the night two years earlier after a local Unionist rally, seems to have used this incident for the opening of her detective novel, *The Nine Tailors*, in which her aristocratic sleuth Lord Peter Wimsey and his valet have a similar motorcar spill in a Fenland ditch. The dashing, handsome young Tory candidate clearly made a favourable impression on her, speaking to her as an adult and sharing her love of French literature; later sending her a second-hand set of Molière's plays as a thank you present. She would return the compliment in December 1915 as Locker-Lampson prepared to sail to Russia with his armoured car division, sending him advanced copies of her first book—a collection of poems—as presents for his officers.

The unflappable young candidate. Oliver Locker-Lampson publicity shot for the 1910 General Election.

Locker-Lampson went on to win the seat in North Huntingdonshire at both of 1910's General Elections, beating at the first contest the sitting Liberal MP, helped by a national swing to the Conservatives. The Liberals, nevertheless, led by Herbert Asquith, were returned to power on a slim majority. Once in parliament on the Opposition back benches he worked hard to get himself noticed. His youthful energy and competitiveness gave him a tendency to arrogance and outspokenness that he never really lost. This coupled with an awareness of the effect his striking good looks had on those whose patronage he needed, both male and female, very soon gained him a reputation. After a weekend party at Conservative Party leader Arthur Balfour's Scottish home, Whittingehame, in October 1910 the future royal secretary and courtier, Alan Lascelles, noted primly in his diary: "I found Balfours innumerable and a bad MP man, Oliver Locker-Lampson—one of the cruder bounders."[7] His reputation was not helped when in February 1911 he was involved in a prank that almost ended his political career only a year after it had begun. Walking through Piccadilly late one Sunday evening with an old Etonian school friend and an unnamed lady, his friend challenged him to a foot race. The sight of two gentlemen in full evening dress running through the crowded, gas-lit streets of London soon attracted attention, which is precisely what his friend had intended. Locker-Lampson had apparently boasted that as an MP it was impossible for him to be arrested. Determined to prove him wrong, he let him get ahead then shouted: "Stop thief! He's stolen my gold watch." A constable stopped him, searched his pockets and found a gold watch with the friend's name engraved on it, which, thinking better of his prank, he admitted to having placed there in order to play a trick. Told to go home quietly and sent on their way, all might have been well until further horseplay, including conducting an imaginary orchestra with their walking canes, nearly knocking off the hats of passers-by, resulted in their arrest. Both men were charged with using insulting words and a breach of the peace and spent the rest of the night in a police cell. The next morning the friend, who admitted to initiating the prank, was fined 5 shillings and bound over to keep the peace. Locker-Lampson meanwhile avoided prosecution by the intervention of the newly appointed Liberal Home Secretary, Winston Churchill, who was asked by the Conservative Chief Whip to have a quiet word with the magistrates to drop the charges. The story, however, got into the papers and questions were asked in the House of Commons as to whether Locker-Lampson had brought parliament into disrepute.[8] If matters had not been handled delicately there was a good chance he would have to resign. Churchill, with a somewhat partial retelling of the incident, assured the House the Honourable Member was the innocent victim of a "senseless and cruel" practical joke by a known prankster and in no way at fault.[9] This and an apology by the prankster printed in the papers probably saved his parliamentary career and earned Churchill Locker-Lampson's undying gratitude. It would prove to be the start of a long friendship.

The gold watch incident had shown he had a reckless, impetuous streak, always ready to rush in where others feared to step, dangerously coupled with a tendency to arrogant boasting. He should have known better than to accept such a challenge from his friend, as his reputation as a prankster was common knowledge in upper-class Edwardian society. His friend was none other than William Horace de Vere Cole, one of the most notorious practical jokers of the 20th century. Bizarrely enough, given Locker-Lampson's later association with Einstein, the prematurely grey-haired and moustachioed Cole was frequently mistaken for him.[10] Cole had been something of a public nuisance since his Cambridge undergraduate days when he had successfully passed himself off to the town's civic and university authorities as the uncle of the Sultan of Zanzibar on a surprise visit to the town. His most famous hoax, however, had occurred a year before the gold watch incident—in February 1910—when he and a group of his Bloomsbury-set friends, including a young Miss Adeline Stephen (the future Virginia Woolf), hoodwinked the Royal Navy into giving them a guided tour of the pride of the fleet, HMS *Dreadnought*, in the belief they were members of the Abyssinian royal family. The prank, dubbed the 'Bunga Bunga' affair in the papers after the made-up language used by the hoaxers, brought forth indignant letters to the papers from retired admirals and questions in the House concerning the security of the Royal Navy and the apparent credulity of its senior officers.

Locker-Lampson was beginning to look to his bosses in the Conservative Party like someone unreliable, a dilettante and a bit of a bounder. For the rest of his political career he would work mainly as a maverick intriguer on his own account or as a behind-the-scenes fixer. His first major test as a wheeler-dealer came in 1912 when Conservative Central Office asked him to draw up a scheme to save the *Daily Express*, whose circulation was falling dramatically in competition with other popular newspapers—in particular, Lord Harmsworth's *Daily Mail*. Central Office feared they were about to lose the only cheap popular national newspaper that supported the Conservatives. His scheme involved putting together a consortium of wealthy Tory supporters to buy controlling shares in the ailing newspaper. Unfortunately for Locker-Lampson, the young Canadian-born Conservative MP Max Aitken, the future Lord Beaverbrook, got wind of his scheme and effectively scuppered it by raising his own capital from an American banker and winning over to his side the paper's brilliant but highly temperamental editor, Ralph Blumenfeld. Locker-Lampson's swagger had not endeared him to Blumenfeld, who felt, probably correctly, that his goal was to place himself as conductor of the *Express* and direct editorial policy, which ironically is, of course, what Beaverbrook would eventually do himself. The Conservative Party leader Andrew Bonar Law, who had at first encouraged the scheme, got cold feet and left Locker-Lampson out on a limb. After an acrimonious exchange of letters he withdrew to lick his wounds.

The fiasco over the failed *Daily Express* coup seems to have been the last time in his political career when Locker-Lampson was employed by Conservative Central Office. He felt, not without justification, that it had got itself into a muddle and had used him as a scapegoat. The affair had long-term repercussions. Throughout the 1920s and 30s Stanley Baldwin repeatedly refused to give him any post or honour because of persistent rumours he had misappropriated Conservative Party funds, despite both Churchill's and Austen Chamberlain's assurances he had acted with complete propriety. From now on he would conduct his own campaigns and develop his own agenda, often at variance with the Conservative Party's official line. One of his most vigorously fought campaigns was against political corruption. His first battle in this arena was over the 'Marconi Scandal', an infamous early example of insider trading. Prominent members of the Liberal Government's front bench, including the Chancellor of the Exchequer, David Lloyd George; the Attorney General, Rufus

Isaacs; and the Postmaster General, Herbert Samuel, were suspected of having bought shares in American Marconi in advance of an announcement the UK Government had awarded the British branch of the company a hugely lucrative contract to build a chain of wireless radio stations linking up the British Empire. Locker-Lampson and a barrister friend, Peter Emanuel Wright, who later became an MI6 agent in Switzerland during the war—like Somerset Maugham's fictional agent Ashenden —hatched a plan to bring the directors of Marconi to court on a charge of defrauding their shareholders, buying one share each in the company in order to become legitimate stakeholders in the case. An act caustically described by the historian of the scandal as being "inspired by the curious altruism of the common informer".[11] So successful was their plan the directors settled out of court to the tune of at least £14,000 in costs alone and probably a good deal more besides—some accounts say £30,000—a very great sum, equivalent to more than £2 million today. He next turned his attention to the matter of the selling of honours. It had become commonplace and almost acceptable for rich businessmen to buy titles and honours by placing large contributions into the governing party's funds. There was said to be a sliding scale of charges from a knighthood to a peerage. Locker-Lampson's Traffic in Titles Bill never received a second hearing, Asquith's Liberal Government having made sure there was not enough time to debate it.

Long before he had a chance to reintroduce the Bill two great political crises occurred that put everything else on hold. First was the crisis over Home Rule for Ireland, which Locker-Lampson as a staunch Unionist was fiercely opposed to, and second, the outbreak of war following Germany's invasion of Belgium in August 1914. It was to be the Home Rule crisis that provided him with the springboard that pitched him headlong into the opening engagements of the war, at the head of his own squadron of the recently developed motorised armoured car. During 1913 the Ulster Volunteer Force (UVF) trained thousands of Protestant Unionists to provide a militia to oppose the introduction of Home Rule, which they feared would lead to the election of a predominantly Roman Catholic, Nationalist government in Dublin. In Britain, Locker-Lampson joined with other Tory 'Die Hards' to provide financial and political support for Sir Edward Carson's UVF. He was even rumoured to have been involved in a secret plan to take weapons and an armed force of English and Scottish Unionists to Ireland to aid the UVF should civil war break out. Locker-Lampson's half-sister Eleanor's husband, Augustine Birrell, was at this time the Liberal Government's Secretary of State for Ireland. How much inside information he may have come by through this family connection is not known but it clearly could have put him in touch with influential parties on both sides of the crisis.

With the declaration of war against Germany in August 1914 the Irish Home

Rule Bill was put on hold, and the UVF was rapidly turned from a potentially insurrectionary militia into the British Army's new 36th Ulster Division, ready to serve King and Country. The official history of the Ulster Division records that Locker-Lampson, described as "one of Ulster's staunchest friends", provided a cheque to cover the cost of kitting out the division.[12] Although he may have been cash rich at this time due to the out-of-court settlement from the Marconi affair, it is unlikely he could have afforded to pay such a bill entirely by himself and in reality he was acting as the conduit for funds from wealthy supporters of the Unionist cause, including Lord Rothschild and Lord Derby. Locker-Lampson was keen to find some war work commensurate with his talents and ambitions. He had toyed at first with the idea of offering his services as an interpreter, as he was an accomplished linguist. When this plan failed he became involved in a scheme to convert private motor cars into field ambulances for use in France, utilising his connections as a director of the Norwich-based motor traders Duff, Morgan and Vermont, which also helped develop prototype armoured cars for use on chassis provided by Lanchester, Rolls-Royce and Ford. Noticing the public interest in the work of a fledgling armoured car unit in France attached to the Royal Naval Air Service (RNAS) and commanded by the swashbuckling Commander Charles Rumney Samson, he hit on a scheme to raise and command his own armoured car company and attach it to the newly raised Ulster Division. The War Office, however, decided it did not want the Ulstermen to have their own mobile armour, fearing it might have trouble getting the machines back after the war when its men reverted to being members of the UVF. The Royal Navy, however, with the support of his friend, the First Lord of the Admiralty, Winston Churchill was keen to accept Locker-Lampson's offer to equip and man a squadron of armoured cars out of his own resources. In December 1914 he was commissioned with the newly created rank of lieutenant commander in the Royal Naval Volunteer Reserve and immediately began to assemble his mobile force.[13]

After a few months stationed in Cromer, where its officers were billeted at his family home at New Haven Court and its non-commissioned men in local families' cottages and seaside boarding houses, the RNAS Armoured Car Division's No. 15 Squadron was despatched to the Front where it was attached to a remnant of the Belgian Army in West Flanders. It was here Locker-Lampson first met King Albert, king of the Belgians, who would later play an important role in the Einstein

Locker-Lampson (seated right) in mourning for his mother, with General Hills-Johnes VC (seated left) and officers of Armoured Car Squadron 15, Flanders, 1915.

story. By the time the squadron arrived in Flanders in 1915 the effectiveness of mobile armour had been totally negated by trench warfare. After a few weeks of ineffectual skirmishing, he learned to his horror the Admiralty had decided to disband all of its armoured car squadrons, an innovation the Sea Lords had never approved of. With Churchill gone from the War Cabinet following the Dardanelles disaster, they were finally free to axe the RNAS's armoured car wing. Facing the loss of his command and transfer to a Whitehall desk job or the trenches of the Western Front, he pulled strings at the very highest level, up to and including King George V, concocting a scheme to get his armoured car squadron not disbanded but tripled in size and posted to the Eastern Front to help bolster Britain's beleaguered Russian ally.

In December 1915, temporarily promoted to the rank of full naval commander, he set sail from Liverpool at the head of the Anglo-Russian Armoured Car Division, bound for Russia, where after several months trapped in the ice in Murmansk, it operated throughout 1916 in the Caucasus against the Turkish Army as a tiny, mobile adjunct to Imperial Russia's vast, sprawling, poorly equipped and badly trained armed forces. In February 1917 Locker-Lampson personally witnessed the revolution that swept Tsar Nicholas II from his throne. His armoured car squadrons continued to fight on the Eastern Front under the nominal direction of Kerensky's Provisional Government until the Bolshevik coup of November 1917 (the October Revolution in the Russian calendar) finally forced his unit's

Keeping his feet dry this time. Locker-Lampson's Rolls-Royce staff car breaks down mid-stream in the Caucasus campaign, 1916.

return to England minus their armoured cars and equipment, which were seized by the Red Army. During this period he acted more like a privateer rather than a Royal Navy officer, carrying round with him letters signed by George V and the Tsar, which he would flourish before any bureaucrat or military official who got in his way, claiming to be a royal emissary. There is substantial evidence, for example, that without any official authorisation from the British Government, the War Office or the Admiralty he transferred his unit from the Caucasus to the Romanian Front in 1916 and then became directly involved in a failed military coup against Kerensky in September 1917, placing his armoured cars at the disposal of the leader of the coup, the Cossack general Lavr Kornilov. It was this affair that seems to have finally brought about his enforced exit from Russia aboard Kerensky's personal armoured train in October 1917, leaving his officers and men to find their own way home. Back in Britain he was appointed the Ministry of Information's Russia liaison officer and became concerned in the organisation of support among the allied Western powers' for armed inventions against the Bolsheviks in Russia's civil war.

After the Armistice Locker-Lampson returned to domestic politics, winning a seat in the newly unified Huntingdonshire constituency in the General Election of December 1918. Soon afterwards he was appointed Parliamentary Private Secretary to the new Chancellor of the Exchequer, Austen Chamberlain. In this capacity he attended the Paris Peace Conference with Chamberlain in 1919. In the General Election of 1921 he left his Huntingdonshire seat to stand as a Lloyd George Coalition Conservative for the Birmingham constituency of Handsworth, which he won. Handsworth was part of the Chamberlain family's political fiefdom. He had in effect tied himself to their political coat tails but his fledgling political career failed to take flight after his chief, Austen Chamberlain, failed to become Prime Minister in 1924, leaving him in the wilderness on the back benches with no government post to expend his still fizzing energies on. Not one to stand still for long, he now turned to helping his brother, Godfrey, Conservative MP for Wood Green and an Under-Secretary of State at the Home Office, in his campaign against the Soviet Union. His experiences in Russia during the war and the financial losses he claimed to have suffered following the Bolshevik takeover in 1917 spurring him on.

For more than a decade he ran a 'Rout the Reds' campaign, organising and leading demonstrations up and down the country against Bolshevism and the influence of the Soviet Union, which he believed had infiltrated the British Labour Movement and was behind the General Strike in 1926. His anti-Red campaign then began to run out of steam, as much of what he had campaigned for was achieved with Britain's breaking-off of diplomatic relations with the Soviet Union in 1927 in the wake of the ARCOS (the All Russian Co-operative

Society) affair. He now became involved in Churchill's campaign against Home Rule for India, believing the status quo of White colonial rule in the British Empire must be maintained. He also continued to campaign for the economic policy of Imperial Preference, which sought to set preferential tariffs on goods sold between member countries of the Empire. During the late 1920s and early 1930s Locker-Lampson became increasingly drawn towards the trappings of fascism, eventually founding his own uniformed patriotic movement known as the Blue Shirts. He also began at about this time to renew his old interest in Zionism and the development of a Jewish hegemony in the British Mandate of Palestine, a cause that paradoxically would lead him to seek out and befriend one of the most famous victims of fascism and anti-Semitism—Albert Einstein.

Notes

1 *Bigham, A Picture of Life, p.15.*

2 *Steve Locker-Lampson, Nothing to Offer But Blood, p.25.*

3 *The Granta, 14 March 1903, pp.251–2.*

4 *Adelson, Mark Sykes, p.63.*

5 *Information courtesy Dr Clare Rider, The Honourable Society of the Inner Temple.*

6 *Coote, Editorial, p.76.*

7 *Hart-Davis, End of an Era, 3 October 1910.*

8 *Daily Mirror, 21 February 1911.*

9 *Hansard, House of Commons Debates, 1 March 1911.*

10 *Downer, The Sultan of Zanzibar, pp.150–1.*

11 *Donaldson, The Marconi Scandal, p.235.*

12 *Falls, The History of the 36th (Ulster) Division, p.5.*

13 *See Perrett and Lord, The Czar's British Squadron.*

The Professor and the Blue Shirt

EINSTEIN'S progress as he crossed the Atlantic had been chronicled almost daily in the US and European press, so by the time the *Belgenland* docked in Antwerp on the 28 March his criticism of the new regime in Germany had been much reported, coupled with speculation about whether he would or could return to the country of his birth. On this he still felt conflicted and not yet ready to make a definitive public statement. While the dangers of returning to Germany to face his enemies had become all too clear, he wanted a little time on solid ground to assess the situation and plan his next course of action calmly and clearly. Beside the danger of assassination or imprisonment after some sort of show trial, his work at the University of Berlin would very soon become impossible, as Jews were about to be barred from holding academic appointments. His homes in Berlin and Caputh had already been desecrated. There was also his family to consider. They might be held hostage or their lives threatened to ensure his silence or some sort of humiliating recantation. More generally, the Nazis were already blaming him for attacks on his fellow Jews by his allegedly traitorous utterances. His every step and public announcement now needed to be thought through in order to minimise the harm to others.

The welcoming party at Antwerp included Camille Huysmans, Burgomaster of Antwerp; Professor Théophile de Donder, a mathematician and physicist at the Free University of Brussels; and Dr Arthur De Groodt, a lecturer in medicine at the University of Ghent. In addition to genuine admiration and concern for his safety, each had strong personal or political motives for their support of Einstein against his Nazi critics. Huysmans, a socialist and pacifist who would become Prime Minister of Belgium after the Second World War, was a staunch defender of Jewish refugees who had settled in Antwerp after the First World War. Professor de Donder was the leading advocate of Relativity theory in Belgium and a personal friend of Einstein's since their first meeting at the Fifth Solvay Conference in Brussels in 1927. Dr De Groodt had his own bitter personal experience of German aggression, having fled to Britain following their invasion of neutral Belgium in August 1914, as indeed had Huysmans. In September 1914 Locker-Lampson had written a letter to *The Times* calling for each UK constituency outside London to make arrangements to take in the anticipated large flow of refugees from Belgium, offering his Westminster office as a clearing house for offers of help.[1] At the same time his mother took in refugees at the family's home in Cromer and organised fund raising to find accommodation for Belgian refugees all over East Anglia until the Defence of the Realm Act forced all aliens out of the region before the end of the year.

Postcard of Cantecroy Castle, Belgium.

According to Einstein's biographer Antonina Vallentin, who knew the Einsteins personally, the couple's first place of residence after disembarking was a students' hostel in Belgium.[2] If so, it would probably only have been for their first night ashore. Sending a telegram to the *Belgenland* as it approached Belgium, De Groodt had invited Einstein and Elsa to stay at his home, Cantecroy, a large, moated, partly medieval castle at Mortsel only a few kilometres from Antwerp—an invitation they now took up. Cantecroy Castle was to be the first in a series of closely guarded locations where Einstein would find temporary refuge until his planned return to America in October. De Groodt and his partner Juliette Adant regularly hosted gatherings of intellectuals there. A friend of Einstein's from his time lecturing at Leiden University, the cultural historian Johan Huizinga—a staunch critic of Nazism—had been a recent guest as had the Indian poet and philosopher Rabindranath Tagore, who had visited Einstein at his summer house at Caputh in 1930, where they had discussed the meaning of truth and beauty, Einstein arguing he did not know whether beauty was universal but truth was, and that was his religion. The day after his arrival *The Times* reported:

> Professor Einstein, who has declared that he will not return to Germany, arrived in Antwerp from America yesterday evening. He stated that he expected to stay in Belgium for five or six months before deciding finally in which country he would live permanently.[3]

Einstein now asked to be driven to the German Embassy in Brussels where he formally renounced his citizenship for the second time in his life, having already sent a telegram to the Prussian Academy of Science in Berlin resigning his professorship. Although this was a time of great anxiety, he could at least feel certain he would not be homeless or unemployed for long. Indeed, as soon as his situation became known a frantic international auction began to win the considerable kudos his presence would bring to the academic institution or country that gave him sanctuary. Over the next few weeks universities in Belgium, Britain, France, Palestine and Spain would all put in bids. In Britain, Frederick Lindemann, Professor of Experimental Physics at the Clarendon Laboratory,

Oxford, later known as Churchill's war-time 'Prof' on all matter scientific, led the British bid, which was immediately matched by the leading advocate of Zionism, Dr Chaim Weizmann, himself a man of science, a chemist, who tried to persuade Einstein to accept a chair at the newly founded Hebrew University in Jerusalem, capital of the British-controlled Mandate of Palestine. Although Lindemann regarded Einstein as one of the few people in the world superior to him intellectually, his feelings about Jewish people were highly ambivalent and his behaviour towards Jews often offensive. He was prone to making snide anti-Semitic remarks and jokes, and was very sensitive to gossip that he was himself a Jew or of Jewish ancestry. Yet, after the Nazis came to power, he made many personal and professional interventions to help Jewish scholars escape Germany.[4] These competing invitations were a source of anxiety for Einstein as he didn't want to close off any options too soon or delay too long and lose a potential escape route. In the meantime, a greater worry was how to get his closest family and associates into places of safety. The list was fairly long. It included his stepdaughters Ilse and Margot, and their husbands Rudolf Kayser and Dimitri Marianoff. Then there were his elder son Hans Albert, his wife Freida and their young sons Bernhard and Klaus, all then in Switzerland, and his personal secretary Helen Dukas and scientific assistant Dr Walther Mayer, who were still in Germany but would soon join him in Belgium. For the time being his sister Maja was safe in Italy and his former wife Mileva, having settled in Zurich, had no intention of moving, especially as their younger son Tete had been diagnosed with schizophrenia and was now institutionalised there.

A day or so later Locker-Lampson's letter, posted in London on 28 March, somehow managed to find Einstein at Cantecroy. As his location was not public knowledge, the hand of a power more instrumental than the British and Belgian post offices seems to have been behind this. He began by recalling the occasion they had first met—in Oxford "when Lord Haldane was still with us".[5] This throwaway remark is intriguing. If true it would date their first meeting considerably earlier than 1933. Richard Haldane, created first Viscount Cloan in 1911, was an eminent Scottish lawyer, politician and philosopher who had held the offices of Secretary of State for War and Lord Chancellor in Asquith's Liberal Government. As a well-known authority on German culture, Haldane had been forced to resign in 1915 after a jingoistic campaign in the British press harassed him for his supposedly pro-German sympathies, including accusations he was secretly married to a German woman and had a pet dog called Kaiser—the latter at least was true. After the war he courageously sought to rebuild cultural bridges with Germany and in 1921 published *The Reign of Relativity*, one of the first non-scientific assessments of the implications of Einstein's theories for society and philosophy. In May and June 1921 he acted as Einstein's host on his first visit to Britain. On the morning of 14 June, Lindemann drove Einstein and Haldane from Haldane's London home in Queen Anne's Gate to Oxford where he was given a guided tour of the Clarendon Laboratory. After lunch Lindemann and Einstein strolled around Christ Church Meadow with the metaphysician and relativity sceptic Professor J. A. Smith, before Einstein and Haldane returned to London by train in the evening.[6]

This was Einstein's first visit to Oxford, which he did not visit again until 1931, by which time Lord Haldane was dead. It is possible Locker-Lampson had simply muddled up Lord Haldane with his brother, the physiologist John Scott Haldane, who did meet Einstein in Oxford in 1931, or indeed his nephew J. B. S. Haldane, who was also a scientist and a Fellow of New College, Oxford, at this time. However, the fact that neither were peers of the realm nor, crucially, deceased when he wrote his letter makes this unlikely. Had he wished to establish a more recent meeting, he might more plausibly have cited 28 October 1930, when Einstein, on a flying visit to London, had sat in the Visitors' Gallery in the House of Commons with his friend Sir Herbert Samuel to listen to an exchange between Prime Minister Ramsey MacDonald and the Leader of the Opposition, Stanley Baldwin, about a change in British policy towards the Mandate of Palestine. However, if his remark is taken as true, Locker-Lampson's first meeting with Einstein could have only been in Oxford during that June afternoon in 1921. As it is improbable they would have met by chance, this suggests a meeting had been set up but facilitated by whom? Despite their falling out many years later over the reason for Einstein's permanent settlement in the United States, Locker-Lampson and Lindemann seem to have been on friendly terms at this period. In December 1924, for example, Locker-Lampson and his wife Bianca vacationed with Lindemann and Lord and Lady Birkenhead in Madeira.

As for what reason a meeting might have been arranged, the answer may lie in Locker-Lampson's role in government at this time. Austen Chamberlain had been appointed Chancellor of the Exchequer in Lloyd George's Coalition Government in January 1919. Locker-Lampson, whom he appointed as his Parliamentary Private Secretary (PPS), accompanied him to the Paris Peace Conference the same month. In March 1921 Chamberlain became leader of the Conservative Party and moved to the non-Cabinet position of Lord Privy Seal and Leader of the House. Locker-Lampson, however, remained his PPS and was kept on at the Treasury in some sort of fact-finding capacity. Twelve or so days prior to Einstein's first visit to Oxford on 14 June 1921, Locker-Lampson had returned to London after a ten-day visit to Germany, where he had been sent by the Treasury to gather data on the effect of war reparations on their economy. On 13 May 1921 he had written from his office at the Treasury to Paul Lemperly of the Rowfant Club—an American book collectors' club based in Ohio named after his late father's famous library—"We have been overwhelmed with the coal

Locker-Lampson, PPS to the Chancellor of the Exchequer, Austin Chamberlain (left) in c.1921.

strike and German reparations, and I have not had much time for other work. I am also obliged to leave at once for Germany for ten days."[7] He was clearly delayed, for on 23 May he wrote to Arthur Clark, bibliographer of the Rowfant Club, apologising for not having replied sooner: "but the truth of the matter is that we have been overwhelmed with work in connection with reparations and the coal strike. ... I leave at once for Germany, but shall be back in ten days' time", so on or about 2 June.[8] He was certainly back by 9 June, when he attended the funeral of the veteran Labour MP Will Crooks in London on behalf of Austen Chamberlain, while on the 13th he made his sole speech in the House of Commons that year—on the provision of council housing for ex-servicemen in his Huntingdonshire constituency.

Could it be that Locker-Lampson, a fluent German speaker, was sent to Oxford by the Treasury to sound out the views of Einstein on reparations? The suggestion is not as far-fetched as it sounds. Einstein had been closely involved in the reparations debate, as had Lord Haldane. Four months earlier Einstein had visited the headquarters of the International Trade Union League (ITUL) in Amsterdam as a delegate of the German human rights pacifist group, the *Bund Neues Vaterland* (New Fatherland League), accompanied by the League's founder, Otto Lehmann-Russbüldt, who thirteen years later, on the run from the Nazis, would seek out Locker-Lampson with intelligence on German rearmament and proposals for establishing a right of asylum for refugee Jews in Britain.[9] In 1921 Einstein's mission was to persuade the ITUL to attend a reparations conference due to be held in London in May and advocate the setting of non-punitive terms that would not cripple the German economy.[10] His efforts were in vain and he described the mission to his friend, the Austrian physicist Paul Ehrenfest, as a "quixotic political scheme".[11] Pressure from the French Government in particular led to reparations being set in April 1921 at 132 billion gold marks plus interest—equivalent then of more than £6.6 billion or $33 billion. Austen Chamberlain had argued, unsuccessfully, for the setting of more achievable terms, fearful a bankrupted Germany would be the breeding ground for extremist politics, leading to European instability, perhaps even to a Bolshevik-style revolution in central Europe. Another of Locker-Lampson's political mentors, Lord Birkenhead (F. E. Smith) was also an advocate of setting less punitive terms. Meeting Einstein in Oxford rather than at Haldane's London home may simply have been politically expedient, given Haldane was still associated with Asquith's non-Coalition Liberals and moving closer politically to the Labour Party, becoming Lord Chancellor in Ramsay MacDonald's first Labour Government in 1924. The following year Einstein wrote to Haldane to urge him to support a more sustainable reparations plan but Haldane reported that the Treasury was not interested.[12]

Having established some sort of acquaintance, however tenuous, Locker-Lampson went on to sympathise with Einstein's plight:

> My purpose in writing is above all motivated by the desire, my dear Professor, to reassure you that a great many of my countrymen sincerely sympathise with you and those of your faith in Germany at the wrongs that you have had to endure. The news that 'Einstein is homeless' has moved me deeply and perhaps this may serve as justification for the suggestion which I, a humble MP, am almost afraid to make to the world's greatest man of learning.[13]

His suggestion was simply this: that he and Frau Einstein make use of his "*kleines Haus*" in London should they wish to seek refuge in England. He was, in fact, being somewhat modest in his description of his London home, especially when it is compared with Einstein's cosy Berlin apartment, now ransacked and boarded up by Göring's secret police. His London residence in North Street, Westminster, comprised, in addition to the usual amenities, an entrance hall, dining room, living room, drawing room, master bedroom, two guest bedrooms and three staff bedrooms. He reassured Einstein he would of course live rent-free, including the cost of the staff's wages. He concluded his letter with a somewhat clumsy play on words, hoping "the 'Ether-Atmosphere' of England's love of 'Fair Play'", might help him to explore still deeper "the 'Mysteries of Relativity'". Locker-Lampson was not a scientist and was perhaps unaware Einstein had disproved the existence of a cosmic ether a quarter of a century earlier. Whether England's love of fair play would also prove to be a chimera remained to be seen.

Einstein either declined the offer or didn't respond, at least, no reply has been found. Several newspapers, however, reported he had said the offer might need to be taken up at some later date but meanwhile his fellow Jews in Germany had greater need of refuge than him.[14] It was, Einstein may have thought, rather too generous an offer to come entirely without strings attached. Locker-Lampson, after all, was a politician and might reasonably be suspected of having a hidden agenda. Given his distaste for starched-collar formality, it is also possible the mention of a small brigade of domestic servants might have alarmed Einstein. His previous stays in grand establishments had caused him acute embarrassment when having to deal with the domestic staff. He famously disliked wearing formal attire, and preferred to have his meals sent in on a tray so he could continue with his work while he ate. It was in any case a rather slight acquaintance to call upon, and it must be doubted whether Einstein would have had anything but the vaguest recollection of a man he may or may not have met very briefly almost twelve years earlier. Although his opening gambit in the great international game to save Einstein had failed, Locker-Lampson was not a man to give up easily. By a mixture of dogged determination, organisational skill, high-level contacts and considerable personal charm, he would manage, over the next six months, to bring Einstein to England twice, introduce him to some of Britain's leading critics of the Nazis and help bring the plight of Germany's Jewish population to the public's attention through the press and at two major public platforms—the House of Commons and the Royal Albert Hall.

Over in Belgium one of his hosts at Cantecroy Castle, Juliette Adant arranged a short-term lease on the Villa Savoyarde, a pretty, two-storey, white-painted holiday chalet situated on Shakespearelaan (Shakespeare Avenue) in Le Coq-sur-Mer (present-day De Haan) on the Belgian coast about 6 miles (9 km) north of Ostend. The house consisted of a living-room and kitchen on the ground floor with three small bedrooms above, in one of which a table by the window acted as Einstein's desk. Adant and her husband, Arthur De Groodt, would continue to keep an eye on Einstein from La Maisonnette, a self-contained flat next door. Almost from the start Einstein's seaside refuge was characterised by a mixture of high security and intense public curiosity. Antonina Vallentin, who visited Albert and Elsa at this time, found a typical out-of-season seaside resort:

> The spring was slow in coming that year. A grey, wintry sun hung over the coast. The silver dunes were swept by a sharp wind. Leaden waves beat against the shore; there was something desolate in the salt air that irritated the lungs.[15]

A short piece of cine film exists showing Einstein strolling along the windy promenade at Le Coq-sur-Mer in his familiar dark overcoat. It was presumably shot during the colder weather in April and from his demeanour he does not appear to have welcomed the attention.[16] Here for the next five months Albert and Elsa enjoyed the status of VIP guests of the Belgian Government; guarded day and night by armed gendarmes, while plain-clothed detectives mingled among the town's holidaymakers on the lookout for anyone acting suspiciously. It was a scenario, comic if it wasn't so serious, that might have sprung straight from the pages of one of Hergé's adventures of the Belgian boy detective Tintin. Indeed, bizarrely enough, Einstein had met the model for Hergé's goatee-bearded Professor Calculus, the Swiss physicist Professor Auguste Piccard, at the Fifth Solvay Conference in Brussels in 1927.

Locker-Lampson, as Einstein probably did not yet realise, was a friend of his friend, King Albert, whom he had first met in the trenches of West Flanders in 1915, where the squadron of RNAS armoured cars he commanded was briefly attached to the remnants of the Belgian Army under the King's direct command. Albert had crawled into his trench one day and asked to be shown how to use one of the unit's Lewis guns. It was only very gradually that he realised this tall, fair-haired Belgian officer was the king of the Belgians. Locker-Lampson was awarded the Order of Leopold for his wartime service in the defence of Belgium and his relationship with the king after the war was more than mere acquaintance—they met regularly at the Swiss ski resort of Mürren. Writing after Albert's death in a climbing accident in 1934, Locker-Lampson claimed it was he who had taught the king to ski in remote Alpine locations. Albert, anxious not to be recognised, went incognito under the name Herr Blum. On one occasion the chivalrous monarch gave his jersey to an unnamed female travelling companion of Locker-Lampson's described as his niece—he had several—who was shivering in the cold mountain air, and later carried her skis down the "dangerous and precipitous paths". Locker-Lampson recalled making tea and toast and cooking the king poached eggs in his chalet and playing the rousing old Cumbrian ballad 'D'ye ken John Peel' on the piano while the king sang along with the choruses. The cosy hideaway he provided for King Albert in Switzerland in the 1920s curiously foreshadows the refuge he would later organise for another Albert—Albert Einstein— including a piano and young female companions.[17]

Locker-Lampson, ski instructor to royalty, with Queen Elisabeth and King Albert at Mürren in Switzerland.

For Locker-Lampson, the spring of 1933 was a busy as well as a sad time. A month before writing to Einstein, he had suffered a shocking family bereavement. On 2 March his twin sister Maud died suddenly and unexpectedly aged 52. She had been found by her maid, having apparently died in her sleep at her home, Puck's Hill, in Roughton—the north Norfolk village that would play such a significant a part in the Einstein story later that year. According to newspaper reports he had travelled 300 miles to attend a dinner at the Savoy Hotel in London in honour of the Friends of Palestine in Parliament only to be met by Godfrey, who told him their sister had died "without a minute's illness".[18] Maud's death was his second close bereavement in a little over three years. His first wife Bianca had died in hospital on Christmas Day 1929 aged 30, also while he was hundreds of miles away, having been taken ill while a house guest of their friends Lord and Lady Birkenhead. To lose his wife and then his twin sister must have impressed upon him the fragility of human life and his own mortality. It is tempting to speculate whether his experience of grief modified his political outlook at this time. The dinner for the Friends of Palestine in Parliament had been organised by the British section of the Jewish Agency, a Zionist organisation set up under the British Mandate in Palestine to advise the administration there on the settlement of Jewish immigrants in the Jewish national homeland, a provision of the 1917 Balfour Declaration. The key speaker at the dinner, Chaim Weizmann, told the assembled guests, including members from both Houses of Parliament:

> In the hour of their trial it is well that our fellow Jews in Germany should know that they do not stand alone, but that the full weight of enlightened opinion in all civilised countries, and especially in England, is behind them in their struggle against the forces of reaction.[19]

Locker-Lampson's acceptance of an invitation to this dinner seems to have been the first public occasion at which he had publicly indicated his pro-Semitic or at any rate pro-Zionist sympathies since Hitler's appointment as Reich Chancellor in January. It marked a turning point in the direction of his political campaigning. From this date onwards the frequency of his public utterances on the menace of his old foe, the Soviet Union, declined in inverse proportion to his attacks on the activities of the fascistic regimes in Italy, Germany and Romania. His taking up of pro-Semitic causes in 1933 is all the more remarkable considering that throughout the 1920s and early 1930s he had been moving politically further and further to the right, to such an extent he had even begun to interest the Nazis as a potential British Führer long before Oswald Mosley caught their attention. What brought about his rejection of this role and change in political direction? There is no simple answer. It can hardly have been opportunism. His outspoken criticism of the Nazis in the 1930s was out of step with both the trend of public opinion, fearful of provoking another war, and his own Conservative Party's policy, which for much of the decade sought to appease Hitler and Mussolini for the same reason. Nor can it have been the result of any lingering anti-German sentiment from the war. He was in fact very much a Germanophile; he spoke the language fluently, visited the county frequently and had several old friends there, including Dr Karl Ott, who would later become, unbeknownst to himself, Einstein's Norfolk *Doppelgänger*. In common with many British politicians, including Churchill, he had at first admired Hitler as a political strongman and staunch anti-communist. Neither is it evident that prior to 1933 he saw himself as a champion of the Jews. Indeed, his uncritical support for the White forces that committed atrocities against Jews during the Russian Civil War cannot be overlooked.[20]

Hansard does not record a single speech by Locker-Lampson in parliament on any Jewish-related issue before July 1933. Despite this, Jews and Jewish affairs had long been a factor in his political and personal makeup. Before the war, his campaign against political corruption, especially over the Marconi share-dealing scandal in which Herbert Samuel and the Isaacs brothers Godfrey and Rufus were implicated, had brought him within the ambit of the anti-Semitic British controversialist Cecil Chesterton, brother of the novelist G. K. Chesterton.[21] Later, Locker-Lampson's attitudes towards the Jews and their place in the world was shaped by the Balfour Declaration published on 2 November 1917, which had stated it was the British Government's intention to support the creation of a Jewish homeland in Palestine, provided it did nothing to affect the rights of the existing, non-Jewish population, primarily the Arab peoples of the Muslim faith. Shortly after the Declaration the *Zionist Review* canvassed Locker-Lampson's opinion on Zionism. He replied: "I have great sympathy for the movement and entirely approve the policy expressed in Mr Balfour's letter. ... I can only hope that the Jewish People may be accorded every facility to return to Palestine and that every nation will cooperate in the achievement of this object."[22] That December while still a serving naval officer as well as an MP, he was invited to speak by the Brighton and Hove Zionist Society, which he was happy to do, though he does not seem to have made it. Underlying his support for the Balfour Declaration was a belief particularly strong among Conservative politicians that the establishment of a Jewish homeland in Palestine would set up a strong bulwark against the spread of Bolshevism into the power vacuum created by the collapse of the Ottoman Empire in the Middle East. There was also a belief among British politicians on the right and left that it would be better to divert eastern European Jewish immigrants away from Britain's shores to remote corners of the Empire in order to forestall anti-Semitic unrest in Britain and encourage the establishment of a British Empire-friendly 'White' race in those parts of the Empire without any dominant Anglo-Saxon rulers.[23] Before Palestine was settled on by the Zionists as the Jewish homeland serious thought had been given by British politicians to facilitating the settling of Jewish colonies in parts of the Empire, in Cyprus, Egypt and East Africa, for example, but these ideas had come to nothing.

From a personal point of view Locker-Lampson seems to have held none of the anti-Semitic prejudices then common to someone of his class and education. From youth he had had a number of Jewish friends, including Lady Constance Battersea, a Rothschild by birth, who was his near neighbour in north Norfolk until her death in 1931. In 1935 her biographer asked perceptively: "I wonder whether Commander Locker-Lampson's memory of Lady Battersea partly acted as an incentive to his generous and enthusiastic support of Professor Einstein and the Jewish refugees?"[24] At Cambridge the Jewish aristocrat Edwin Montagu was his co-editor of *Granta*. Later a prominent Liberal statesman, he would take an opposite stance to Locker-Lampson on the Balfour Declaration. It is also worth noting that he was an admirer of Benjamin Disraeli. His Blue Shirt organisation owed a great deal to the model established by the Primrose League, a grassroots Tory organisation named after Disraeli's favourite flower, which at its height before the First World War had more than 2 million members. It was friendships and enthusiasms such as these that British anti-Semites such as Arnold Leese would later highlight as accounting for his otherwise, to them, unaccountable pro-Semitic sympathies. Yet, despite Locker-Lampson's public enthusiasm for the cause of a Jewish Homeland and sympathy for the plight of Germany's persecuted Jews the shadow of anti-Semitism lurks worryingly in some of the political causes and military circumstances he was associated with in his highly eventful career up to this date. He had been made all too aware of the murderous consequences of anti-Semitism while serving on the Eastern Front during the war. During the retreat of the Russian Army in July 1917 he had witnessed a pogrom in Kozowa in Galicia (now part of Ukraine) carried out by Cossack troops after a rumour had spread that local Jews collaborating with the Austro-Hungarian Army were to blame for the shelling of the town's railway depot, which had destroyed a huge armaments dump. Locker-Lampson had, perhaps understandably, refused to allow his isolated and comparatively small British force to intervene to protect the town's Jewish population when asked for help by the area's Russian Army commandant. The extreme anti-Semitism found among all echelons of Russian society, from peasant to royal family, was notorious. In Petrograd, he had associated socially with malcontent Russian aristocrats and anti-Semitic politicians such as Prince Felix Yussupov and Vladimir Purishkevich, the principal conspirators in the assassination of Rasputin, among whose alleged 'crimes' was his defence of the civil rights of Russian Jews. Indeed, he would later claim under oath in a British court that he had been invited by them to take part in their murder plot but had declined, realising that while he had acted more like a privateer than a Royal Naval officer on many occasions on the Eastern Front, this was a step too far even for him.[25] Another hair-brained plot, this time to rescue the Tsar, was, however, planned and very nearly carried out by Locker-Lampson until the Tsar refused to escape to Britain without his family.[26]

While in Russia in 1917 Locker-Lampson had been closely associated with the *Morning Post*'s Russia correspondent, Victor Emile Marsden, whom he had first met in a restaurant where he was helping one of his armoured car officers order a meal in Russian. They had quickly become friends. Laid low by pneumonia following the February Revolution, he had recuperated in Marsden's Petrograd apartment. That June, he returned the favour by writing a preface for Marsden's projected book on the causes of the Russian Revolution, which was initially accepted for publication by British publisher Constable until its lawyers and the official censors deemed it unpublishable in wartime under the provisions of the Defence of the Realm Act. Following the 1917 October Revolution Marsden was arrested and imprisoned in the notorious Peter and Paul fortress in Petrograd and not released until late 1918, his freedom partly engineered by Arthur Ransome, Russia correspondent of the *Daily News* who went on to write the classic children's story *Swallows and Amazons*. On his return to Britain Marsden asked Locker-Lampson to write a revised preface to his proposed book on the Russian Revolution. In common with many intellectuals on the right, Marsden was convinced the Bolshevik Revolution was being controlled by an international Jewish conspiracy. In an article in the *Morning Post* published in December 1918, 'The Jews in Russia', he listed 447 Jews he alleged were leading officials in the Bolshevik regime, including Leon Trotsky ("real name Lev Bronstein") and Lenin, whom he categorised as an "Asiatic Jew". In his preface to the revised typescript for Marsden's Russian Revolution book written in 1919, Locker-Lampson helped reinforce this view, stating without corroborating evidence that the murderers of Captain Francis Cromie, the British naval attaché assassinated at the British Embassy in Petrograd in August 1918, had all been Jews.[27] This libel was repeated in the anonymous preface to Marsden's English translation of *The Protocols of the Learned Elders of Zion*, a notorious anti-Semitic Russian forgery first published in Britain in 1921 that purported to be the blueprint of a Jewish conspiracy to achieve world domination. His accusation echoed others then current, such as the allegation that the executioners of the Tsar and his family at Yekaterinburg in July 1918 had all been Jews. Fortunately for Locker-Lampson's subsequent reputation, Marsden's history of the Russian Revolution was not published and his death in 1920 obscured Locker-Lampson's part in this tawdry affair.

Throughout the post-war years until 1933 Locker-Lampson's hatred of Bolshevism seemed to have blinded his better judgement and led him down a path towards fascism. During this period his constant harrying of the Soviet Union in the press, in parliament and at public meetings gained him a reputation that some found patriotic and others ridiculed as the rantings of a crank. Before long his belligerent, anti-communist rhetoric attracted the attention of fledgling British fascist groups. From 1926 to 1931 members of Rotha Lintorn-Orman's British Fascisti regularly acted as stewards at his 'Rout the Reds' rallies, where they sometimes used strong-arm tactics to quell hecklers. Newspapers reported the novel spectacle of women stewards dressed in blue and silver uniforms strong-arming hecklers out of meetings and engaging in rough-house fighting. At some of his anti-communist meetings members of the British Fascisti or British Fascists as they were renamed in 1924 also provided an honour guard of Union Jacks as he and the other speakers marched to the podium: a scene that disturbingly prefigures the mass rallies of Oswald Mosley's black-shirted British Union of Fascists a few years later. It is also disturbing to note the taint of anti-Semitism in the language he used at these meetings, such as in a speech he made in Eastbourne in September 1926 in which he described the recent General Strike as: "planned, plotted and nourished by the shekels of the Soviet" and his repeated use of the phrase "scarlet shekels" at other anti-Bolshevik public meetings at this time, which echo the view of anti-Semites like Marsden that the Russian Revolution was a Jewish conspiracy.[28]

Between 1929 and 1932, Locker-Lampson experimented with the creation of his own right-wing uniformed populist movement—the Blue Shirts—picking up on the blue-shirted uniform of the British Fascisti. His own blue-shirted phalanx now provided the honour guard and security at his rallies, which continued to be marked by violence: "the meetings are rowdy. Uniformed fascists are there to support him. Probably that is why they are rowdy."[29] The movement was designed to appeal to disillusioned Conservatives, Protestant Unionists and Empire loyalists, many of them former servicemen, as well as to middle-class women who found the various other quasi-fascistic groups either too full of uncouth bully boys or paradoxically too left-wing, such as Oswald Mosley's New Party, Mosley having previously sat as a Labour MP from 1924 to 1931. Their political platform was based on support for the status quo: the primacy of the Church of England and the monarchy, White rule in the British Empire and overseas trade based on Imperial Preference (preferential tariffs that favoured imports from the British Empire's colonies). Above all the movement was anti-socialist and anti-communist. With his characteristic drive and sometimes arrogant self-confidence he threw too much of his own money into promoting the Blue Shirts, designing uniforms and insignia such as cuff links, ties, hat pins, lapel badges, ladies' brooches and car radiator badges, which were then produced for sale by mail order or at their rallies. He even issued a 78 rpm recording, 'March On', of what he hoped would be a rousing anthem to drown out the singing of the socialist anthem 'The Red

BUY OUR BLUE SHIRT BADGES

[Whoever purchases these loyalist emblems is pledged thereby to personal service and national discipline.]

		Price	Postage
1.	The music of our battle song "March On!" which will drown the "Red Flag"	1/-	½d.
2.	The record of "March On!" sung by Harold Williams. Reverse: "March On!" Dance Tune played by Savoy Band	3/-	6d.
3.	The record of "March On!" sung by Harold Williams. "Reverse: "Night Song in Camp" sung by Harold Williams	3/-	9d. for two
4.	The music of "Night Song in Camp"	3d.	½d.
5.	Cuff Links with loyalist motto: (see crest on cover). Silver or Gilt	2/6	1½d.
6.	Badges: Ladies or Gentlemen	6d.	1½d.
7.	Ladies' Hat Clips	2/6	1½d.
8.	Car Badges	5/6	Post free

APPLY:

"BLUE SHIRT" HEADQUARTERS,
St. Stephen's House,
Westminster, London, S.W. 1

Telegraphic Address: "Combative Parl, London."

Blue Shirt merchandise.

Flag'. The music, a brisk foxtrot, was based on music by Walter Collins used in the 1929 futuristic film *High Treason*, which was based on a screenplay by an eccentric former RNAS officer and far-right politician, Noel Pemberton Billing, about a fascistic European super state on the verge of war with a militaristic North American alliance. The lyrics, written by Locker-Lampson, included such deathless verse as:

Let others scream their Hymns of Hate,
And work to undermine the State.
Our heritage is builded high
On faith and love, they will not die.
March on! March strong!
The bugles of loyalty call.
Blue shirts be brave,
Fight on to save
Honour and freedom for all.[30]

Locker-Lampson recorded a spoken introduction to the song outlining his movement's aims, including to "tap into" the English people's "latent fund of loyalty" and instil a faith in the future of their destiny and their need for self-sacrifice in the cause of liberty and order. His surprisingly soft, almost mincing voice is not what one might expect, sounding more like a clergyman delivering a sermon than a potential British Führer.

The Blue Shirts as an inchoate British fascist movement lacking any real object of hate, other than the 'Reds', did not attract any significant levels of support beyond Locker-Lampson's loyal, mostly female, acolytes. Ultimately, it amounted to little more than a failed marketing exercise—'cocktail party fascists'—whose political stance, in the words of Arnold Leese, leader of the virulently anti-Semitic Imperial Fascist League, was no more than "Conservativism with knobs on". Left-

Locker-Lampson (left) electioneering with his Blue Shirts, 1931.

wing critics, such as the German socialist Wolf Zucker, were equally dismissive. In an essay published in 1931, he noted: "The Blue Shirts of that old reactionary Locker-Lampson, a kind of Salvation Army with added fanfare and jazz bands, are trying to recruit from the intellectual youth of England, twenty years after we on the Continent woke up to Nietzsche's dangerous philosophy."[31] Zucker had a point when one considers reports in the British press of events such as the "All Blue Gala" Locker-Lampson organised at the Chantilly Club in Trafalgar Square in July 1931. Ten young women led by his private secretary and a future guard of Einstein, Barbara Goodall, danced and performed cabaret skits in shiny blue pantomime uniforms, while waiters wearing blue bow ties offered guests blue-coloured cocktails, blue cigarettes and even bread rolls dyed blue. The guests included the exiled King George II of Greece and his brother and future king of Greece, Prince Paul, as well as Conservative Party grandee Lord Birkenhead and a scattering of wealthy industrialists, aristocrats, minor British film stars and society debutantes.[32]

Embarrassingly for Locker-Lampson, his Blue Shirt movement attracted unwelcome interest from the Nazi Party; a contact that came, bizarrely enough, via an intelligence-gathering operation organised by MI6. In the early 1930s a former RAF officer, Group Captain Frederick Winterbotham, was working for the Secret Service, gathering information on Germany's covert development of an air force, an arm of the military that had been specifically banned under the terms of the Versailles Treaty. To this end he sought to make contact with prominent members of the Nazi Party, who, while not yet in power were considered potential future leaders of Germany. Posing as a still serving RAF officer, Winterbotham invited the leading Nazi theorist and publisher Alfred Rosenberg to England. Rosenberg, a Baltic German, was a pseudo-intellectual whose hare-brained theories helped prop up the Nazis' racist ideology. He had been an early member of the National Socialists and had even briefly led the party in 1923 when Hitler was imprisoned following the failed Munich Beer Hall Putsch. The precise date of his first visit to London is uncertain. His first official visit occurred in 1933. Rosenberg, who had been the Nazis' spokesman on foreign affairs in the Reichstag before Hitler came to power in January 1933, had been appointed head of the *Aussenpolitisches Amt* (the German foreign affairs bureau) in April. During a visit to London in May he committed a diplomatic gaffe, possibly contrived by his arch rival Joachim von Ribbentrop, when he laid a wreath adorned with a swastika on the Cenotaph. Official permission had not been sought and the subsequent publicity caused a public outcry. Hostility to anything German was still very strong among large sections of British society.

By an odd coincidence given Locker-Lampson's Norfolk connections, the public's sense of outrage at Rosenberg's unauthorised wreath-laying was given public expression by James Edmonds Sears, then living in Aylsham in north Norfolk. On 11 May 1933, accompanied by two others, he drove slowly past the Cenotaph in Whitehall at the ceremonially significant time of 11 a.m. Stopping briefly, Sears leaned from the car and slashed the swastika off the wreath with a knife; returning later on foot he snatched it up and threw it into the car, which drove off without him. He then submitted himself for arrest to a policemen stationed outside the Home Office. At Cannon Row Police Station Sears was charged with theft and wilful damage of the £5 wreath, which was later recovered from the Thames by the River Police. While he was fined £2 for the damage, the more serious charge of theft was dismissed. Sears, aged 57, was a respectable pillar of the community and not the sort of person expected to go around vandalising wreaths. A former captain in the Royal Army Service Corps and veteran of the Great War having volunteered as a private in 1915 aged 40, he was chairman of the Aylsham branch of the British Legion, managing director of a Norfolk-based building construction firm and the Labour Party's prospective parliamentary candidate for London's South West St Pancras constituency. In court Captain Sears read a statement:

> What I did was as a deliberate protest against the desecration of our national war memorial by placing on it a wreath by Hitler's emissary, especially in view of the fact that the Hitler Government are contriving to do those very things and foster those very feelings which occurred in Germany before the War, for which many of our fellows suffered and lost their lives in the War.[33]

Rosenberg's wreath sparked off a rash of similar protests and counter-demonstrations. Later the same day a chaplet of tulips and gardenias bearing a white card with the inscription "This wreath is placed here in sincerity by a British citizen who resents the insult to our glorious dead", was placed on the spot where Rosenberg's wreath had been. The card was later torn off by a pro-Nazi supporter; an altercation ensued and further arrests were made.[34] Some days later Dr S. M. Marcus, a former US Army major and grandson of a prominent Chicago rabbi, placed a single lily on the Cenotaph with a card denouncing Hitler as a "murderous dictator". In September, following Einstein's flight to England, Dr Marcus, via Locker-Lampson, offered Einstein the protection of a bodyguard of one hundred medical students he had assembled from the University of London. These later became the nucleus of the large body of students who acted as stewards at the Royal Albert Hall meeting addressed by Einstein in October.[35]

While the May 1933 trip was the first and last visit to Britain that Rosenberg made as an official representative of the Nazis, a number of earlier private visits do seem to have been made. In Winterbotham's first published account of his adventures as an MI6 agent, *Secret and Personal*, he stated that Rosenberg visited London in November 1931. [36] In his retelling of the story in *The Nazi Connection*, the date of this visit had become the autumn of 1932.[37] Hitler had been interested in forging links with fledgling British fascist groups since the mid-1920s. Winterbotham's plan was to exploit Locker-Lampson's status as a Conservative MP and leader of the Blue Shirts, which Rosenberg believed was a full-blown fascist movement, in order to convince Hitler he was a man with useful contacts with influential, pro-German figures in the British establishment. Apparently unaware he was being used as a stalking horse, Locker-Lampson accepted Winterbotham's invitation to meet Rosenberg at the Savoy Hotel, where they discussed politics over an expensive lobster dinner. Rosenberg was suitably impressed and enthusiastically commended Locker-Lampson for his anti-Red campaigns. He returned to Germany pleased with the contacts he had made; so pleased in fact that he sent Locker-Lampson the gift of a gold-plated cigarette case, no doubt embellished with swastikas. To his credit he returned the gift, not wishing to be compromised by association with a foreign political party. If this happened towards the end of 1932, then there was only a matter of a few months between his partaking of lobsters with a man who had briefly led the Nazi Party and his acceptance of an invitation to a pro-Zionist dinner. His rapid *volte face* is partly explicable in the context of the rapid turn of events in Germany, though there were other factors both personal and political that need to be explored.

During March 1933 there was a growing sense of unease among British Jews at the worsening situation in Germany. On Sunday 26 March the British Board of Deputies discussed what steps should be taken to help their fellow Jews in Germany, debating then rejecting a call to boycott German goods, mindful of the need not to provoke the Nazis into even worse action at this time of heightened tension.[38] Few people at this stage could have imagined the horrors of the Holocaust to come, even though the first concentration camps were even then being prepared. Meanwhile, Locker-Lampson had been temporarily distracted from the plight of Germany's Jews by his old bugbear, the Soviet Union. The latest issue to exercise him concerned a group of six British subjects, employees of the engineering firm Metropolitan Vickers, who had been arrested in Russia on charges of spying, industrial sabotage and bribery. In the House of Commons he asked the Government to issue a warning to Britons in Russia against the dangers of "improper arrest" and renewed his call for the Prime Minister, Ramsay MacDonald, to impose an embargo on the importation of Soviet goods into Britain.

On Tuesday 28 March, the day Einstein arrived in Antwerp and Locker-Lampson wrote inviting him to stay in his London apartment, the British newspapers carried reports of the German Government's decree that Jewish shops and goods were to be boycotted by its 'Aryan' citizens. The pro-Nazi press noted this was an act of defence against attacks being made on Germany by Jews living abroad, clearly alluding to Einstein's recent anti-Nazi statements in the United States. In the British press it was reported that Jewish leaders in Germany were being coerced by Göring and Goebbels into urging their fellow Jews abroad to desist from making any anti-Nazi statements under threat of unleashing a general pogrom. Behind the scenes the British Foreign Office agreed to the German Government's offer to withdraw the boycott if leading Jews in Britain and the United States were to make public announcements that reports of atrocities perpetrated against the Jews in Germany were false. The former Foreign Secretary, Sir Rufus Isaacs, who had been one of those targeted by anti-Semitic slurs when he was Attorney General during the Marconi share-dealing scandal before the war, agreed to do so on behalf of British Jewry.[39] Later that day, spurred on by the mounting crisis, a Labour MP asked the Foreign Secretary, Sir John Simon, a question similar to Locker-Lampson's question of the previous day concerning the safety of British citizens in the USSR, only this time concerning the safety of British Jews in Germany. After being reassured that there was no cause for alarm, the House returned to its main business, debating proposals for reform of the governance of India. Whatever might be happening elsewhere in the world, Britain still had an Empire to run.

On 30 March Locker-Lampson made his first speech in the House on the situation in Germany, asking Sir John Simon to bring the question of Jewish nationality and the persecution of the Jews in Germany before the next meeting of the Council of the League of Nations. Sir John replied that there was nothing in the Covenant of the League that would allow the British Government to raise such a question. Strictly speaking he was correct as the League was set up to resolve international disputes, not to debate the internal policy of nation states towards their own citizens. Resort to the League of Nations would, in any case have been futile. Six months later Hitler stage-managed Germany's withdrawal from the League, ostensibly over France's refusal to disarm. Nevertheless, at the time it appeared that morally, the British Government was washing its hands of the whole matter, secretly fearful of the large number of refugees that might come to Britain. That evening an estimated three thousand people filled the Kingsway Hall in London to protest against acts of "ferocity and violence committed by the Hitler Government in Germany", passing a resolution appealing to the British Government to grant the right of asylum to "the victims of these unparalleled atrocities and to grant facilities to those refugees desirous of entering Palestine".[40] The principal speaker, Dr Moses Gaster, Chief Rabbi and vice-president of the English Zionist Federation, said: "Germans must learn that the Jews who did so much for their progress were one of its arteries which could not be cut without bleeding for it." Prophetic words. It was the expulsion of intellectuals like Einstein and thousands of other Jewish men and women of talent and learning —'Hitler's gift'—which would greatly help hand victory to the Allies in the Second World War. Twenty-six Nobel Prize-winning scientists, for example, fled German and Italian anti-Semitic persecution before 1940, mostly to the USA.[41]

Einstein, having renounced his German citizenship and resigned from the Prussian Academy of Science, had caught the Nazis off-guard. They were particularly incensed that he had voluntarily distanced himself from the Third Reich before they had had a chance to expel him themselves. In revenge they confiscated his savings account and personal property from his Berlin apartment, including his beloved violin, as well as seizing his holiday home and sailing boat in Caputh. Fortunately, not all was lost; his elder step-daughter Ilse and her husband, Einstein's first biographer, Rudolf Kayser, had for some time been secretly smuggling his personal and academic papers from his Berlin apartment into the French Embassy, from where they were sent to Paris by diplomatic bag. Shortly afterwards the apartment was sealed by the Gestapo. Ilse then fled to Paris. Meanwhile, Einstein's younger step-daughter, Margot, had already moved to Paris with her husband, the Russian-born journalist Dimitri Marianoff.

Einstein's devoted secretary, Helen Dukas, and his scientific assistant, Dr Walther Mayer, then quietly slipped over the border and joined Einstein in Belgium. His sister Maja was, for the time being, safely in Italy, while his former wife Mileva and younger son Eduard remained in Switzerland. On 10 May as the last vestiges of opposition in Germany, the trade unions and the Social Democrat Party, were suppressed, a bonfire was lit in Berlin on which Einstein's publications along with thousands of other books were burned to the jeers of the mob.

For a refugee Einstein was in the fortunate position of having a number of options for where to settle. He could, if he wished, have returned to Switzerland, although it was probably rather too close to Germany for comfort. Moreover, with his former wife Mileva living in Zurich, it is unlikely Elsa would have been keen to move there. There were offers, all of which he had provisionally accepted, to give a series of lectures in Britain, France and Spain, but the offers had come with strings attached, trying to bind him to accept a professorship that would bring renown to the university which won him but would, he feared, place unwanted administrative burdens on him personally. In addition, Locker-Lampson had offered him his London home free of charge for a year, Professor Lindemann was keen to get him to Oxford University and Dr Weizmann was urging him to join the staff at the Hebrew University in Jerusalem. Although he was a committed Zionist Einstein refused to contemplate going to Palestine on the grounds that he believed the Hebrew University there was at this time being badly managed. In any case there was no need to make his mind up where to settle until the following year. Abraham Flexner, the director of the Institute of Advanced Study in Princeton, had invited him to take up a temporary post in October, which he had every intention of accepting, as long as he could persuade them to accept his condition that they employ his mathematical assistant Dr Walther Mayer, who being a Jew would not have been able to find another job commensurate with his abilities in Germany. Until then he decided to stay put in Le Coq-sur-Mer. Here, among the sand dunes, while the world went mad about him, he and Mayer resumed work on the Unified Field Theory, one of the most intractable problems in physics.

Notes

1 *The Times*, letter, 2 September 1914; *Eastern Daily Press*, letter, 4 November 1914.

2 Vallentin, *Einstein*, p.155.

3 *The Times*, 29 March 1933.

4 See Birkenhead, *The Prof in Two Worlds*, pp.23–4; Harrod, *The Prof*, pp.107–111 and Stevens, *The Dispossessed*, pp.126 & 226.

5 Albert Einstein Archives, The Hebrew University of Jerusalem: AEA 50-804.
6 Harrod, The Prof, p.20; Robinson, Einstein on the Run, pp.198–9.
7 Brown University Library, Hay Manuscripts: Ms.52.184.
8 Library of Congress Manuscript Division, Washington, DC: AC 9426.
9 Furness, 'The Moral Imperative of Exile', pp.71&74–5.
10 Fölsing, Albert Einstein, p.486.
11 Nathan and Norden, Einstein on Peace, p.45.
12 Ibid., p.652.
13 Ibid. 5.
14 Birmingham Daily Gazette, 6 April 1933.
15 Ibid. 2, p.163.
16 www.youtube.com/watch?v=lGw8zFSKp2A
17 Steve Locker-Lampson, Nothing to Offer But Blood, ch.18 passim.
18 Eastern Daily Press, 3 March 1933.
19 The Times, 3 March 1933.
20 Collins, 'Clear out the Reds!'
21 Donaldson, The Marconi Scandal.
22 Oliver Locker-Lampson Papers, Norfolk Record Office: OLL 2311.
23 Defries, Conservative Party Attitudes to Jews, pp.43–5.
24 Cohen, Lady de Rothschild and Her Daughters, p.218.
25 Napley, Rasputin in Hollywood.
26 Ibid. 17, pp. 198–200.
27 Ibid. 22: OLL 1727.
28 Eastbourne Chronicle, 2 October 1926.
29 Manchester Guardian, 17 May 1929.
30 From the published sheet music, courtesy Steve Locker-Lampson.
31 Zucker, 'Weidersehen mit England'.
32 Daily Mirror, 9 July 1931.
33 The Times, 12 May 1933.
34 Ibid.
35 Chicago Daily Tribune, 12 September 1933.
36 Winterbotham, Secret and Personal, pp.24–9.
37 Winterbotham, The Nazi Connection, pp.24–35.
38 The Times, 27 March 1933.
39 Woodward, Documents on British Foreign Policy, pp.14 and 19.
40 The Times, 31 March 1933.
41 Medawar and Pyke, Hitler's Gift, App. I.

Homeless on Shakespeare Avenue

ON April Fool's Day 1933 as Albert and Elsa settled in at 5 Shakespearelaan, Le Coq-sur-Mer, Oliver Locker-Lampson turned from harrying his old foe, the Soviet Union, to express his frank disappointment at Hitler's treatment of Germany's Jewish citizens. Deploying his well-honed flair for creating headline-grabbing attention he published an open letter to Hitler in *The Times*. He began by admitting he had long admired him:

> As a member of Parliament and former officer who has always and openly stood for Germany's claims to military equality and territorial revision and who has been for years your sincere admirer I take the liberty of calling your attention to the fact that the decision to discriminate against the German Jews has had a most damaging effect upon good feeling for Germany which was growing stronger and which culminated on your accession to power. We hoped to see Germany strengthened under your leadership. This action against the Jews is making the work of myself and other friends of Germany almost impossible.
>
> Forgive me, Chancellor, for these frank words of an Englishman who has often cheered you in your meetings in Germany.[1]

A few days later the British press announced that a non-party committee of MPs and peers had been set up in parliament to watch actions being taken against Jews in Germany. Inevitably, Locker-Lampson was appointed its secretary.

Locker-Lampson's only previous public utterance on Hitler had been somewhat eccentric. In September 1930 an article—'Adolf Hitler as I know him'—had appeared under his name in the *Daily Mirror*, then owned by Lord Rothermere who also owned the *Daily Mail* and was using both papers to support Hitler. In it he wrote that he had been in Germany shortly after the failed Munich Putsch of November 1923, following which Hitler had been tried for treason and imprisoned. While there he had met some British officers, former prisoners of war, who told him they had met Hitler during the war while he was recuperating in a military hospital near their POW camp. Hitler had watched British soldiers playing cricket and had asked them for the book of rules for this baffling game, which he wished to 'Teutonise' into a military training exercise; for example, leg pads and batting gloves were to be dispensed with as "unmanly and un-German". He had even made up a German team and played a match against the British POWs. The story was a complete fabrication, though whether Locker-Lampson originated it isn't known. Hitler was hospitalised in Germany twice during the First World War, at Beelitz in 1916, where he was treated for a shrapnel wound to his left thigh, and at Pasewalk in 1918, where he was treated for either mustard-gas or shell-shock induced temporary blindness and muteness, injuries which presumably would have prevented him from participating in any field sport, especially as his stays in hospital occurred in October and November. A possible explanation for the story is a photograph of Hitler and twelve other wounded German soldiers posed in white hospital tunics and trousers, looking vaguely like a cricket team. Apart from the nonsense about a cricket-playing Hitler, the article is full of his admiration for the charisma and political savvy of Germany's "legendary hero". It was a very tall tale and one that risked exposing Locker-Lampson to ridicule, were it not that cricket was held in almost religious veneration by many Englishmen of this period as the fountainhead of fair play and gentlemanly conduct; a reputation the infamous 'Bodyline' Ashes Test series in Australia in 1932–3 would call into question.

Locker-Lampson's post-war stance on Germany had not always been as sympathetic as he now made it out to have been. In the years immediately following the war it would have been political suicide to make such views known. In keeping with the public mood for revenge, he had campaigned for re-election to parliament in December 1918 on a manifesto that included the imposition of harsh reparations on Germany. He won with a majority of over four thousand. While his aim in publishing an open letter to Hitler now was clearly to make himself look like a friend offering well-meant advice to an erring ally, the intended audience of the letter was clearly not Hitler but British public opinion. In the fifteen years since the end of the war attitudes towards Germany had begun to shift from a desire for vengeance to a growing acceptance the terms of the Treaty of Versailles had been too harsh and ultimately counter-productive. German reparation payments were formally suspended in 1932. Among many British people, especially on the right, there was a grudging if somewhat apprehensive appreciation of Hitler, the 'gallant corporal' who had restored Germany's pride and unity. Churchill felt ambivalent towards Hitler right up to the Munich crisis of 1938, fearful of the spectre of aggressive militarism rising again in Central Europe but keen to see a strong, united Germany as a bulwark against the spread of communism from the East. As an outspoken opponent of the Soviet Union, it isn't surprising Locker-Lampson admired the same thing in Hitler; it is, however, disturbing to learn he had often cheered Hitler at his meetings. Although Hitler had briefly played down the anti-Semitism in his speeches and writings after the Munich Putsch debacle, concentrating his ire instead on the communists, as a fluent German speaker he could not have failed to understand the extreme anti-Semitism that ran through Hitler's ideology. It is difficult to reconcile this letter with the one he had written to Einstein only a few days earlier, outraged at the wrongs he and his fellow Jews were suffering in Germany. It must be supposed Einstein had no knowledge of it.

On 7 April Locker-Lampson spoke at a public meeting in Birmingham Town Hall alongside his old chief, Austen (now Sir Austen) Chamberlain. Although Sir Austen's political star had begun to dim he remained a loyal acolyte—for now. Birmingham was the Chamberlain family's political heartland and he had held the Handsworth seat there since 1921. In his speech Sir Austen, a former Foreign Secretary and a winner of the Nobel Prize for Peace, surveyed the state of foreign affairs and warned that Britain and other nations would not tolerate Hitler's treatment of the Jews. A prediction that would prove to be woefully mistaken. As Lord Birkenhead said of him: "he always played the game and always lost it". A year later Locker-Lampson would transfer to the team of a different prophet in the wilderness, Winston Churchill, a politician with a much more ruthless will to win. Locker-Lampson spoke next, concentrating on the plight of Germany's Jews, for which he received prolonged applause. According to Leo Amery, another Birmingham-based Conservative MP present at the meeting, the audience's enthusiastic response was not because of any Jewish sympathies; after all, he reasoned, there were not many Jews in Birmingham but because Locker-Lampson had called on the sense of fair play supposed to be inherent in the soul of every true Englishman.[2] In fact there was a sizeable and established Jewish population in Birmingham, which at this date maintained three synagogues. It was not widely known that Amery's mother was of Jewish descent, a fact he sought to conceal throughout his public life. In 1945 his elder son John Amery was executed as a traitor, having supported the Nazis during the war, even setting up a unit of the *Waffen* SS known as the British *Freikorps* recruited from British POW camps. Amery's belief that the warm reception for Locker-Lampson's speech was due to the audience's belief in 'fair play' is indicative of Conservative thinking on German fascism at this time. While its anti-Semitism was misguided, given the right encouragement by their more civilised British cousins and a more benign economic climate it was rectifiable. It was the same sentiment of fair play Locker-Lampson had himself used when trying to persuade Einstein to come to England as his guest only a week earlier and would evoke again in July when introducing a Private Members Bill to extended opportunities for British citizenship to Jews living outside the British Empire, when he would describe the Nazi's treatment of Jews in Germany as "caddish and un-English".

He had used that phrase before. For Locker-Lampson the essential Englishness of a sense of decency and fair play, especially when helping the powerless, cannot be over-stated. He had invoked the same high-minded ideals four years earlier in defence of another persecuted minority—Britain's Roma or gypsy people. In April 1929 several gypsies were summoned to appear at Epsom Police Court for driving their caravans onto Epsom Down in contravention of an order issue by the Epsom Grand Stand Association, a group of wealthy landowners and horse breeders. Gypsies had probably been a traditional feature of the Epsom Derby for as long as horses had been raced there. The vested interests of the course, however, wanted their inconvenient presence expunged. In the press, Locker-Lampson described this as "caddish and un-English", and announced he had appointed himself their champion because they were "homeless and hunted" and unable to defend themselves.[3] His campaign was supported by Lady Eleanor Smith, a student of Romany lore who later wrote a series of melodramatic novels based on gypsy life and the circus some of which were turned into films. The daughter of Locker-Lampson's old political mentor, Lord Birkenhead, she was a close friend of his first wife Bianca and later dedicated her first novel *Red Wagon* to her after her sudden death at Christmas 1929.

In the coming struggle with totalitarianism a call for fair play would not be enough. Two days after his Birmingham speech Locker-Lampson addressed a meeting of the Association of Jewish Friendly Societies at the New Scala Theatre in London. Here he argued Jews had been among those opposing the humiliation of Germany after the war; a point he was to make again when introducing his Jewish Citizenship Bill in the House of Commons in July. The following day he joined Churchill to protest in the House at the London Metropolitan Police Commissioner's decision to remove posters from the streets calling for a retaliatory boycott of German goods following the Nazis' imposition of a state boycott of Jewish goods and shops. Meanwhile, he had not forgotten his mission to get Einstein over to England under his personal protection. At the end of April Elsa received a letter from him that was to cause her husband some embarrassment. Almost a month had now passed since Locker-Lampson had offered Einstein free use of his London apartment. He now wrote to Elsa that their mutual friend Professor Yahuda had passed on her request he find them: "a small house on the coast from the start of July until possibly October, in a quiet spot not too distant from London".[4] He was happy to oblige but wondered just how far from London they wished the cottage to be situated, joking that "not too distant", relatively speaking, probably meant something different in England than it did in Switzerland or Germany. He looked forward to meeting them when they came to Oxford in June and asked that they let him know as soon as they arrived so they could meet and discuss arrangements. It is interesting to speculate how he knew of their planned visit. Had perhaps Professor Lindemann kept him informed? Einstein replied at once. He regretted Yahuda had put him to so much trouble in vain. He had certainly not authorised him to make such a request, indeed he had no intention of spending the summer in England. He suspected Yahuda wished to have him in close proximity for reasons of his own. Just what they might be he did not say, but clues can be gathered from the subsequent correspondence exchanged between Einstein, Locker-Lampson and Yahuda later that summer.

Abraham Shalom Yahuda was an eminent Jewish scholar and linguist. He had been a delegate at the first Zionist Congress in Bern in 1897 and in 1915 had been appointed professor of Rabbinical Studies at the University of Madrid, thought to be the first Jew to hold a university chair in Spain since the expulsion of the Jews in 1492. Two days after Einstein's arrival in Belgium he published a letter in *The Times* under the heading 'Einstein and Hitlerites'.[5] In it he pointed out that far from being a traitor to Germany Einstein had actually done much to enhance Germany's position in the world after the war. He recalled attending Einstein's lecture at King's College London in 1921, when he had courageously chosen to speak in German (Einstein's English at this period was adequate though he preferred to use German when talking in public on purely scientific matters) at a time when the war was still fresh in people's minds and all things German were still anathema to many Britons. A fortnight after Einstein's arrival in Belgium Yahuda personally brought him the offer of a Chair in physics at the University of Madrid, to commence the following spring. Einstein initially welcomed the offer but later turned it down after hearing of anti-Semitic attacks on him in ultra-conservative Spanish newspapers. It was a wise decision in retrospect, given the civil war that broke out in Spain three years later. Despite his having accepted the Chair only provisionally, on 11 April *The Times* reported Einstein had formally accepted the position, causing him further embarrassment.

When Einstein eventually declined the Madrid chair, Yahuda seems to have decided to bide his time and concentrate on arranging for him to acquire British citizenship with the minimum of publicity while being closely guarded somewhere in England, where he might better control his movements and his visitors. In this enterprise he may have recruited Locker-Lampson, who had long-standing contacts with members of the Zionist movement in Britain dating back to his support for the Balfour Declaration in 1917. Although a leading Zionist, Yahuda was anxious to prevent Einstein accepting Weizmann's offer of a chair at the Hebrew University in Jerusalem. Yahuda was a vocal opponent of what he saw as Weizmann's more militant form of Zionism, which he believed was too hostile towards the indigenous Arab population in Palestine. Yahuda may also have had personal as well as professional reasons for holding a poor opinion of the Hebrew University, piqued perhaps it had turned down his application for a professorship.[6]

At the beginning of May Locker-Lampson went to Sennen near Land's End for a short break from the political hurly-burly at Westminster. Before leaving he wrote a brief note to one of his secretaries, Barbara Goodall, whom he would later marry. In their private language of love she was his "Barbarossa" (she had light auburn hair), his "little goatherd & playmate" (an allusion to the Roughton camp with its small flock of nanny goats to supply him with milk) and he "the Old Campaigner".[7] This was a side of him few saw: affectionate, playful and full of a longing for intimacy. Their burgeoning romance was hampered in his eyes by their age difference—he in his early fifties, she in her early twenties. Although in love and lonely since the sudden death of his young wife Bianca three years earlier, he felt Barbara should find a husband of her own age and encouraged her to do so. At that period, public knowledge of a romantic relationship between them, though both were unmarried, would have damaged his political career and her reputation, so they were treading on eggshells all the time. On 15 May the *Western Morning News* reported Einstein may be coming to stay with Locker-Lampson in Cornwall, mentioning his close association with Sennen.[8] This was followed up by a longer article in *The Cornishman*, which reported a rumour Einstein was to settle in Cornwall, describing his friend Commander Locker-Lampson as: "a brilliant and versatile man, distinguished in the realms of politics, journalism and sport".[9] There can be little doubt of the source of the stories—Locker-Lampson himself.

As he continued to plot to bring Einstein to England, Einstein himself was beginning to adapt to his enforced exile in Belgium. He had first visited the country in 1911 to attend the First Solvay Conference in Brussels and more recently in 1927 to attend the Fifth Solvay Conference, which is said to have been the greatest gathering of human brain power in the history of humanity. It seems to have been during this visit the Belgian royal family first cultivated his friendship, especially Queen Elisabeth, who shared his love of music making and was, moreover, like him a southern German by birth. He had visited the royal couple again in 1930, writing to Elsa about how he had played in string quartets and trios with the Queen at the palace and afterwards dined with the royal couple on a simple vegetarian meal of potatoes, spinach and hard-boiled eggs.[10] They had met most recently in 1932 when Einstein attended a planning meeting in Brussels for the Seventh Solvay Conference scheduled for October 1933. Such was the informal closeness of their friendship Queen Elisabeth one day paid an unannounced call to the Villa Savoyarde, frightening an old carpenter working in the house, who hid in the lavatory until she had gone.[11]

Postcard of the Villa Savoyarde and La Maisonnette, Le Coq-sur-Mer.

"I am sitting here in most comfortable exile with Professor Mayer", is how Einstein began a letter to Lindemann in Oxford, dated 1 May 1933, about his planned visit to Britain in June.[12] However, the idyll of sunbathing and undisturbed work at Le Coq-sur-Mer in the company of his mathematical assistant was not to last long. He soon received news from Mileva in Switzerland that the mental health of Tete had deteriorated dramatically. After completing a series of lectures in Brussels Einstein travelled to Zurich to see his son for what would prove to be the last time. Then, at the end of May, he travelled directly from Switzerland to Britain in order to give a series of lectures. Arriving in Oxford he wrote to a friend, the physicist Max Born, about the desperate situation for Jewish scholars in Germany. His low opinion of Germans had now gone lower than he could ever have imagined. He confessed he had wanted personally to create a "university of exiles" but that was now impossible as all of his money had been taken away from him by the Nazis. In fact not all his savings had been lost as fortunately he had wisely deposited his foreign earnings from academic posts, lectures and book royalties in a savings account outside of Germany. Nevertheless, the loss of his German savings was a serious blow.

On 1 June he was given a warm welcome by the audience assembled for Lord Rutherford's Boyle Memorial Lecture, before which he gave a short speech. Over the next three weeks he gave three public lectures on theoretical physics, two in Oxford and one in Glasgow, his only recorded visit to Scotland, where he went to receive an honorary doctorate. His friend and host in Belgium, Professor De Groodt, had lectured in medicine and pathology at Glasgow University while a refugee during the war, and a former colleague of De Groodt's, the eminent surgeon Professor Archibald Young, was Einstein's host on this visit. On arriving at Glasgow railway station Einstein got caught up and disorientated by a large crowd, which he assumed was there to meet him but had in fact come to glimpse the American actress Thelma Todd, chiefly remembered today as a *femme fatale* in Marx Brothers' films. When informed what had happened Miss Todd is said to have remarked: "I wish I'd known, I'd have lent Einstein some of my crowd", a riposte worthy of Groucho himself. She was to meet a sad end a few years later, found gassed in the back of her car. Although the official verdict on her death was that it was accidental, rumours persisted she was murdered because of her ex-husband's connections with the Mafia. Just at the moment Einstein had his own mob to worry about.

On his return to Belgium Einstein found himself in trouble again, this time from his erstwhile colleagues in the pacifist movement over his change of mind on the question of compulsory military service. While he had been lecturing in Britain a controversy had blown up in Belgium concerning two young conscientious objectors who had been imprisoned, awaiting trial, for refusing to be conscripted into the Belgian Army. Many leading pacifists now called on Einstein to speak on their behalf, which presented him with a dilemma. For some time now, following Hitler's coming to power, he had been struggling with his belief in absolute pacifism, which included the doctrine all military forces should be abolished, even defensive ones. He now believed the refusal of a country to defend itself against the sort of aggressive expansionism inherent in Nazism was tantamount to national suicide. Nevertheless, he still found the state's right to force its citizens to bear arms repugnant. As a guest in a foreign country he felt reluctant to intervene in such a politically sensitive matter and yet feared his silence would look as though his pacifist idealism had been bought off by the Belgian state with the security it was providing him.

As he pondered how to resolve the problem he received a coded message from the Royal Castle at Laeken that "the husband of the second fiddler" wished to speak with him on an urgent matter. As an accomplished violinist he had often played chamber music with Queen Elisabeth, so the person meant was clearly King Albert. News that attempts were being made to seek Einstein's support for the two conscientious objectors seems to have reached the Belgian secret intelligence service, who were probably monitoring his correspondence at Le Coq-sur-Mer. The Belgian Government was worried Einstein's presence in their country might stir up anti-Belgian feelings in Germany and become the focus for political action by disaffected right-wing groupings within its own borders such as the pan-Flemish fascist movement, *Verdinaso*, and the mainly French-speaking Walloon Catholic Party, out of which Léon Degrelle's pro-Nazi Rexist Party later developed. Both parties, while hating each other along cultural and religious lines, were equally anti-Semitic.

Einstein met King Albert at Laeken in early July and wrote to the King on the 14th, agreeing he would not intervene in the matter of the conscientious objectors. The Belgian Army, he accepted, was not an aggressive force but purely defensive in a time when such a force was essential for national security. Although it would be wrong of him as a guest in the country to intervene, he suggested conscientious objectors should be allowed to perform their national service in useful, non-military work, such as in hospitals; a pre-echo of his remarks about young scientists being employed as lighthouse keepers in his Royal Albert Hall speech later that year. Ten days later the king replied that he welcomed Einstein's attitude towards Belgium's defensive policy and was delighted so distinguished a man had chosen to live in his country. Crisis adverted, for now.

On 20 July, seemingly out of the blue, Locker-Lampson wrote to Lindemann: "Someone has seen Einstein and is bringing him to England and has asked me to put him up at my cottage this weekend."[13] Somehow, after months of trying, it appears he had at last persuaded Einstein to visit him in Britain. It is a mystery who exactly this "someone" was. However, given Einstein had become a political liability in Belgium over the compulsory military service controversy and Locker-

Lampson and Einstein were both friends of King Albert, it doesn't seem too far-fetched to suggest it was the King himself, presumably acting on the advice of the Belgian Government. Having resisted such a trip for anything other than professional, scientific purposes, Einstein seems now to have agreed fairly rapidly it would be a good idea if he went over to England for a while. Locker-Lampson, King Albert's confidential holiday companion, skiing-instructor and the gallant holder of the Belgian Order of Leopold, seemed ideally suited to be his host on this occasion. In his unfinished memoirs Locker-Lampson acknowledged the King's role in securing Einstein's safety, writing he had received a letter from the King "who feared that Professor Einstein's existence in Flanders might embroil him with Germany and lead to the kidnapping of this eminent man".[14]

On Friday 21 July, Einstein took the coastal tram from Le Coq-sur-Mer to Ostend and boarded the ferry for Dover. Once in England he took the train to London, where Locker-Lampson and his sister Dorothy Delmar-Morgan met him at Victoria Station. They then drove down to Esher in Surrey where Locker-Lampson had rented a small farmhouse for the summer. Winterdown Cottage sat in a secluded wooded spot within a large country estate. The set-up here would prove to be a dress rehearsal for the camp in Roughton in September. Locker-Lampson had installed a small thatched wooden hut in the garden for Einstein's use, complete with a piano, just as he was to do at Roughton, and just as was to happen there, the press were incongruously invited to visit the 'secret' retreat. A photograph of Locker-Lampson and Einstein, looking suitably sun-tanned and relaxed, appeared in the *Daily Mirror* and *Daily Herald*. Another report, in the *Belfast Telegraph*, helpfully noted: "the professor eats very little, does not like to attend social dinners and luncheons, and finds it difficult to work after large meals".[15] There had clearly been a great deal of planning involved in this set up, which suggests Locker-Lampson entertained hopes Einstein's stay would last longer than the mere week he planned to spend in England before returning to Belgium or he would get him back there for a longer stay later in the year.

The next day they motored down to Chartwell, Churchill's home in Kent, where Einstein again had his photograph taken with Churchill in the garden, still wearing his by now rather crumpled white linen suit, while Churchill wore his famous overalls and a panama hat, having no doubt just broken off from a spot of bricklaying, one of his favourite hobbies, to greet his guests. Their chief topic of conversation was the growing military menace posed by covert and by now blatantly overt German re-armament. Later that day Einstein wrote to Elsa that Churchill was "an eminently clever man, and I fully realized these people have made good preparations and will act resolutely soon".[16] It seems likely Professor Lindemann was present at this meeting and also Brendan Bracken,

Churchill and Einstein at Chartwell, 21 July 1933, by unknown photographer.

though neither they nor Einstein signed the visitors' book for some reason. In his letter to Lindemann written on 20 July Locker-Lampson had said he was bringing Einstein to "Winston's on Saturday. I do hope you are likely to be there."[17] In his account of these years, *The Gathering Storm*, Churchill wrote that he and Lindemann received several eminent visitors from Germany who "poured out their hearts in their bitter distress". In a letter dated 7 May 1933 Einstein had warned Lindemann the Nazis were "collecting war materials and in particular aeroplanes in a great hurry. If they are given another year or two the world will have another fine experience at the hands of the Germans."[18]

During his stay in England that July Einstein was also taken by Locker-Lampson to visit his old political chief Sir Austen Chamberlain and the former Prime Minister David Lloyd George. No record of Einstein's meeting with Sir Austen on this occasion has come to light. According to his published diary letters he was staying at his summer retreat at Lytchett Heath near Poole all that week, so presumably this is where they met. Locker-Lampson was on less sure ground in calling on Lloyd George. Before the war he had been a thorn in his side with his constant harrying of the Liberal Government over its alleged involvement in the Marconi share-dealing scandal and the sale of honours. Despite this they seem to have met on easy terms socially after the war. The reason for this rapprochement was probably that Locker-Lampson through his allegiance to Austen Chamberlain was a supporter of Lloyd George's Coalition Government. In April 1920 Locker-Lampson had been a house guest at the Villa Haslihorn, King Albert's private chalet in Lucerne, which he had made available for Lloyd George's use. There, Lloyd George had lived up to his reputation as the Welsh mountain goat by leading his guests to the top of a nearby hill before breakfast. After the Coalition Government fell in 1922 Locker-Lampson continued to cultivate Lloyd George's acquaintance, particularly through his personal secretary and mistress, Frances Stevenson. Locker-Lampson frequently worked his charm on her when he needed a favour from the great man, and was usually successful.

An incident during Einstein's visit to Lloyd George's home at Churt near the Surrey—Hampshire border would be observed by Locker-Lampson and used to make a telling point in the House of Commons two days later. According to telegrams preserved in the House of Lords Library, Locker-Lampson asked Lloyd George if he could bring Einstein to lunch or dinner on Monday 24 July. Dinner was offered and Locker-Lampson telegrammed to confirm the arrangements: he and his unnamed "friend" would travel down by train to Guildford in the evening, where, it seems, they were to be met by Lloyd George and his driver. Locker-Lampson had politely informed Lloyd George "we shall not be dressed". Einstein had an aversion to formal attire and had in any case probably come over with just the clothes he wore throughout his stay: a light-coloured linen suit, appropriate for the unusually hot weather England was experiencing that July.[19]

Before dinner Lloyd George would no doubt have given Einstein a guided tour of his extensive house and gardens, as he did for most of his visitors, conducting it at his normal break-neck speed. The tour usually concluded in front of two enormous glass-fronted cabinets stuffed full of memorial caskets and medallions given to him by various allied countries and institutions for his war work. These he would show to his visitors, remarking with sardonic irony: "I have been honoured for killing my fellow man".[20] This may have been the first time the two men had met. An earlier opportunity, during Einstein's first visit to England in 1921, had been missed when Lloyd George, perhaps reluctant to be seen associating with a German socially so soon after the war, declined an invitation from Lord Haldane to meet him, though oddly according to the *New York Times*' report of the visit they did in fact meet. Before leaving Churt, Einstein signed the visitors' book. In the column for his address he wrote in German *Ohne*, meaning 'without one'. That same day, Locker-Lampson took steps to try to ensure Einstein's assistant, Dr Mayer, would not be homeless too, writing to Lord Moynihan, president of the Royal College of Surgeons and a prominent figure in the Academic Assistance Council (AAC), recommending 'Professor Myer', as he called him, for a British university post. Moynihan passed the request on J. H. Jones, professor of economics at Leeds University and a member of the Leeds Academic Assistance Committee, where it presumably got lost in the bureaucracy. Walther Mayer would travel to the United States with Einstein in October.

Wednesday was traditionally the day on which members of parliament might introduce a Private Member's Bill under the Ten Minute Rule. Such Bills had very little chance of becoming law unless backed by the government, and as such were primarily regarded as a means of airing a topic on which an MP felt strongly. As MPs were allowed so short a time to speak, powers of oratory had to be brought to play to interest the few MPs who stayed in the House of Commons chamber to hear the speech and any newspaper reporters still in the House. Locker-Lampson was a past master at this sort of thing and supplemented his rhetorical skills with expertise in amateur dramatics, stage managing the occasion to perfection. On the afternoon of 26 July Locker-Lampson strategically placed Einstein in the Visitors' Gallery in view of the assembled MPs and gentlemen of the press. He wore the same light-weight summer suit he had worn throughout his visit, its whiteness and his shock of sun-bleached grey hair helping to draw attention to him as he sat in the diffused light of the Visitors' Under Gallery. The assembled reporters seemed mesmerised by his presence and particularly fascinated by his suit, though none could agree on its material. The *Daily Express* described him "coolly dressed in tussore", while the *Manchester Guardian* described it as "light shantung" and the *Daily Telegraph*, more prosaically, as "a white linen suit". It was the hottest day of the year so far, with temperatures in London reaching a sweltering 90° F (32.2° C), which was excessively warm for England even at the height of summer. At 4.05 p.m., amid the airless, stiflingly oppressive heat of the House of Commons chamber and with a hint of electricity in the atmosphere, Locker-Lampson rose from his seat and addressed the Speaker of the House. Beginning with the customary words on these occasions: "I beg to move that leave be given to bring in a Bill", going on to outline his proposal for an Act of Parliament that would "promote and extend opportunities of citizenship for Jews resident outside the British Empire".

Locker-Lampson guiding Einstein into the Houses of Parliament, 26 July 1933.

Locker-Lampson continued by emphasising: "I am not personally a Jew. I do not happen to possess one drop, so far as I know, of Jewish blood in my veins ...". His point was that one did not need to share the faith or race of the persecuted in order to hate the tyranny that oppressed it. "I hope I only require English birth and breeding to loath the oppression of a minority anywhere. It is un-English, it is caddish ...". In his next rhetorical flourish he sought to establish he was not motivated by "anti-Germanism" but was, on the contrary and in common with many in the House of Commons, "almost pro-German", still a daring statement at that time. Referring back to the war, he felt the German people had been misled by their leaders and unfairly treated after the war. As an example he cited the fact the French Army had billeted Black African troops in the house in Weimar of the great German poet, Goethe, an act he described as "a terrible humiliation". The racially motivated moral panic about Black French soldiers stationed in Occupied Germany, sometimes known as 'The Black Horror on the Rhine', gained considerable traction in the right-wing press in Britain and North America in the 1920s and 1930s and was ruthlessly exploited by the Nazi's propaganda machine. His remark, tacitly agreeing the act was self-evidently insulting, shows even high-minded advocates of racial tolerance like Locker-Lampson had a blind spot when it came to their attitudes to non-White races. While opposing anti-Semitism in Europe he continued to be a firm advocate of the status quo of White supremacy in the British Empire, especially in India where, like his friend Winston Churchill, he actively opposed Indian Home Rule.

Locker-Lampson continued by stating it was the German Jews who had persuaded him by their tireless advocacy that Germany should be treated fairly by England after the war. It is not obvious which German Jews he is referring to here. He was perhaps thinking of politicians he may have met there, such as Einstein's friend the Jewish politician Walther Rathenau, whom he may have met on his reparations fact-finding mission to Germany in 1921. At that period Rathenau was Minister of Reconstruction in the Weimar Republic. He later became Foreign Minister and negotiated the Treaty of Rapallo, re-establishing diplomatic relations and ending financial war-claims between Germany and the Soviet Union. Rathenau paid a terrible price for daring to reach the pinnacle of political power in Germany when he was assassinated by ultra-nationalists in 1922.

Locker-Lampson continued his speech by arguing Germany was turning on its Jews and driving out "not her cut-throats and blackguards" but the cream of her culture, including "her most glorious citizen—Einstein". At this point, although it is not noted in Hansard, Locker-Lampson seems to have gestured towards the very man seated in the Visitors' Gallery. The *Daily Express* correspondent noted that members of the House cheered when they saw him, a very rare privilege seldom accorded to 'strangers' by MPs. According to Hansard, the first mention of Einstein in a speech in the House of Commons occurred on 18 November 1919, coincidentally also during a debate on immigration during the third reading of the Aliens Restriction Bill, which sought to extend the Government's wartime control over the movement and employment of immigrants, particularly those who were former enemy aliens like Einstein. One of those seeking to amend the bill to allow Germans of talent like Einstein to enter Britain was the Liberal MP Captain William Wedgwood Benn, who like Locker-Lampson had served in the Royal Naval Air Service in the war. Benn had remarked with irony:

> While I am on the field of science, there is an enemy alien called Einstein who has discovered a new theory of light. I am glad to say that owing to this Bill we shall prevent the dumping of any German science in this country. We shall be able to have an all-British law of gravity.[21]

"Einstein", Locker-Lampson continued, "is without a home"; going on to quote the German word for without—*Ohne*—that Einstein had written in Lloyd George's visitors' book. While "the road hog" of Europe had plundered his home and even stolen his violin, England could be proud it had given him shelter temporarily at Oxford. In a word that seems to imply a foreknowledge of the coming Holocaust, Locker-Lampson spoke of "the same spirit of frightfulness which overwhelmed small Belgium … is now turned upon a helpless handful for extermination".

What then should be done to help alleviate the suffering of Germany's Jews? He suggested the League of Nations send a commission of inquiry and issue international passports so Germany's Jews might escape their persecution. Failing this, the British Empire should "help fulfil the Messianic miracle" and extend citizenship within the British Mandate of Palestine to all Jews deprived of their citizenship anywhere in Europe. The phrase "Messianic miracle" is a curious one, and it is uncertain whether Locker-Lampson meant Britain should act in a Christian way and help the oppressed or Britain should act as a new Moses and lead the Jews to the Promised Land. In any case Jewish immigration in Palestine was already a fact. The setting-up of a Jewish national homeland in Palestine had been an aim of the British Government outlined in the Balfour Declaration of 1917, partly in return for the promise of Jewish support for the Allies' war aims. Article 6 of the Mandate set up by the League of Nations after the war and administered by the Jewish Agency in British-controlled Palestine put the Balfour Declaration into force. By 1933 the number of Jews who had settled in Palestine, mainly from Russia and south-east Europe, had grown from less than 10,000 in 1918 to about 200,000. The influx had led to widespread resentment among the Arab population, something the Balfour Declaration had warned against, and this had spilled over into riots in the 1920s. Locker-Lampson continued by reminding the House of Commons that many Jews, subjects of the king, had fought and died for England in the war. England for him, as for most people of his class, meant the same thing as Britain and the United Kingdom. He recalled in particular one Jewish family from his "village" (meaning Cromer) who had lost three sons in the war. This family was almost certainly the Levines, who owned a jewellery business in the town. They had in fact lost two sons in the war, not three: Cyril, who died of wounds at Arras in 1917, and Myer, a RAF officer who was killed in a flying accident in 1918.[22] In conclusion, he observed that he had seen English and Jewish blood spilt on many battle fronts "and I have noticed that the colour of the blood is the same". Germany, he said, had once described the British Expeditionary Force as "contemptible" but it had lived to beat it. The Jews were Germany's new contemptibles and they too would win in the end with British support. The Bill was then voted on, accepted and a second reading set for 7 November, which did not happen. Knowing his Bill stood little chance of becoming law, his primary aim was to win over the public's sympathy for the plight of Germany's Jews and its detestation at the Nazis' anti-Semitic policies by calling on what he imagined was the British public's innate sense of decency and fair play. Einstein was a valuable pawn in this strategy. However, while sympathy for the celebrated scientist was fairly easy to achieve, getting the public's support for a policy of providing refuge for a mass influx of Germany's Jews was always going to be much more difficult.

The British press were on the whole sympathetic to Einstein's plight. Only the *Daily Mail* chose to ignore the events in parliament altogether, being at this time editorially pro-fascist and a supporter of Hitler and a resurgent Germany. The German press, now under the control of Goebbels, were unequivocally hostile. Alfred Rosenberg wrote in *Der Völkischer Beobachter* that it had been no more an "Einsteinian Jew Show", while "Sir Oliver Locker-Lampson", as he insisted on calling him, was merely "the knight of opportunism".

As Einstein's ferry steamed back to Ostend, Locker-Lampson probably felt he had good reason to congratulate himself. He had finally managed to get Einstein to come to England as his guest, and had used his presence to raise awareness of the plight of Germany's Jews to the newspaper-reading public and with an influential group of statesmen. However, as to whether he had helped or hindered the cause of Einstein personally was not yet clear. The intense media interest surrounding Einstein's visit to parliament clearly worried Yahuda, who wrote to Locker-Lampson on 28 July, complaining the publicity surrounding news of Einstein's arrival in England was in his view a "ghastly indiscretion", which he assumed was not to his taste either.[23] He had clearly not yet got the measure of the man. Worse followed when much of the British press throughout the whole of the first week of August unambiguously stated he was seeking naturalisation as a British citizen in news reports that invariably mentioned Locker-Lampson's role as his champion. Although it was one of Yahuda's ambitions for Einstein that he acquire British citizenship, he was anxious all discussion of the subject remained low key. Einstein was still a Swiss citizen after all, and the Swiss authorities were still trying to negotiate with the authorities in Berlin for the return of his confiscated property. His enemies in Germany, moreover, would simply seize on this as further proof Einstein was a renegade and a traitor. Yahuda urged Locker-Lampson to use his influence with the press to have it put about it was he and not Einstein who had opened discussions with the Home Office on naturalisation because he wished to offer Einstein the protection of a strong country.[24] On the same day he wrote to Einstein urging caution on the subject of British citizenship.[25] Einstein replied on 1 August that he had never given Locker-Lampson authority to assert in public he was seeking British citizenship. In fact that was not his intention, exclaiming in exasperation, "God protect me from the intentions of my friend".[26] For now Einstein intended to remain in Belgium for the rest of the summer. Locker-Lampson, however, chose to believe he had received Einstein's promise he would visit him again before he returned to America in October. If true, it is likely Einstein envisaged a visit lasting no more than a couple of days in London. Fate had other plans.

Notes

1 *The Times, 1 April 1933.*

2 *Barnes and Nicholson, The Empire at Bay, entry for 7 April 1933, p.292.*

3 *'Will the Gypsies Survive?', Peterborough Standard, 13 September 1929.*

4 *Albert Einstein Archives, The Hebrew University of Jerusalem; AEA: 50-805.*

5 *The Times, 31 March 1933.*

6 *Clark, Einstein, p.448.*

7 *Letters used with kind permission of Steve Locker-Lampson.*

8 *Western Morning News, 15 May 1933.*

9 *The Cornishman, 18 May 1933.*

10 *Hoffman and Dukas, Albert Einstein, pp.164–5.*

11 *https://focusonbelgium.be/en/facts/albert-einstein-lived-de-haan-1933*

12 *The Cherwell Archive, Oxford University; cat. ref.: D57/6.*

13 *Ibid. 12: D57/22.*

14 *Steve Locker-Lampson, Nothing to Offer But Blood, p.219.*

15 *Daily Mirror, 25 July 1933; Daily Herald, 26 July 1933; Belfast Telegraph, 22 July 1933.*

16 *Fölsing, Albert Einstein, p.677.*

17 *Ibid. 13.*

18 *Ibid. 12: D57/12.*

19 *UK Parliamentary Archives, GB-061; Lloyd George Papers: LG/G/11/3.*

20 *Rowland, Lloyd George.*

21 *Hansard, House of Commons Debates, 18 November 1919.*

22 *Cromer Museum, Oh The Mud!, pp.42–3.*

23 *Ibid. 4, AEA: 39-560.5.*

24 *Ibid.*

25 *Ibid. 4, AEA: 30-560.9.*

26 *Ibid. 4, AEA: 39-560.6.*

Murder in Marienbad

DURING the summer of 1933 the pressure of events and the strain these put on him began to affect Einstein's ability to concentrate on his work. Life at the Villa Savoyarde had become fraught with tension and disturbed by frequent interruptions by a seemingly constant stream of visitors. The area surrounding the seaside chalet, a mixture of hotels, cafes, holiday homes, sand dunes and marram grass, was patrolled by plain-clothed detectives on the lookout for suspicious activity, while uniformed members of the Belgian *Gendarmerie* on guard at the Villa checked all who called there day and night. According to Einstein's stepson-in-law Dmitri Marianoff, who visited the Villa from his own exile base in Paris, there were also "two Scotland Yard men" sent by the British Government to guard Elsa and Einstein throughout their stay; however, no evidence for this has been found.[1] The gendarmes were not authorised to prevent the admittance of anyone the Einsteins wished to enter nor was their mail vetted—at least not officially. Einstein had long been the recipient of crank letters but now they increasingly took on a more sinister tone. One man wrote claiming to be a disgruntled ex-Nazi with secret information to sell. Elsa, fearing he might be an *agent provocateur* but worried in case he really did have important information about a kidnap or assassination plot, agreed to see him. His rambling, semi-coherent account of himself persuaded her he was mentally disturbed and knew nothing of value. This sort of thing hardly made for a calm domestic atmosphere. A rumour Hermann Göring's younger brother Albert was staying in Le Coq-sur-Mer also caused alarm. It would not have been generally known at the time that Albert Göring was anti-Nazi and did what he could to help Jews escape persecution and death.[2]

During August Einstein had cause to correspond with Locker-Lampson again. A German lawyer and outspoken critic of the Nazis, Alfred Apfel, had visited him on 10 June and stayed in Le Coq-sur-Mer for a week. Apfel was then based in Paris, having fled Germany in fear for his life and was now telling everyone by way of a cover story that he was collecting material for an erotic novel he planned to write in order to make some money.[3] He had been among those rounded up for interrogation following the Reichstag fire in February, for no other reason than he was Jewish, politically on the left and a prominent anti-Nazi lawyer. Some non-German newspapers at the time had even reported he had been tortured and killed. In 1930 he had defended Albrecht Höhler, a communist accused of murdering a minor Brown Shirt member, Horst Wessel, introducing evidence at the trial to show that far from being a pure, upstanding member of the master race, Wessel was a thuggish petty criminal and pimp. After his death Wessel was elevated by the Nazis into a martyr and Höhler was murdered by the Brown Shirts in a forest near Frankfurt. Apfel later defended the German pacifist and anti-Nazi Carl von Ossietzky, who had exposed covert German rearmament, including the training and building of a secret air force by the ultra-nationalist militia the Black *Reichswehr*, contrary to the terms of the Treaty of Versailles. Ossietzky died in 1938, his health broken by starvation and abuse at a series of concentration camps.

Apfel came to Einstein seeking support for an institute for Jewish emigrants, which he hoped to establish in order to advocate for the rights of Jews and other asylum seekers wherever they found themselves. On the 18 August Apfel wrote to Locker-Lampson asking for his support, both moral and financial, for the proposed institute. Five days later Einstein, who had received a copy of Apfel's letter, wrote to Locker-Lampson. He began by recalling the lovely time he had had with him in England in July, then went on to caution him not to become entangled with Apfel, who had been too forward in his assertion that he was fully behind his project. Apfel, he wrote, was certainly a well-known lawyer and a clever man but in his opinion his reputation was not as spotless as one might wish for the official advocate of so important an enterprise. Einstein referred him to an enclosed separate letter that outlined how he had come to this conclusion. This letter seems to have been lost and it is unclear what this evidence was; possibly, he suspected Apfel had a political rather than a purely humanitarian agenda and his record of defending communists would allow the Nazis to reinforce their assertion that anyone who associated with him was a Soviet agent, an accusation which had damaged him before. In 1941 Apfel died of a suspected heart attack at the US Consulate in Marseilles, where he had fled for asylum following a roundup of "persons of interest" to the Third Reich by their Vichy collaborators.

Recent events had taught Einstein to be cautious of allowing his name to be attached to each and every cause that appealed to him for help. His change of mind about absolute pacifism, national armed defence and compulsory military service had set off a shock wave through the European pacifist movement in July. The War Resisters' International organisation removed as far as possible all mention of Einstein from its literature, while his old friend the pacifist Romain Rolland accused him of having played an intellectual game when he had previously opposed military conscription, noting in his diary: "such weakness of spirit is indeed unimaginable in a great scientist". A few years later he would reluctantly come to accept that Einstein's change of mind had been far-sighted and correct.[4] Throughout August the reverberations rumbled on as the news began to sink in among those committed to the total rejection of military force. He found himself having to write letters almost daily to explain his new position to pacifists who felt either he had been misrepresented by the press or had betrayed the cause. He was also under renewed pressure from King Albert, whose ministers feared Einstein's continued presence in Belgium presented Germany with an opportunity to engineer an international incident while he was under Belgian protection. This scenario would soon prove all too credible. In the first days of September shocking news reached the Villa Savoyarde that intensified Elsa's anxiety for her husband's safety.

Theodor Lessing by Will Burgdorf, 1930.

On 30 August a leading German Jewish academic and author, Professor Theodor Lessing, was assassinated in the Czechoslovakian spa town of Marienbad, where he had fled to escape political persecution organised by far-right elements in his home city of Hanover. It was strongly suspected German-speaking Sudetenland Nazi sympathisers had carried out the killing, either on their own initiative or at the bidding of high-ranking Nazis. Until forced to flee Lessing had been a professor of philosophy at Hanover Polytechnic, where he had long been a thorn in the side of ultra-nationalists and anti-Semites. As a Jew and a critic of the growth of ultra-conservative and extreme nationalist politics in post-war Germany he had become a target for right-wing extremists, including among the students at his own university. In 1925 Lessing had been vilified for the publication of a controversial study of the notorious Hanover serial killer Fritz Haarmann. A series of bizarre murders haunted Germany in the post-war period, leading to a popular fascination with human 'monsters', exemplified in Fritz Lang's 1931 film *M*, in which Peter Lorre had his first major screen role as a sinister yet pathetic child killer. Lessing's book, *Haarmann –The Story of a Werewolf*, is a serious psycho-social study of a murderer and the press and public's hysterical reaction to his crimes.[5] Following Haarmann's execution in December 1924 by beheading, then still the most common form of execution in Germany, Lessing argued he had been judicially murdered as he was clearly insane and so not responsible for his actions. He also poured scorn on sensationalist stories being put about by the anti-Semitic press that Haarmann's crimes, which had included elements of cannibalism, paedophilia, mutilation, sadomasochism and vampirism, had in fact been the acts of Jews, perpetuating the old Blood Libel, a pernicious myth that had its origins in the discovery of the body of a murdered Norwich boy, William, on Mousehold Heath in the 12th century. It was a subject Locker-Lampson was to challenge himself in 1934 when he was instrumental in having the British fascist Arnold Leese prosecuted for publishing similar anti-Semitic libels.

In 1932 Lessing again enraged ultra-conservatives and extreme nationalists in Germany when he publicly queried the wisdom of the 84-year-old General Paul von Hindenburg standing for re-election to the presidency of the Weimar Republic. Far-right student groups had organised protest rallies in Hanover and enforced boycotts of his lectures, while some of his academic colleagues called for his dismissal from the faculty. Lessing had previously let it be known he had opposed Germany's involvement in the 1914–18 war and done all in his power to avoid military service. Such comments enflamed nationalistic elements in the press; flames fanned by the Nazi's chief propagandist Josef Goebbels and the Brown Shirt's leader Ernst Röhm. Hindenburg was still widely regarded as a war hero and father of the nation, and his venerable status was subsequently used by Hitler as a stalking horse to gain acceptance for his appointment as Reich Chancellor in January 1933, which was somewhat ironic as Goebbels had described Hindenburg in a speech in the Reichstag in 1932 as the preferred presidential candidate of "the party of deserters", as he called the left-wing Social Democratic Party.

On 1 March 1933, faced with mounting persecution, including death threats, Lessing boarded a train for Prague. His daughter Ruth accompanied him, while his wife Ada stayed behind to sort out their affairs before joining them. Prague, with its large German-speaking population, was rapidly becoming the asylum of choice for exiled German intellectuals. Soon after arrival Lessing was offered accommodation at a hotel in Marienbad, the Villa Edelweiss, owned by a Czech Social Democratic Party delegate. Here the Lessings opened a school for German refugee children. The Prague left-wing, German-language newspaper, *Das Prager Tagblatt*, which had already published some of Lessing's work, asked him for further

Villa Edelweiss, Marienbad.

contributions and Lessing continued to write articles criticising the growth of the politics of extreme nationalism and anti-Semitism in Germany. In June several Czech German-language newspapers published a story that a reward of 80,000 Reichmarks (equivalent to around £5,600 or $19,000 at that time) had been anonymously offered to anyone who would kidnap Lessing and bring him back to Germany to stand trial for treason. After this the Czech police provided him with protection. The similarity with Einstein's present predicament was striking: outspoken criticism of the Nazi regime, a campaign of provocation and persecution against him, flight to seek refuge in a neighbouring country and, once there, death threats, a price placed on his head and the need to accept police protection.

On 30 August Lessing left the Villa Edelweiss and drove to a Zionist meeting in the town. At some point in the evening for reasons never fully explained he left the meeting prematurely and returned to his hotel without informing the police guard there he had returned. At about 9.30 p.m., as he was writing in his study on the first floor, two shots rang out. His wife rushed into the room to find him slumped over his desk bleeding profusely. A car quickly took him to hospital where he died shortly after arrival. The police found a ladder against the wall beneath the Lessings' apartment, possibly placed there as a marker, and holes made by high-velocity bullets through each of the two study windows. A tracker dog picked up a trail that led to the edge of the forest and then disappeared. A local forester informed the police of his suspicions concerning the recent movements of another forest worker, Rudolf Max Eckert. Eckert was a well-known local poacher and a noted marksman, and was known to be involved in the Sudeten–German Nazi movement. Directed by the forester the tracker dog now picked up the scent again, leading the police to the cottage of Eckert's brother. Rudolf Eckert, however, was nowhere to be found and it was suspected he had fled across the border into Bavaria. An accomplice was also sought as forensic evidence suggested two different calibre rifles had been used. Witnesses told the police Eckert had frequently been seen in the company of Rudolf Zischka, who had also vanished shortly after the shooting. Zischka had earlier been seen in the company of a mysterious foreigner known only as "Prince Henriet", who was posing as an exiled Russian aristocrat. Witnesses claimed he wore a small golden swastika on a bracelet round his wrist.

Before the Munich Agreement consigned Czech Sudetenland to Nazi rule and the Lessing murder investigation was closed down by the Gestapo, Czech detectives traced Eckert and Zischka to Munich, where they had changed their names and joined the Brown Shirts. An informer now passed the police information that the assassination had been planned by a man named Hoffmann, thought to be a leader of the Brown Shirts' *Gruppen* 4, with the full backing of Röhm. After Liberation in July 1945 the Czech police reopened the case and with the help of the US Army arrested Eckert near Marienbad. During interrogation he confessed to the murder and named a third accomplice, Karl Hönl. Zischka and Hönl had originally planned simply to kidnap Lessing and claim the reward for his rendition to Germany but had been persuaded by a Nazi agent, possibly Hoffmann or the mysterious 'Prince Henriet', to assassinate him instead. Eckert was sentenced to 18 years imprisonment. Released after 13 years he disappeared into West Germany. Zischka and Hönl were never caught and were believed to have died on the Eastern Front during the war. Röhm, who may have sanctioned and financed the plot, was murdered by the SS during the 'Night of the Long Knives' purge in the summer of 1934.[6]

The day after Lessing's murder the English translation of a book detailing Nazi atrocities was published with Einstein's endorsement printed on the dust wrapper. The book had first been published in Paris in August. The violent reaction to it in Germany, much of it directed towards Einstein's alleged part in its authorship, together with the news of Lessing's murder, may have provided the final impetus that drove Einstein to England. *The Brown Book of the Hitler Terror and the Burning of the Reichstag*, to give it its full title, had been prepared for publication by the World Committee for the Victims of German Fascism, a predominately left-wing grouping of opponents of Nazism. Although he had not written a word of it, Einstein had agreed his name could appear in the Preface as a member of the committee that drew up the evidence. The title *Brown Book* was no doubt chosen to draw attention to the colour predominately associated with the Nazis at that time due to the uniform of the Brown Shirts. Indeed the jacket of the first German language edition, designed by the German Surrealist artist John Heartfield, featured an image of a grotesque, axe-wielding, blood-splattered Brown Shirt. *The Brown Book* was intended to shock and still has the power to disturb, with its descriptions of torture and beatings, graphic photographs of the victims' wounds and lists of the murdered. The book's impact was immediate. One Nazi-supporting German paper called it "Einstein's newest infamy", and suggested he was next on the list for execution as a traitor. All of this was too similar to the events leading up to the murder of Lessing to be ignored by Einstein's family, friends and protectors. Intriguingly, just nine days before Einstein would become a big local news story in Norfolk, *The Brown Book* and Einstein's part in it was thought sufficiently newsworthy for the *Eastern Daily Press* (*EDP*) to provide an editorial analysis for its readers:

> *The Brown Book of the Hitler terror* which has just been published is one of the most terrible records of political madness that has ever appeared. It is impossible to dismiss it as a piece of fantasy, malignant or otherwise. That it appears under the authority of such a spectator of all time and existence as Professor Einstein is a guarantee that it is not a fabrication, and behind Professor Einstein there are others whose names are pledges of truthful intention.[7]

The article goes on to argue, in the best traditions of British fair play, that the Nazis should be given the opportunity to reply to the accusations but even if they were only partially true "it brands the Nazi leaders as reckless, irresponsible criminals". The appeal to fair play leads one to suspect Locker-Lampson's hand in this, as *The Brown Book* was really not the sort of publication a provincial newspaper like the *EDP* usually took much interest in. If he was behind its appearance it suggests he was preparing the ground for Einstein's flight to Norfolk at least two weeks before it happened. The conclusion of the article mirrored the attitude of the British Government and probably most of the British people at this time, which was one of caution. The Nazis might be vile but they did not represent the real Germany. Government needed to be vigilant but also patient. No one wanted to get into another war and it was widely believed Hitler's regime could not last very long. It was a view shared by Einstein at this period. In a letter to Yahuda written on 1 August he said he was sure Nazism wouldn't last long in Germany and an "enlightened Despot" would soon succeed Hitler who would present a much lesser threat to peace.[8] Whom he had in mind is not clear.

Meanwhile, Yahuda was keeping up his campaign to persuade Einstein to take up a professorship at Madrid University. On 26 August he wrote to Lindemann in Oxford to try to clear up a false impression being reported in some quarters of the press that following his exile from Germany Einstein was greedily scooping up university chairs at inflated salaries in Britain, France, Palestine, Spain and the USA. In fact, Yahuda claimed, Einstein did not wish to take on any position that would make extra demands on his time, nor did he wish to take posts and salaries that might otherwise be offered to other refugee scholars. The only chairs he had provisionally accepted, he wrote, were as a visiting professor at the Sorbonne (it was in fact at the Collège de France, a research academy rather than a teaching one) and at the University of Madrid, and only on the understanding these positions did not interfere with his work and, in the case of Madrid, a second chair be created for a German scientist whom he would recommend. Einstein was in fact genuinely fearful these extra demands on his time would finish him off as a creative physicist. Writing to his friend Maurice Solovine in April, he had remarked: "I have more professorships than useful ideas in my head. The devil shits on the biggest pile."[9]

The long, warm summer showed no sign of ending. Tucked away in Le Coq-sur-Mer, Einstein, assisted by Dr Mayer and his ever-loyal private secretary Helen Dukas, tried to do some useful work while enjoying the continuing good weather. Photographs taken at this time show a smiling Einstein and Mayer sat on a sand dune enjoying the sun. However, the storm clouds gathering over Europe could not be ignored for very much longer. The reverberations that had followed the publication of *The Brown Book* had ratcheted up the febrile tension at the Villa Savoyarde several more notches. The scenario at times approached farce, like an Alfred Hitchcock thriller set in the world of *Mr Hulot's Holiday*. As streams of *vacanciers* made for the beach, plain-clothed detectives scoured the dunes, tripping over sun bathers and courting couples, and questioning sightseers who strayed too near the Villa. Armed and uniformed gendarmes, when not on guard duty, slept on chairs in the corridor or sat on the stairs. Einstein tried to work through it all as best he could but Elsa was nearing her breaking point.

Notes

1 *Marianoff and Wayne, Einstein, p.153.*

2 *Vallentin, Einstein, pp.168–9.*

3 *Schwing, Alfred Apfel, p.301.*

4 *Brock, Twentieth-Century Pacifism, pp.131–2.*

5 *Lessing, Haarmann.*

6 *Information on the investigation of the murder of Lessing from 'Der Mord an Theodor Lessing'; accessed online in 2003, no longer available.*

7 *Eastern Daily Press, 2 September 1933.*

8 *Albert Einstein Archive, Hebrew University of Jerusalem; AEA: 39.560.6.*

9 *Einstein, Letters to Solovine.*

September Blow Soft

... till the fruit's in the loft (old English proverb)

NEWS of Lessing's murder reached the Villa Savoyarde on 1 September. It is said to have turned Elsa's normally rosy complexion white the moment she heard it. Although he was neither a close friend nor an academic colleague, Einstein valued his work for Jewish causes in Germany, his advocacy for the creation of a Jewish Homeland and his outspoken criticism of extreme nationalistic rhetoric. In 1922 Lessing had published an article ironically titled "On 'Einstein's error'", in which he forensically analysed the flaws in non-scientific critical attacks on the Special and General theories of Relativity, which he noted inevitably began by fundamentally misunderstanding them and then debunked them based on the author's original misconception.[1]

The following day, a Saturday, Einstein received a visit from a woman who would later become legendary in British left-wing circles as the indefatigable supporter of the Jarrow March, a protest by unemployed shipyard workers in north-east England who walked to London in 1936. Ellen Wilkinson, the child of a Manchester cotton mill worker, was quick-witted, brave, energetic and shrewd. She had been elected Labour MP for Middlesbrough East in 1924 when her physical appearance—diminutive with vivid red hair—and her socialist principles had earned her the nickname the 'Fiery Particle'. Since losing her parliamentary seat in 1931 she had devoted much of her energy to journalism and anti-fascist causes. She was a member of the British branch of the World Committee for the Relief of the Victims of German Fascism, the organisation promoting *The Brown Book of the Hitler Terror*, and had herself written a pamphlet for them exposing Nazi terror tactics.

The 'Fiery Particle', Ellen Wilkinson, 1926.

She had met victims of their brutality during a number of visits to Germany, was well aware of the type of person they were using to win political power and knew no one who opposed them was safe. In April she had written in the radical weekly magazine *Time and Tide*:

> … neither personal eminence nor past public service could save a man if he be a Jew or a Socialist. The life of an Einstein is at the mercy of hysterical lads of eighteen or tough slum gangsters provided with revolvers with the warm approval of Captain Goering …[2]

Following the Reichstag fire in February she had helped the Committee organise an enquiry into the causes of the fire: a direct challenge to the dubious probity of the official investigation, which had put the blame squarely on Jews and communists. Her anti-fascist activities made her an object of Nazi opprobrium—their mouthpieces in the German press dubbing her "the Jew of Jews".[3]

Wilkinson visited Einstein now ostensibly to offer him the opportunity of resigning from the Committee and having his name removed from its stationery. According to the cover of the British edition of the *Brown Book* published by Victor Gollancz, Einstein was president of the Committee. Einstein never denied this though his position was purely honorary. On the face of it this was an odd offer, given the withdrawal of such a high-profile supporter at this stage would hardly have mollified the Nazis and would undoubtedly have provided them with more ammunition for their anti-Einstein propaganda. Knowing the character of the man, she had presumably calculated it was unlikely he would be willing to withdraw his support. Wilkinson had in fact been commissioned by the Beaverbrook press to write an account of Einstein in exile. She described the scene that confronted her at the Villa Savoyarde in "Einstein the man", published by the *Daily Express* on 12 September:

> Einstein sat and talked to me in his little sitting room, dressed in a pair of old trousers and a well-worn pull-over. We knew his life was threatened. The detectives stood at his gate. He had made his simple will. … I implored him to resign, to let us take his name off our notepaper. 'No,' he said, quietly, 'They shall not force me to do that. The work your committee has done is good.' His wife sobbed. … I realised what that simple 'No' might mean. The life of the best brain of the world is at the mercy of the bullet of a fanatic.[4]

Tension at the Villa had been stoked up by an album received anonymously through the post in which photographs of so-called 'enemies' of Germany were printed above lists of their alleged crimes against the Fatherland. Under Einstein's photograph was printed:

> Discovered a much-contested theory of relativity. Was greatly honoured by the Jewish Press and the unsuspecting German people. Showed his gratitude by lying atrocity propaganda against Adolf Hitler abroad. (Not yet hanged.)[5]

It was also about this time an old friend of the Einsteins, the biographer Antonina Vallentin, visited the Villa Savoyarde. In 1931 Einstein had provided the foreword for her biography of his friend Gustav Stresemann, the late Chancellor and Foreign Minister of the Weimar Republic and a joint Nobel Peace Prize winner with Locker-Lampson's old chief, Austen Chamberlain. The official purpose of Vallentin's visit was to bring a message from the French Minister of National Education, Anatole de Monzie, reminding Einstein of his offer of a professorship at the Collège de France in Paris, which he had made in person at Le Coq-sur-Mer in August. Her real mission, however, was to urge him to leave Europe as soon as possible, working, if necessary, on Elsa's anxiety if Einstein proved to be imperturbable. She had done the same at their summer home at Caputh the previous year, passing on a warning by a prominent right-wing politician, General Hans von Seeckt, a former head of the German Army, who had told her she should urge all her Jewish friends, Einstein in particular, to leave Germany as "His life is not safe here any longer".[6] Considering it is now known that General Seeckt had been instrumental in setting up the secret Black *Reichswehr* terrorist corps after the war, charged with eliminating suspected communists and collaborationists in the Occupied territories, his warning could be taken as serious. By the early 1930s the Black *Reichswehr* had been revived by the Brown Shirts and had become more overtly anti-Semitic in its choice of targets under the name the *Fehme*. According to Vallentin, recalling her visit in her biography of Einstein twenty years later, Elsa was by now thoroughly alarmed; her fears leading to sleepless nights, alert to every creaking floorboard and, inevitably, given the stress they were under, to heated arguments in which she begged her husband to at least seek temporary safety in England. "A threatened man lives longer" was his defiant response but she would not be brow-beaten this time—he had to go.

Einstein's hasty flight to England in September 1933 closely paralleled an episode almost ten years earlier, in November 1923, when he had fled over the border into Holland during Hitler's failed Munich Beer Hall Putsch. The similarities are striking, including the fomenting of ultra-nationalist hysteria by the press, mounting political tension, death threats and the assassination of a leading Jewish intellectual. In 1923 it had been the Weimar Republic's Foreign Minister Walther Rathenau, in 1933 it was Professor Theodor Lessing. Einstein's decision to leave Belgium at this time may, however, have had been given another, more private impetus. Given the revelations concerning his private life that have emerged in recent years, the possibility exists that fears for his safety, while primary, were not Elsa's sole concern. After Elsa's death in 1936 Einstein confessed to close friends to having had a number of extramarital affairs. Among the visitors to the Villa Savoyarde that summer was a married Viennese Jewish friend, Grete Lebach. Nearly sixty years later, Einstein's godson, Micha Battsek,

6 years old in 1933, recalled happy days spent with his parents visiting Einstein at Le Coq-sur-Mer. He particularly remembered Helen Dukas feeding him chocolates and "a very nice-looking lady" who often seemed to be in Einstein's company around the town and at the beach much more than Elsa, whom he hardly remembered.[7] Years later his parents told him that she was Einstein's lover, Grete Lebach. Born Margarete Bachwitz in 1885, she had been a regular visitor to the Einsteins' summer home at Caputh just outside Berlin, bringing boxes of Viennese pastries. There was gossip in the neighbourhood arising from Einstein's unaccompanied outings with 'the Austrian woman', sailing on the nearby Havel Lakes while Elsa was away in Berlin. On one occasion, after Einstein and Lebach had been sailing, a woman's bathing costume, evidently too small to fit Elsa, had been found in the small cabin on his boat and this had been brought to Elsa's attention. It is now accepted by Einstein's biographers that Grete Lebach was one of the more enduring of his lovers. A letter Einstein wrote from Oxford to his stepdaughter Margot in May 1931 all but admitted the affair: "Out of all the women, I am in fact attached only to Mrs. L. who is absolutely harmless and decent."[8] It was apparent to close friends Elsa knew what was going on and her anger sometimes led to rows. Lebach's reappearance on the scene in Belgium at this time may therefore provide another reason for the heated arguments Elsa told Antonina Vallentin about. It was not the end of their relationship. Greta Lebach was photographed sailing with Einstein on his small sail boat *Tinef* in Long Island in 1937, the year after Elsa's death. Following the Nazi's annexation of Austria in May 1938, he tried to arrange for her and her husband to move to America permanently without success. Meanwhile, the Battsek family continued to keep up with her in Austria. According to Micha's parents she died of cancer in Vienna in August 1938 after the Nazi-controlled hospitals there refused to give her medical treatment because she was a Jew.

The various forces now moving behind the scenes to effect Einstein's flight to England are difficult to disentangle. The whole business was characterised by a baffling mixture of secrecy and publicity. At least three parties seem to have been involved: King Albert and the Belgian Government, anxious to avoid an international incident; the Beaverbrook-owned newspapers, the *Daily Express* and *Sunday Express*, looking for a scoop that would put clear blue water between them and the fascist-supporting Harmsworth press; and Locker-Lampson, still vigorously pursuing his own agenda of securing Einstein under his protection in England as a propaganda tool. Stories subsequently arose he had been smuggled out of Belgium on Locker-Lampson's yacht, which had landed him on either the Kent or Norfolk coast. It was also rumoured he had fled to South America, a story possibly planted in the press by the Belgian authorities as a red herring.[9] Locker-Lampson, perhaps knowing Einstein was about to be moved, seemed to be doing his best to spread misinformation. On Friday 8 September the *Eastern*

Daily Press, in which he seems to have been able to place stories at will, included a brief report Einstein was in hiding and Mrs Einstein was "very perturbed" in Blankenberge, which is about 6 miles (9 km) up the coast from Le Coq-sur-Mer. In fact both were still at Le Coq sur-Mer. That morning Irish journalist Patrick Murphy knocked at the front door of the Villa Savoyarde, having shown the gendarmes his credentials. According to an account he published many years later, he had been despatched there by the editor of the *Daily Express*, Beverley Baxter, who had heard of Einstein's predicament at Le Coq "by some mysterious means".[10] There can be little doubt the source was Locker-Lampson via Lord Beaverbrook, of whom Baxter said "He is Allah, and the rest of us are his prophets"[11]. Murphy's report appeared two days later in the *Sunday Express*. The door was opened by Elsa. To begin with she was cautious, telling him the professor was out, which she invariably did with visitors she did not know. "Never have I seen more eloquent terror in a woman's eyes", he wrote. Then, after a whispered word from one of the detectives, who had clearly been briefed to verify him, she admitted her husband was at home after all and would see him. A few minutes later Einstein came into the room "smiling like a shy schoolboy".

Murphy began by asking Einstein about his security at Le Coq-sur-Mer—a gifted linguist, he spoke in German. While agreeing it was an impossible situation, Einstein still seemed reluctant to leave. Everyone had been more than nice, he explained, he had even had a letter from King Albert saying "Belgian soil is honoured by your presence", telling Murphy that to flee to England now would be discourteous to his host. Losing her temper at this point, Elsa shrugged her shoulders in despair, blurting out: "He does not understand the danger. He does not understand. He is a man and also he is just a boy. Someone must look after him. There are reasons why I cannot leave. Where will he be safe and secret?"[12] Elsa then asked Murphy if he would make a telephone call to "A great friend. A noble friend in England", having presumably either remembered Locker-Lampson's offers of refuge, which Einstein had declined earlier in the year, or been prompted to do so by the well-briefed Murphy, who said he would call him immediately—he presumably had his London or Cromer phone numbers

Patrick Murphy, the Irish reporter who brought Einstein to England.

with him—offering to accompany him to England. Elsa then told Einstein: "I think the young man is right. You should go to England with him." She again made it clear she was unable to go with them. Her reasons for staying have never been explained. Given her fears for his safety, fully justifiable by recent events, it seems strange she was now prepared to let him out of her sight. Nothing seemed to tie her to Belgium at this time. Her daughter Margot's husband, Marianoff, believed there had been a plot by the Nazis to kidnap both Ilse and Margot in March while they were still in Berlin but both were now safely out of Germany.[13] Indeed, by staying behind Elsa exposed herself to the possibility of being kidnapped and held as a hostage to secure Einstein's silence or a humiliating retraction of his anti-Nazi statements. A Reuter's report the following week stated that the armed guard was withdrawn from the Villa Savoyarde after Einstein's departure but Mrs Einstein was now surrounded by relatives—Ilse and Margot. During their journey to London Einstein told Murphy that his wife had "another worry on her mind almost as great as that which concerns my safety". The worry was perhaps connected with her own health or more likely the health of Ilse, although there seems to have been no confirmed diagnosis at this date of the cancer that would kill her the following year or of the kidney disease that would hasten Elsa's death three years later. Additionally, she may have been concerned about relatives still in Germany or simply anxious over the arrangements for returning to America in the autumn.

Late the following afternoon Murphy and Einstein took the little coastal tram to Ostend, where they boarded the Dover ferry, on which a private cabin had been reserved. The reason they didn't catch the morning ferry might be explained by the fact that in the morning Ostend had been occupied by a party of six hundred French- and German-speaking 'New Belgians', including a choir and a full marching band, who were travelling to England to lay a wreath at the Folkestone war memorial in honour of British soldiers who had lost their lives to liberate Belgium in the Great War. The 'New Belgian' cantons of Eupen and Malmedy, where the majority were German-speaking, had been ceded to Belgium from Germany in 1920 under the terms of the Treaty of Versailles. Had the Belgian secret service judged it unwise for Einstein to have been associated, if only accidentally, with such a demonstration? The issue was still highly controversial, even more so since the coming to power of Hitler. A large number of the cantons' German-speaking population were active revanchists, agitating for reunion with a newly resurgent, nationalistic Germany. It was just the sort of coincidence the Nazi press would have pounced on had it become known.

During the crossing Murphy observed that Einstein had the air of a schoolboy off on his holidays, recalling Elsa's description of him only the day before. No wonder; he had just been plucked from a seething cauldron of political intrigue and domestic tension, and could now look forward to a few weeks of restful, undisturbed work before leaving for America in October. During the crossing Einstein spoke to Murphy of how bad matters had become in Germany, both for himself and for his fellow Jews. Hitler had, he thought, some sort of inexplicable appeal for the masses but he was not intelligent and would probably not last beyond the following summer. He feared, however, he would be succeeded by someone just as bad. Expressing his faith in Zionism, Einstein was convinced the Jews would never be free of fear until they had their own country. They must organise in order to be able to help themselves. As for himself, he was a fatalist: "If tomorrow I should wake, finish my little work, and then find that I was to be shot—well, what could I do about it?"[14]

Having said his piece, Einstein pulled out some papers from his briefcase and worked on them in silence until they reached Dover. Here Einstein and Murphy boarded the train for London. Murphy noted that once in the carriage Einstein's boyish good humour returned, observing mischievously "English trains are fast, yes? We must be patient, I suppose." His thoughts then turned to Elsa and her anxiety over his safety. Murphy observed that women were often selflessly brave when it came to their own perils but terror-stuck when a loved one was in danger. To this Einstein replied that he didn't know what to say about women, except that even though they took two huge trunks with them when they travelled together, his wife always managed to have a little extra paper parcel with her. Did he perhaps mean this both literally and metaphorically? That with women in general or his wife in particular, there was always a little additional psychological baggage that troubled and confounded his equilibrium?

At Victoria Station a press photographer was waiting. The pictures that appeared in the *Sunday Express* the next day showed Einstein dressed in a dark three-piece woollen suit with a soft wing-collared shirt and loosely knotted tie. Stepping from the train in the early evening he wore a black felt hat and carried a check-lined mackintosh over one arm and a valise in the other hand. Also waiting for him on the platform were Locker-Lampson and his private secretaries, Margery Howard and Barbara Goodall. He had been in Cromer when Murphy's telephone call came through on Friday and he had travelled down to London the following morning. In keeping with the air of secrecy surrounding the trip he had to wait for instructions telling him when and where Einstein would arrive. At some point in the afternoon he received a telegram from Belgium that he would arrive at Victoria Station at about 6 p.m. More than forty years later Margery Howard recalled the scene:

> I was too young to know the significance of his visit, and when he did arrive there was nothing to make me realise the seriousness of the occasion. He stepped from the train in the early evening on his own [Murphy had presumably left the scene

> to phone through his story], carrying nothing but a violin case. He was a paunchy little figure wearing a dark suit with a large black sombrero hat over his head of white curls.[15]

Her mention of a violin case is odd, as it was repeatedly reported that his violin had been stolen from his Berlin apartment by the Nazis. After shaking hands with each of the secretaries Einstein spoke to Locker-Lampson in German, which Barbara and Margery did not understand. At some point Einstein realised he had mislaid a small packet of books, which was a somewhat ironic, one might almost be tempted to say Freudian, accident when one considers his remark to Murphy about his wife's excess parcels. A search of the train was made but nothing was found. The matter was put into the hands of the railway police who reported they had searched for the books at Dover and on the ferry but nothing had been found. From Victoria the party drove to a boarding house in Eardley Crescent, Earls Court, run by one of Locker-Lampson's former housekeepers, Mrs Hildred Varney, where they spent Saturday night.[16] On Sunday morning Einstein wrote to Elsa to let her know he had arrived safely and was going on to Cromer on the north Norfolk coast. He also wrote to his private secretary, Helen Dukas, who had stayed behind with Elsa, complaining to her about the attacks being made on him by his erstwhile colleagues in the pacifist movement over his refusal to publicly oppose military service in Belgium. It was an issue that seemed to preoccupy him more than his own safety during these last few weeks he spent in Europe. Meanwhile, the first news of Einstein's flight broke in a front-page article in the *Sunday Express* under the banner headline "Einstein flees to England, dread of Nazi murder threat" and a photo-montage showing Einstein standing behind a superimposed silhouette of a figure making the stiff-armed Nazi salute. Beneath was a caption quoting from Psalm 23: "Yea, though I walk through the Valley of the Shadow of Death …".

After breakfast they set off by car to Norfolk. While Barbara and Margery sat in the front and shared the driving, Locker-Lampson and Einstein sat in the back, talking in German almost constantly throughout the journey. Locker-Lampson later told Margery they had discussed everything from metaphysics to women. At one point she turned round and offered Einstein some chocolate, at which he looked surprised. According to an account of the journey related to one of Einstein's biographers by Barbara, they stopped at Newmarket for lunch.[17] Margery, however, recalled they stopped at a pub in Thetford.[18] Both towns would have been on the route they were taking to north Norfolk. Later that afternoon Einstein found himself being driven up a narrow, rutted cart track to the secret camp beside Roughton Heath, where preparations had been made to greet him. Here on a fine early autumn afternoon they had tea served outside with a small party of guests, including at least one local reporter. Given Einstein's presence in Norfolk was meant to be a secret, Locker-Lampson seems to have

Locker-Lampson and Einstein taking afternoon tea at the Roughton camp soon after arriving, Sunday 10 September 1933.

taken great pains to publicise it. Although Roughton was not mentioned in the first reports, it would not have been too much difficulty to discover the camp's location given the Commander's local celebrity. He was a well-known personality and his camp beside the Heath was common knowledge in the area. Reports of Einstein's first afternoon in Norfolk containing very similar details appeared in Norfolk's two principal newspapers, the weekly *Norfolk Chronicle* and the *Eastern Daily Press*, as well as a number of national papers, suggesting the story was sold on to the nationals. The reporter described a relaxed Einstein smoking his pipe on the veranda of one of the huts, the North Sea visible to the north-east as the late afternoon sunlight poured through one of the hut's glazed windows. Here Einstein made the first public statement after his flight:

> All I want is peace and could I have found a more peaceful retreat than here in England? … My great friend has invited me here, and I hope to stay in England for a month. No one will know where I am until October when I go to America to lecture. I can live quietly working out my mathematical problems.[19]

At this point Locker-Lampson interrupted to explain that the professor was engaged on a new theory, at which Einstein smiled but declined to offer any details. A little later he was whisked away by car to Cromer. Although he would spend the majority of his time at the Roughton camp, this excursion was to be the first of several to New Haven Court, where a room had been reserved for him. Here he could receive and post letters, use the telephone, enjoy an evening meal and take a bath. That evening a reporter observed Einstein and Locker-Lampson strolling around the grounds, stopping to watch tennis being played on the covered court. Each autumn, before his first wife Bianca's sudden death in 1929, they had hosted a private tennis tournament here featuring a sprinkling

Sketch of New Haven Court, Cromer, showing the covered tennis courts (right) where Einstein watched play, Sunday 10 September 1933.

of star players: the French Wimbledon Champion Suzanne Lenglen, the British Grand Slam player Bunny Austin and Jacques Brugnon, one of the legendary 'Four Musketeers' of French tennis had all played there.[20] The reporter noted Einstein was having trouble lighting his pipe and offered him a cigarette, which he declined, asking instead for a penknife to unblock his pipe. Once he had got it going again he told the reporter he would be staying in England for about a month. He had, he said, brought a number of books (presumably, he had not lost all of them on the journey) and intended to work quietly on a new problem he was engaged in. Locker-Lampson then confirmed the Nazi threats to the professor's life had had "an indirect influence" on his movements that weekend but the stories of a price being put on his head were incredible, adding "It has to be explored, however".[21] After this Einstein and Locker-Lampson were driven away to an undisclosed location, which the reporter rightly guessed was the Commander's "secret camp". Einstein's Norfolk adventure had begun.

Notes

1 *Lessing, "Zu 'Der Irrtum Einsteins'".*

2 *Time and Tide, 1 April 1933.*

3 *Vernon, Ellen Wilkinson.*

4 *Daily Express, 12 September 1933.*

5 *Clark, Einstein, p.443.*

6 *Valletin, Einstein, p.145.*

7 *Highfield and Carter, The Private Lives of Albert Einstein, pp.213–14.*

8 *Albert Einstein Archives, The Hebrew University of Jerusalem; AEA: 143-291.*

9 *Michelmore, Einstein, p.171.*

10 *Patrick Murphy, 'I Saved Einstein from the Nazis', Daily Mail Weekend Magazine, 8 December 1971.*

11 *Chisholm and Davie, Beaverbrook, p.227.*

12 *Sunday Express, 10 September 1933.*

13 *Marianoff and Wayne, Einstein, p.144.*

14 *Ibid. 12.*

15 *Interview with Margery Osborn née Howard in the Dominion Sunday Times (Auckland, New Zealand), 27 July 1975. The author is grateful to Steve Locker-Lampson for this cutting.*

16 *Thanks for this information are due to Eddie Anderson who corresponded with Mrs Varney in the 1980s.*

17 *Ibid. 5, p.465.*

18 *Ibid. 15.*

19 *Norfolk Chronicle, 15 September 1933.*

20 *There is British Pathé newsreel film of Suzanne Leglen with Oliver and Bianca Locker-Lampson at New Haven Court, Cromer, in 1925; see www.britishpathe.com/video/incomparable-suzanne-1/query/suzanne+Lenglen+cromer*

21 *Eastern Daily Press, 11 September 1933.*

The Syrens' Song and the Doppelgänger

TRAVELLING to Cromer on the A140 Norwich Road there comes a point when the blue of the sky ahead deepens, a sign the North Sea is close, soon to be visible perhaps over the horizon. Immediately after this harbinger, the road passes a sign for Roughton, then dips into an unexpected valley. The topography hereabouts is unusually hilly for 'flat' Norfolk due to the Cromer–Holt ridge, gouged out of the terrain by a retreating glacier 400,000 years ago. On high ground to the east of the road, isolated from the present-day village since the Black Death, is the parish church of St Mary the Virgin with its Saxon round tower, evidence of an isolated farming community here before the Norman Conquest. The character of the parish had little changed a millennium later. A 1920s pamphlet appealing for the church's restoration fund described Roughton as "a scattered agricultural parish containing some 550 inhabitants, the majority of whom are engaged on the land. We are a poor community …".[1]

On the west side of the road at the bottom of the long slope is the village pub, the New Inn, and a little further on the village school, St Mary's, direct

Postcard of Roughton church.

descendant of a charity school established here in 1694. In 1933 it consisted of three plain, whitewashed rooms, inadequately heated by tiny coke stoves and hot water pipes and dimly lit by gas light. Instruction was supplied by a head teacher and a deputy headmistress, supported by two uncertified teaching assistants. Pupils were not expected to do more than follow in the footsteps of their parents and grandparents into agriculture labouring or domestic service. The curriculum consisted of the three 'Rs' alongside instruction in domestic hygiene, gardening and rural science.[2] The Norwich Road cuts Roughton in two, making either end of the school day an anxious time for parents as they shepherd their children into waiting cars. Traffic thunders through the village, turning left by the school for Sheringham, Blakeney, Wells-next-the-Sea and all points west, or goes straight on to climb the long, low hill across Roughton Heath to Cromer. At the top of the hill Cromer's cliff-top lighthouse can be glimpsed, at this distance still only a chip of white on the horizon, its beam still flashing at intervals day and night, as it did when Einstein saw it in 1933, almost exactly a hundred years after it was built.[3]

Place-name authorities do not agree on the meaning of Roughton. Some claim it derives from the Viking words for a rye farm, others from the Anglo-Saxon words for a settlement by rough ground, which by a strange coincidence echoes the etymology of Rowfant (a rough fern brake or thicket), seat of the Locker-Lampsons' principal home in Sussex.[4] Evidence of human habitation predates Roughton's Saxon and Norse settlers considerably. Flint tools suggest the land was intermittently hunted over during the Stone Age, when woolly rhinos roamed across Doggerland before the North Sea came south. Four millennia later, people of the Bronze Age Beaker culture built large earth mounds here, which would mystify antiquarian diggers and delvers four millennia after them. Until the 20th century, large tracts of the Heath had never been under the plough. As a consequence many of its tumuli remained relatively intact. Topped with little woods, they have evocative local names—Hares Hill, Kidney Hill, Rowhow Hill. People have long regarded such mounds as supernatural places, both inhibiting and stimulating a desire to uncover and possess what has been deliberately hidden; a psychic tension explored by M. R. James in several of his ghost stories, some of which are set in East Anglia.

James was yet another of the Locker-Lampson family's literary acquaintances. In 1923, Oliver Locker-Lampson was the first to publish 'The Haunted Doll's House' in *The Empire Review*, a magazine he had just purchased control of.[5] Part of the story is set in an hotel on the East Coast. James stayed at New Haven Court or the part of it known as the Royal Cromer Hotel in Cromer on a number of occasions, noting in a letter that while it was a very nice hotel, his host preferred to sleep "in a tent on a heath 3 miles off".[6] In the 1850s an amateur archaeologist, the Rev. Greville J. Chester, prototype of one of James's dangerously obsessive antiquarian scholars, excavated a number of the large earth mounds on Roughton Heath to discover what lay within.[7] Using the crude archaeological methods of his day he hired labourers to dig deep pits into the hillside. He discovered no Saxon crown like James's unfortunate treasure hunter in 'A Warning to the Curious', instead large quantities of charred bone and a few small jet beads shaped like hogshead barrels were turned up, as well as one large, virtually intact, pie-dish shaped burial urn, similar to the type studied with profound metaphysical curiosity by the Norwich-based 17th-century doctor, philosopher and antiquarian Sir Thomas Browne. Musing on how to gauge the antiquity of similar cinerary urns excavated in Norfolk, Browne had memorably mused: "What Song the Syrens sang, or what name Achilles assumed when he hid himself among women, though puzzling Questions, are not beyond all conjecture."[8]

In September 1933 Einstein would similarly hide among the women as the syrens' song of politics lured him from his abstruse mathematical voyages. Over the years since then many Norfolk residents have found the story of Einstein's visit either too far-fetched to be credible or too inconsequential to merit investigation. Compared with De Haan (the present-day name of Le Coq-sur-Mer), which has made Einstein's stay there in 1933 a matter of civic pride, north Norfolk seems to have been notably indifferent. The Roughton village sign, which stands on the east side of the main road on a small triangle of grass, was the focus of a local debate in the 1990s about what should go on it. Elaborately carved village signs became popular in Norfolk after Edward VII liked the look of one near the royal estate at Sandringham. It took Roughton ninety years to get around to putting up one of its own. When suggestions were sought as to what aspects of village history it should depict, the parish committee received a number of suggestions that it include a reference to Einstein's visit—the equation $E = mc^2$, for example. The story made it into the local newspaper under the headline "Villagers sign up Albert Einstein".[9] There were some, however, who doubted he had ever been there and after due parochial deliberation it was decided the sign would depict St Mary's and the Cromer to Norwich 'lobster' stage coach either side of a scroll depicting the will of Robert Brown, which had established the village's free school in 1694. Einstein didn't get a look in and it wasn't until 2005 that a blue plaque sponsored by the *Eastern Daily Press* (*EDP*) commemorating his visit was placed on the wall of the New Inn.[10] Interestingly, a letter published in the *EDP* by the son of the couple who kept the New Inn between 1942 and 1965, claimed the "cloak of secrecy" surrounding Einstein's stay was such that they had never heard it mentioned or had any inkling of it.[11] The only other tangible reminder of Einstein's visit to north Norfolk today is a mural depicting him enjoying a mug of coffee on the wall of a beach-front cafe in Sheringham.[12]

One might be tempted to conclude Roughton's attitude to Einstein's visit has seldom wavered beyond incredulity or indifference but that would be wrong. Speak to local people and you will find a sense of quiet pride about the village's role in the life of its famous visitor. The village pub used to keep a folder under the counter full of clippings about Einstein. It may still do so. People will tell how local children used to be taken on school walks up the lane, known as Eastoe's loke after the gamekeeper who helped guard Einstein and lived in a small, isolated cottage near the camp, to be shown the spot where Einstein had stayed. It is even said British and American pilots flying inland from the North Sea during the Second World War used Eastoe's cottage as a landmark, calling it 'Einstein's house'. Personal recollections of Einstein's time in Roughton, however, need to be treated with caution. Dates, the duration of his stay and the events surrounding his visit sometimes do not tally with the verifiable facts of his very well-documented life.

Many who had grown up in Roughton before the Second World War were convinced they had seen him there at dates when he simply could not have been there and these recollections need to be explained. Several years ago elderly residents were asked for memories of their childhood in Roughton for a history of the village school. Two brief recollections of Einstein were included. Horace Rump was the son of the local midwife, 'Granny' Rump, who drove about the county's lanes in a donkey cart delivering babies and administering natural remedies like cinder tea to colicky infants. A relative wrote that a few years before Horace died he recalled seeing Einstein: "During the War … living in a log cabin on the Heath—he used to walk into the village to the pub and I can still see his grey flannels with the worn knees that he used to wear." Another resident, Joan Wayte, a former pupil at Roughton School, remembered: "Einstein living up on the Heath and walking down into the village", also associating this memory with the Second World War when soldiers trained on the Heath and London evacuee children lived in the cricket pavilion at Gunton Hall.[13] Another story, which appeared in the letters page of the *EDP* after the blue plaque was installed at the New Inn, related how Einstein and Locker-Lampson once rode into the village where Einstein's horse bolted. Disaster was averted when a quick-thinking local lad, Gordon Aldis, grabbed the reins and brought the horse to a stop. More stories from local people appeared in the *EDP* in 2005 during the centenary year of Einstein's Special Theory of Relativity, including those of Elizabeth Crouch, who as a schoolgirl was invited to the camp with a friend to take tea with its special guest but became frightened when she realised he was a German and she found a chest of drawers in a hut stuffed full of guns, and Norman Young, who cycled over to the camp from Overstrand Post Office where has father was the postmaster, with a telegram for Einstein, which he delivered into his hand and received a sixpence.[14]

In 1979 the *EDP* published what seems to have been the first account of Einstein's stay in Norfolk to have appeared in the local press since he left Roughton more than forty-five years earlier.[15] After outlining the events that led up to Einstein's arrival and the role of Locker-Lampson, the journalist quoted from an interview with Albert 'Lal' Thurston. Lal's story is important as it appears to be the only one known to have come from a Roughton-dwelling eyewitness who was an adult at the time of the visit and could plausibly have met Einstein because of his family connection with Herbert Eastoe. He said he was employed by the Commander to guard Einstein at night, patrolling the camp with his shotgun and being paid in glasses of beer. He thus gained access, to both the guarded 'secret' camp and its guest, that most villagers were denied. Lal had another good reason to remember 1933, as this was the year his first child, Robert, was born. His wife Violet was the daughter of Herbert Eastoe, the gamekeeper who appears in a number of the photographs of Einstein at Roughton. Robert was born in March 1933. Lal recalled carrying his son in his arms when he was only a few days old up the loke to the huts, where he showed him to Einstein: "Einstein loved children. He touched my son on the forehead and said, 'Double crown, he'll go a long way.'"[16] Lal later told the same story on television for Anglia TV's *Bygones* series. Lal was sure Einstein was there for much longer than three weeks, estimating his stay to have lasted "the best part of twelve months". He was also sure Einstein was there in the spring of 1933 after his son was born and the gorse was in bloom on the Heath. Roughton women were once known locally as 'yellow aprons' because of the extraordinary profusion of gorse flowers on the Heath that stained their clothes when collecting the peat-like turf for 'firing' their kitchen ranges.[17] Lal recalled talking to Einstein about some pheasant chicks he had found, which would be around mid-June. He also recalled his mother-in-law, Mrs Eastoe, baked Einstein a cake for a surprise birthday party. Einstein, he said, was so touched by this he cried. A charming story, seemingly corroborated by the local nature lore that a countryman such as Lal would have absorbed with his mother's milk, until one realises Einstein was in America on his birthday in March 1933 and never returned to England after sailing to America later that year. Who then had the cake been baked for? Whom had Lal met and spoken to between March and June? The strange truth is Einstein had a Norfolk *Doppelgänger*, whose role in the story of his visit to Roughton in 1933 has not been previously suspected.

The story began in 1896 when Locker-Lampson's recently widowed mother employed a private tutor to coach him in German during the summer holidays from Eton. It would have seemed a useful skill for him to acquire if he was to take up a career in the Diplomatic Service, as his older brother Godfrey was to do briefly a few years later:

> Mother decided on a German tutor and advertised. She interviewed a few but none were to her satisfaction. Then came along compact, dark Dr Ott with bandaged brow which put her off. Mother dreaded drink. 'You have not, I pray, been involved in an unseemly row.' 'I hope not,' he shyly murmured, 'Yet I hardly like to explain—I know appearances are against me.' 'They are, but please explain.' 'I should let my head heal before seeing you. You see, one day I played your cricket. I stood at the end of the pitch—you call it so I hope—and the ball struck me on the head.' A German who had played cricket scored a bull. He became our tutor and our best friend and turned up three times a year for 40 years [so until 1936].[18]

Locker-Lampson's interest in cricket-playing Teutons seems to have started here!

According to Philip Coleman, who lived in Roughton in the 1930s, Dr Ott often used to walk into the village from the camp to visit the village shop or drink a glass of beer at the pub. On one occasion he visited the village school to learn about English elementary school teaching methods, being a lecturer in educational theory in Germany. He almost certainly stayed at the camp in 1933 and probably returned the following year, which may account for Lal's memory of meeting Einstein when he could not have been there and of his being there for twelve months. A photograph published in the *EDP* in 1979 purporting to show Einstein on Roughton Heath wearing an overcoat and woollen hat as he received a birthday cake was identified in an interview with the author by Philip Colman without prompting or mention of the name as showing not Einstein but Dr Ott. Close examination of the photo does indeed show it is clearly not of Einstein. Ott's birthday was in January, which presumably accounts for the winter coat and hat. However, there is just enough similarity between Ott and Einstein's facial appearance, in particular their moustaches, to account for some of the memories that placed Einstein in Roughton when he simply could not have been there. Additionally, they both had southern German accents and for those who would have had very little idea who Einstein was, one German professor living in a hut on Roughton Heath might well have been remembered as another more famous one later on.

Einstein's Doppelgänger, Karl Ott, receiving his birthday cake outside Eastoe's cottage Roughton Heath, c.1933.

Karl Ott was born in Mainwangen close to the Bodensee (Lake Constance) in 1873 about 63 miles (100km) from Ulm, Einstein's birthplace. The son of a teacher, he studied history and modern languages—like Locker-Lampson—at Heidelberg and Leipzig. He must have been a good teacher as Locker-Lampson soon became proficient in French and German. The two regularly visited each other's homes. Ott was even recorded in the 1901 Census as a visitor at Rowfant. In his memoirs Locker-Lampson describes a walking holiday he took in southern Germany in June 1914 when he visited Dr Ott at Karlsruhe in Baden. On his way there a "flat-faced" German baron "insinuated himself" into his company, "seductively suggesting they might travel together". At this moment of intense political tension in Europe, he suspected the German authorities thought he was on a spying mission and had sent this man to keep an eye on him. However, when he mentioned he was visiting a school teacher, the baron said whereas he might associate socially with an English MP he could not associate with a mere pedagogue, at which Locker-Lampson suggested they part company as he could not abide a snob. Once in Baden, he used his status to cadge a trip in an airship, probably at the Graf Zeppelin works in Friedrichshafen, where the airship's captain remarked to him cryptically: "We shall meet again in England, and sooner than you think". Indeed, in February 1915 Locker-Lampson, as commander of a RNAS armoured car squadron based in Cromer, got off a few shots at a Zeppelin raiding the north Norfolk coast. During the First World War, despite the fact he was now an enemy national and it contravened the Defence

Karl Ott and Locker-Lampson on Roughton Heath.

of the Realm Act, he maintained a channel of communications with Dr Ott in Germany, arranging for his friend to receive the *Times Literary Supplement* regularly via neutral Switzerland. After the war Dr Ott resumed his annual visits to England, spending a portion of each vacation with the Locker-Lampsons at their family homes in Sussex and Norfolk. Savin in his history of Cromer listed Dr Ott among the notable visitors to New Haven Court. In 1934, Ott was dismissed from his professorship at Karlsruhe Technical College because of his anti-Nazi views. He made further visits to Norfolk in the late summers of 1935 and 1936, when he spoke to fellow Rotarians in Norwich about his efforts to set up friendly meetings between German, Austrian and French Rotary Clubs. In 1937, the Nazis banned Rotary Clubs in Germany, after which his visits seemed to stop. After the war, he helped restore democracy and rebuild the education system in Baden before his death following a stroke in 1952.[19]

Notes

1 *Roughton Parochial Parish Council, An Appeal, 1926, Norfolk Studies Library.*

2 *Hayes, St Mary's.*

3 *Long, Lights of East Anglia, ch.1, passim.*

4 *See Ekwall, The Concise Dictionary of English Place-Names and Mills, Oxford Dictionary of English Place-Names.*

5 *James, The Haunted Doll's House.*

6 *James, Letters to a Friend, p.139.*

7 *Chester, 'Account of the discovery of ancient British remains near Cromer'.*

8 *Browne, Hydriotaphia.*

9 *Eastern Daily Press, 21 January 1994.*

10 *Keiron Pim, 'Hut-ching a plan to remember Einstein', Eastern Daily Press, 10 November 2005.*

11 *S. W. Lanes, letter, Eastern Daily Press, 30 March 1979.*

12 *Blackburn, Threads, pp.55–61.*

13 *Ibid. 2, pp.91–2.*

14 *Keiron Pim, 'The Day I Met Albert Einstein', Eastern Daily Press, 28 October 2005.*

15 *Clement Court, 'Man who guarded Einstein in Norfolk', Eastern Daily Press, 22 March 1979.*

16 *Variations of this story appeared in Ibid.14 & 15. Recollections of 'Lal' Thurston courtesy his son Mr Robert Thurston.*

17 *Eastern Daily Press, 3 June 1933.*

18 *Steve Locker-Lampson, Nothing to Offer But Blood, p.58.*

19 *Muller, Biography of Karl Ott.*

Splendid Solitude on the Heath

THE camp lay half way along a rutted cart track known locally as Eastoe's loke, which ran between Thorpe Market Road and North Walsham Road to the east of Roughton Heath. The loke was bordered on each side by overhanging trees and thick hedgerows planted to act as a wind break and to keep cattle from straying. Through a gap in the hedge on its west side visitors would have seen something that looked like a paddock or 'pightie' in the Norfolk dialect, enclosed by fencing. On the north side of the camp was a row of wooden huts ranging in size from a large garden shed to a substantial log cabin with glazed windows, which had been thatched with Norfolk reed and clad with split pine trunks to make it look more rustic. A long, narrow grassed area to the north of the huts faced Roughton Heath and by all contemporary accounts had views at that period over the Heath to the North Sea. The other huts were plainer, though Locker-Lampson would later have these thatched and log-clad too. To the south of the huts on the rougher grass of the pightie stood a pair of large white canvas bell tents.

So far, nothing too usual. The Heath was often used for camping and farm outbuildings much like these were a common sight. However, the people there this September did not look like typical campers or farmers. Throughout the

Rare view of the Roughton camp taken before Einstein's stay there. 'Einstein's hut' (far left) has not yet been thatched or clad with pine logs.

day two young women dressed in riding boots, jodhpurs and polo shirts might have been observed walking about, rifles slung over their shoulders on leather straps. Another man, immaculately turned out in a gamekeeper's full rig and sometimes accompanied by a dog might have been spotted, particularly at dawn and dusk, his double-barrelled shotgun at shoulder arms like a guard on sentry duty. From one of the huts the smell of cooking periodically wafted across the camp, followed by the bizarre spectacle of a waiter in a black tail coat and white gloves treading circumspectly across the grass bearing a laden silver tray. From another hut came the incongruous sound of live music being played on a piano. At other times the horn of a wind-up gramophone projected the scratchy sound of classical music, most probably by Einstein's favourite composers Bach and Mozart. Amid it all, a slightly stout, middle-aged man with an unkempt mane of greying hair seemed to be the centre of everyone's attention as he lounged outside in an armchair, often bare-chested, as he soaked up the late summer sun or strolled about the camp, sometimes stopping to talk to a small flock of nanny goats or to pat a sleepy looking horse switching flies with its tail. At other times he might have been glimpsed inside one of the huts, scribbling away as he puffed on his pipe, a disordered pile of papers and notebooks strewn over a card table and spilling onto the floor.

Something about living outside in a tent or a hut seems to have appealed to the eternal boy scout in Locker-Lampson's psyche. In an article published in August 1930, "If I Were a Millionaire", he wrote: "What I like best is a tent on a heath, plain viands, a glass of beer and the sweet communion of my darling books and dearer friends."[1] He seemed determined to project this image. In November 1930 he was featured in the popular weekly tabloid *The Bystander* shaving in the open air beside one of his tents with the caption "Oliver Locker-Lampson has gone into winter quarters at Roughton".[2] One of his first huts had been erected in the partly wooded grounds of New Haven Court. In 1909 his friend the explorer Sir Ernest Shackleton used it while writing *The Heart of the Antarctic.*[3] After Shackleton's death in 1922, Locker-Lampson had a commemorative plaque placed on the hut. In September 1918 with suspected T.B. after the rigours of his Russian campaign, under doctor's orders to sleep in the open air, he set up a camp in a wooded area between West Runton and Cromer known locally as the Roman Camp, recruiting several of his former armoured car men to help him clear the ground and build some huts.[4] In 1926 his Shackleton hut burnt to the ground under suspicious circumstances and it seems to have been after this that he had another hut built on Roughton Heath. As local by-laws did not permit permanent structures on the Heath, the parish council informed him he had to remove it. He rebuilt it only yards away in a farmer's top field. In time he had several more huts built, accommodating eventually a canteen, a library, additional dormitories and a privy, all the work of Cromer-based contractors

Girling & Smith. Although he would later buy the field, in 1933 he was renting it from Farmer Colman of Hill Farm. Amenities were basic. Water and other necessities were brought up by horse and cart from the farm or the village. Other provisions were brought over from Cromer by car or purchased locally.

While there was a local tradition of living in similar temporary structures, they were generally regarded at this time as the homes of the itinerant and poor rather than fashionable 'glamping' abodes. One has only to think of the Peggottys' home made out of an upturned boat on Yarmouth beach in *David Copperfield*. After the Great War, migrant agricultural workers took over disused railway carriages to live on the verges of roads and common land. The custom had been noted by Lady Battersea, who had known Locker-Lampson since he was a boy and lived in the nearby seaside village of Overstrand: "During the season the inhabitants … live in strange little makeshift dwellings, even in railway carriages, standing at the rear of their houses, the latter have been given over to the lodgers and made as fit for their reception as circumstances will permit."[5] One hut, fitted-up to look like a log cabin, was for Einstein's personal use. A second, slightly larger hut provided accommodation for Einstein's bodyguards, Barbara Goodall and Margery Howard. A third, used as a canteen, was occupied by the cook Mona. Other members of Locker-Lampson's entourage to visit the camp included Tom Wilson, a general manager at the Royal Cromer Hotel (otherwise known as New Haven Court); the hotel's butler; his Cromer-based secretary, Miss Billing; and his niece, Dorothy's daughter, Jane Delmar-Morgan, who brought Einstein a violin from W. E. Hills of Bond Street to replace the one stolen by the Nazis.[6] Some biographers of Einstein have claimed Dr Walther Mayer stayed at the camp for a few days but there does not seem to be any evidence for this and letters Einstein and Mayer exchanged during this period suggest Mayer remained in Belgium the whole time.

On fine days meals and high tea were served *al fresco*, while on damp or cool days meals were taken inside one of the huts. Mona was an object of curiosity for the local lads who rarely met young working-class women from outside the village, let alone a brash Cockney who spoke her mind and wasn't afraid to sneak them tots of rum and whisky from the Commander's drinks cabinet. Locker-Lampson, when he stayed at the camp slept in one of the bell tents erected near the huts. In addition to the huts, the camp had a raised viewing platform, originally intended for taking pot-shots at the local wildlife but now used to keep a watchful eye on the surrounding countryside. Einstein used this for sunbathing, dressed only in baggy woollen swimming trunks. A small wooden privy completed the camp, and it is tempting to imagine the great man sitting there, smoking his pipe as he contemplated the mysteries of the universe.

The first week

Monday 11 September

Monday was Einstein's first full day in Norfolk; a day of perfect late summer weather, sunny and cloudless, with the daytime temperature still in the low 70s Fahrenheit, tempered by a light cooling sea breeze. It had been a long, dry summer. Moorland and forest fires had been reported all over the country and Roughton Heath was a tinder box.

As its distinguished visitor began his first week at the camp, the local community got on with its seasonally allotted tasks. The harvest had only just been gathered in and down at Hill Farm, Farmer Colman and his 17-year-old son Philip were using the time they now had in repairing the farm carts and machinery. At some point during this first morning the local gamekeeper Herbert Eastoe walked across their farmyard with an extraordinary piece of news. His words were recalled by Philip Colman sixty-four years later:

> "Master Colman, Master Colman, I got you a little job you can earn some money from. Have you heard? They got an old Jarman up at the huts. Locker, silly old bugger, he wants a horse to ride so he can guard this old Jarman they got up there. They say there's a price on his head of a thousand pound. I wouldn't mind a bit of that but yew mustn't tell anyone he's up there. It's a secret."[7]

Herbert Eastoe, in his mid-50s, married with one grown-up daughter, had worked on Lord Suffield's nearby Gunton Hall estate man and boy but was now only employed there part-time. In the 1890s Lord Suffield had hosted extravagantly lavish shooting parties attended by the Prince of Wales but those days were long gone. The estate had been losing money for decades and was gradually selling off land and buildings to pay its debts. Its decline meant the loss of jobs and incomes in the local community, and Eastoe felt himself lucky to even have been kept on part-time. According to Philip Colman, all that year in 1933 he had been eking out his reduced wages by cultivating a few rows of vegetables, rising at dawn to tend them in a secluded corner of a nearby field so his neighbours wouldn't see him, an estate gamekeeper, humbling himself with agricultural toil. Any extra income he could garner was like gold dust. From time to time when Locker-Lampson wanted a bit of rough shooting he paid Eastoe to carry and load his guns. Philip Colman recalled how, not having a trained retriever, he used to tip Eastoe a shilling for each bird he brought to him. Unfortunately, he was not a good shot and keen not to lose the tips Eastoe would hide pre-shot birds in the undergrowth, disappear behind the nearest hedge and reappear minutes later with a pheasant in hand. Now he wanted him to mount an armed guard at the camp to protect an important guest. It was money for old rope as far he was concerned. He had been promised £1 a week, which was as much as he was getting at Gunton Hall, and unlike the work there, which was several miles away, his cottage at the top of the loke was almost literally a stone's throw from Locker-Lampson's camp, so home comforts would be close at hand when he went out on night patrol. His only problem was actually getting hold of the money. Locker-Lampson seldom carried any and usually referred local tradesmen to the appropriately named Miss Billing for payment. Eastoe could not have imagined this little job was about to achieve for him the kind of fame a lifetime's keeping could never bring him. Within days his photograph would appear in both the local and national newspapers as he guarded the "old Jarman" on Roughton Heath.

While news of Einstein's flight first appeared in the *Sunday Express* on 10 September, it was Monday's newspapers, local and national, that first revealed his refuge was in Norfolk, somewhere near Cromer. For a location that was supposed to be secret, a great deal about it was being made public knowledge. On at least one occasion, towards the end of Einstein's stay, a newspaper actually revealed that the camp was in Roughton.[8] Locker-Lampson might have hidden Einstein more simply and possibly more safely at his well-appointed and spacious London apartment or at either of his family's large homes in Norfolk and Sussex. Presumably, the wooden hut complete with piano he had set up at considerable trouble and expense for Einstein's use near a rented cottage in Escher, Surrey, in July was not available that autumn. He realised the publicity surrounding Einstein had to be constantly fuelled and fanned in order to keep his plight in the public eye. Einstein living in a log cabin on a remote Norfolk heath, guarded by a gamekeeper and young women armed with shotguns was clearly a more colourful story for the papers to report than Einstein holed up in a stuffy hotel or country house.

On Monday the main daily Norfolk newspaper, the *Eastern Daily Press* (*EDP*), printed a couple of columns on an inside page it normally devoted to foreign news reporting the story of Einstein's sudden departure from his "holiday home" in Belgium, his unexpected appearance in Cromer on Sunday afternoon and his current "peaceful retreat" in a small wooden hut at a secret location "facing the North Sea". The rest of the article was padded out with syndicated Reuter's stories on Elsa's fears for her husband's safety and on Einstein's letter to Belgian campaigners against compulsory military service, explaining his painful decision not to support them, a stance regarded by many in the pacifist movement as a betrayal. On the same page, in the paper's regular 'London Letter' column, its correspondent provided a pen portrait of Einstein's host: "Attractive in appearance and personally popular, he is a persistent advocate of the causes he takes up. He has the gift of epigram and has inherited literary grace from his father Frederick Locker, the poet, through who he is related to Mr Birrell."[9] Locker-Lampson's brother-in-law, Augustine Birrell, a retired Liberal politician, barrister and author, lived until 1932 in Sheringham, about 8 miles (13 km) from Roughton. Ill-health eventually forcing him to move to his home in Chelsea where he died in November 1933 aged 83.

From a photograph in Tuesday's edition of the *EDP* it is evident Locker-Lampson had invited the press to the camp on Monday. No photographs are known to exist of Einstein in Cromer, which he had first visited on Sunday evening when it had perhaps been too dark for outdoor photography. Additionally, he probably felt having the backdrop of a log cabin on a heath rather than a grand house and a tennis court were essential elements in creating the whole *mise-en-scène* of the exiled genius. The photograph does indeed look carefully stage managed. Einstein, wearing baggy flannel trousers and a light-coloured cardigan over his clearly shirtless, slightly portly torso, is sitting in a low armchair outside a hut. On his feet are shoes but no socks. Lal Thurston, who shared guard duties at the camp with his father-in-law Herbert Eastoe, recalled in the 1970s that Einstein had told him his big toes made holes in his socks when he was a boy so he never wore them.[10]

In another photograph taken from a slightly different angle and not published at the time, Herbert Eastoe can be seen near this group, his shotgun lent against his shoulder. In yet another photograph, Einstein and Locker-Lampson are

The small horse group again, showing the bell tents at Roughton Heath camp. Left to right: Locker-Lampson, Barbara Goodall, Einstein, Margery Howard, Herbert Eastoe.

standing side by side outside the same thatched hut, clearly sharing a joke about something. The ubiquitous Eastoe can be seen behind them with his shotgun, the gorse-covered Heath stretching away to the horizon behind him. This photograph appeared alongside a report in the *Norfolk Chronicle* that a British schoolboy had been beaten up by Brown Shirts when he failed to salute their swastika banner in the street. After a strongly worded protest by the British Foreign Office, the Nazi Party claimed the assault had in fact been carried out by communist spies disguised as Brown Shirts.[11] Whether the various photographs at the Roughton camp were taken by one photographer and then syndicated or by a group of photographers from different papers is not known. It is clear, however, that Locker-Lampson's plan was to gain maximum coverage rather than give an exclusive to one paper, something the Beaverbrook-owned *Express* papers were presumably unhappy about given their scoop in being the first to publish the news of Einstein's flight. In a further set of photographs almost certainly taken on the same day given the identical clothes worn by the subjects, Einstein, Barbara and Margery, and Eastoe are gathered about Locker-Lampson seated on a small horse. Given all he had been through over the past few days it is remarkable how relaxed and good humoured Einstein appears to be. The Norfolk air clearly agreed with him.

Another view of the small horse group, Roughton Heath camp, September 1933. Left to right: Margery Howard, Einstein, Tom Wilson, Locker-Lampson, Barbara Goodall.

Having distanced himself from the tense, overheated atmosphere at the Villa Savoyarde, Einstein's thoughts turned again to the pacifist dilemma of how a small democratic county like Belgium could defend its freedom from a militarily aggressive country like Germany. This is clear from a letter he wrote on Monday in which he expressed his views more cogently and uncompromisingly than he had felt able to do before. The letter was addressed to the biologist Professor G. C. Heringa of the University of Amsterdam, a leading pacifist campaigner and a friend and colleague of Dr De Groodt, Einstein's host at Cantecroy in March. Heringa had written to Einstein before he left Le Coq-sur-Mer to express his disbelief in a story circulating that he had renounced his adherence to the doctrine of absolute anti-militarism. In reply, Einstein explained that the threat to peace and personal freedom posed by the Nazis was of such a magnitude nations and individuals needed do all they could to defend themselves while seeking to change Germany's aggressive foreign policy by diplomacy backed up by superior military strength. Disarmament and passive resistance were, he felt, no longer viable options: "To prevent the greater evil it is necessary the lesser evil—the hated military—be accepted for the time being."[12] The seeds were perhaps sown here of his support for the development of the Atom Bomb in America in order to counter the possibility of a viable atomic weapon being developed by the Nazis before they had been defeated.

Turning from the international arena to more parochial matters, the news of Einstein's arrival in north Norfolk had clearly raised a few eyebrows among members of Cromer's Urban District Council. On Monday evening, as the news of his sudden appearance in the area broke in the local and national press, the Council met to discuss such topics as the cost of illuminating the municipal pitch and putting green in the evening and the nuisance caused by private motor vehicles using the bus station forecourt. At the end of the session under any other business a question on whether they should honour their distinguished visitor in some manner was raised. His visit was, all the councillors agreed, a wonderful advertisement for Cromer as a holiday resort and one suggested the acting chairman of the Council, Councillor Rust, visit the camp where Einstein was staying and formally welcome him. The suggestion seems to have given rise to some mirth, leading to questions such as wasn't his visit supposed to be secret and was it not the case he was living in a hut? Might it not be better in the circumstances, asked one councillor, if the professor was instead brought down to the Council's offices, as there was a danger Councillor Rust might be mistaken for one of those who were after him and be shot at? In the end, deciding discretion was in order, Councillor Rust replied that there was really nothing they could do as it was, after all, a private visit.[13] One can only imagine the potential for confusion if Einstein had been informed that a Herr Rust wished to meet him, for, by chance, this was the name of the current Nazi-appointed Minister for Cultural Affairs in Prussia, Bernhard Rust, a man who at that very moment was enforcing new laws that were driving thousands of Jewish teachers and lecturers from their academic posts. Only that April he had demanded Einstein's former colleagues at the University of Berlin denounce him as a traitor: "It is less important that a professor make discoveries than he train assistants and students in the proper view of the world", echoing the Nazi's view that Einstein's theories were merely "Jewish science".[14]

Reports of the Cromer Council meeting appeared in the *EDP* on Tuesday and in the weekly *Norfolk Chronicle* on Friday. Such items in the local press, despite their potential to turn the circumstances surrounding Einstein's presence in the area into farce, seemed to be grist for the mill as far as Locker-Lampson was concerned. He needed to balance his desire for maximum publicity for Einstein's plight with the necessity to keep Einstein safe from the unhinged and the wicked. The calculation he probably made was that the risk to his guest's security in north Norfolk was probably not high, though it was good publicity for the cause to pretend it was. In reality, anyone living in the area could easily have discovered where the camp was located. Locker-Lampson might as well have erected signposts. Fortunately, Nazi assassins seem to have been in short supply in north Norfolk that September and locals likely to be antipathetic to his political stance were thin on the ground and not yet well organised. British Union of Fascist (BUF) branches had recently been set up in King's Lynn, Downham Market and Hunstanton in the west of Norfolk but there is no evidence they were interested in Einstein's presence in the county despite all the publicity. A year later it might have been different; by then branches had also been set up closer to Roughton in Cromer, North Walsham, Norwich and Sheringham, and the BUF had become much more openly anti-Semitic and pro-Nazi.[15]

Further reactions to Einstein's flight from farther afield, mainly culled from Reuter's stories, were also published in the local and national press this week. It was reported the chairman of the Reichstag Fire Committee, the anti-Nazi coalition that Ellen Wilkinson had helped organise, had declared if a hair of Einstein's head was touched, certain Germans who had been identified in Paris, would answer for it. Meanwhile, still ensconced at Villa Savoyarde, Elsa Einstein told a reporter: "We have nothing to do with politics; a savant should be left in peace. Nobody knows what we have been through this last week." Elsa was wrong. Like it or not, everything Einstein said and did was now subject to political interpretation.

Tuesday 12 September

The weather turned somewhat cooler on Tuesday morning, with now and again the barest rumble of thunder from far out over the North Sea. Although

Einstein had stayed up talking with Locker-Lampson at the camp until 1 a.m., he rose at 7 and continued to work on his current mathematical problem. Although not dated, a manuscript containing a closely hand-written page of calculations seems to have been begun by Einstein this day. Headed *Dienstag* (Tuesday), the work concerned what he called the electricity problem of his Unified Field Theory. The notes were addressed to Dr Mayer, Einstein's 'calculator', who had remained in Belgium. Einstein and Mayer had been working that summer on finding a way of explaining the existence of two electrical charges in an atom of equal charge but differing mass. The work would ultimately prove to be a dead end with the discovery of the positron, the electron's anti-particle. Before coming to the maths, Einstein provided Mayer with a pen-sketch of his present situation, extoling the "*Herrliche Einsamkeit auf der Heide!*" ("Splendid solitude on the heath!")[16] The phrase has a poetic feeling to it, reminiscent of a Schubert song. In a letter mysteriously headed "24, Cromer, England" and signed "Papa", Einstein tried to explain his present predicament to his younger son Tete. Death threats, he wrote, had driven him out of Belgium to England where he was currently staying on the coast in a tiny wooden hut: "That an old fellow like me should have no peace!", it was nothing other than a revolution of the stupid against the rational and sadly it seemed the stupid currently formed a sizeable majority in Germany.[17] In April Tete had been admitted to the Burghölzli Psychiatric Hospital in Zurich, where he would remain for the rest of his life, dying there in 1965. Einstein, who had last visited him there in May, would never see him again.

Fascinating details of the arrangements at the camp during these first few days can be gleaned from the local newspapers. Despite the fact the camp was supposed to be secret and well-guarded, local reporters seem to have had no trouble finding it and gaining access. On Tuesday or possibly Wednesday afternoon with the news of Einstein's arrival beginning to become stale, a reporter from the north-Norfolk-based weekly *Norfolk Chronicle* visited the 'secret' camp in search of an interview:

> Two days after the first excitement of the Professor's visit had somewhat abated I was fortunate enough to penetrate the stronghold where the great scientist is in retreat ... and learn the whole story concerning the Professor's movements. So keen are the watchers that the moment I got in view of the encampment I was accosted and requested to produce my credentials. After a brief wait I was taken to Commander Locker-Lampson and cordially received in his comfortably appointed cabin.[18]

On being asked whether he might see the professor, Locker-Lampson said "no—he was guarded like the Crown Jewels and must have quiet and be undisturbed so he could work". When strangers were about, he explained, Professor Einstein remained in his cabin working on his new mathematical theory but when the coast was clear he would sometimes slip out of his hut and into another where he played delightful music on a piano specially installed there for his use. The piano, a baby grand, had been hired from Norwich after Einstein had expressed an interest in playing during his stay. By day Locker-Lampson and his staff and friends were always on the alert for any threat to Einstein's safety, although he believed he was quite safe in England where he was welcomed everywhere. At night armed guards patrolled the perimeter. He was happy to report there had been no intruders so far and the only night-time disturbance had been when the gamekeeper's dog tried to catch a hedgehog outside Einstein's hut. While there is no evidence that the local policeman PC Emery was actively involved in guarding Einstein, it would seem unlikely he was unaware of his presence given his official position in the village. While reports in the British press make no reference to local police involvement, a report in some US newspapers said: "local police are aware and can be summoned instantly if necessary to aid private guards".[19]

According to Locker-Lampson, who by now seems to have appointed himself Einstein's official spokesman, Einstein had decided not to attend any public function or visit anyone or receive visitors while he was in Norfolk but to devote his whole time to his one all-absorbing passion—his work. As it turned out, this was far from true as he would receive at least three visitors at the camp and on one occasion even paid a call on a Cabinet minister vacationing in the area. Meanwhile, according to Locker-Lampson, the professor was enjoying the country air, which was a tonic and no doubt accounted for the fact that two of England's greatest men of action, Oliver Cromwell and Horatio Nelson, came from the Eastern counties. Oliver Locker-Lampson had something of an obsession with Cromwell. Having chosen Cromwell's home county, Huntingdonshire, to contest for his first parliamentary seat in 1910, he set about convincing the electorate his parents had named him after the great English parliamentarian and that he was related to the family of Cromwell's wife via a great grandfather, the Reverend Jonathan Boucher. Another great grandfather, William Locker, had been Nelson's 'Sea Daddy'.

The *Norfolk Chronicle* reporter sought to place Einstein's Jewish identity in a local context, noting since the death of Lady Battersea, an old friend of Locker-Lampson's parents and a member of the Rothschild family, there was only one Jewish family in the area—the Levines, who owned a jewellers in Cromer. Their shop had recently been robbed of £2,000 worth of jewellery and antiques while shut for lunch. When told of the crime Einstein is said to have expressed a wish to meet the family and offer his condolences before he left Norfolk. The report mentions the Levine family had lost two sons in the Great War. This was the same family Locker-Lampson had referred to when introducing his Bill to extend

British nationality to Jewish refugees in July. The reporter went on to note that Einstein had been greatly impressed by the many fine church buildings he had seen in his journey through Norfolk, especially their distinctively English style of architecture. The spacious interior of Cromer church had especially impressed him.

A curious little tailpiece to the report in an adjacent column noted the professor had made great friends among the few people he had met since arriving in Norfolk and everyone who had met him had said afterwards "what a lovable man". The article concluded with this final, throwaway remark: "He is also on friendly terms with the Commander's old horse Abraham." An appropriate name given Abraham, the biblical patriarch, was the leader of the Israelites out of captivity into the Promised Land. This horse was clearly not Tom, Hill Farm's small beast of all work. Photographs taken at the camp show Locker-Lampson astride a black hunter with a cropped tail. Could this be Abraham?

Wednesday 13 September to Sunday 17 September

The weather continued to feel a little cooler than at the beginning of the week, largely because of a fresh wind that was getting up along the coast. Einstein seems to have spent the remainder of his first week at the camp inside his hut working on his mathematical problems and occasionally playing the piano. On Thursday morning the wind increased speed markedly. A British steamer, *Porthcawl*, with a cargo of esparto grass that had caught fire drifted out of control along the Norfolk coast, "bobbing in the big seas like a cork" towards the treacherous Haisbro' Sands. The Cromer lifeboat *H. F. Bailey*, skippered by its legendary coxswain Henry Blogg, was launched at about 4 p.m. to assist as holidaymakers gathered on Cromer pier and along the cliffs to watch the unfolding drama.

Meanwhile, the Norfolk press continued to be fascinated by the county's distinguished visitor. An editorial in the *EDP* on Wednesday, picking up perhaps on the minutes of the recent Cromer Town Council meeting, concurred that his visit was indeed a good advertisement for the resort. It was a fine conclusion to a good summer season: "Even the presence of a film star could hardly exceed the value of the town's latest visitor ... it all happened so suddenly and so unexpectedly that a little embarrassment may well be excused." Einstein fever was to be found outside Norfolk too. During a lecture on the expanding universe given by Sir Arthur Eddington at a British Science Association meeting in Leicester, an unknown man had risen at the mere mention of Einstein's name and called for a vote of sympathy to be sent to him. It was Eddington who in 1919 had helped provide conclusive proof of Einstein's theory that light was susceptible to gravity and time was therefore relative to the observer.

Elsewhere in its pages the *EDP* reiterated that Einstein was still at work on his latest mathematical treatise under armed guard "somewhere in Norfolk". The report is basically a condensed version of one that would be published at greater length on Friday in the weekly *Norfolk Chronicle*: "He sits in a hut by himself with Commander Locker-Lampson, M.P., keeping a watchful eye for intruders. At night keepers and some men who served with the Commander on his last Russian expedition form a guard and patrol round the grounds with sports guns."[20] Other than former RNAS petty officer Tom Wilson, the names of the Locker-Lampson's armoured car men from Cromer who helped guard Einstein have not been recorded—nearly thirty had been under his command on the Eastern Front in 1916–17. Asked if it was true he had insured Einstein's life, Locker-Lampson laughed and denied it; the moment captured perhaps in the photograph of the two men laughing outside one of the huts, a facsimile copy of which, signed by both men, Locker-Lampson later gave away as a souvenir to those who had helped look after Einstein.

Warmer weather returned towards the weekend, with temperatures rising into the mid-70s Fahrenheit on Sunday; real Indian Summer weather for England in September. During this quiet interlude, with the press's attention lessening and with few or no visitors, Einstein continued to work on the application of the Dirac Equation to solve a fundamental problem of Quantum physics. His solution covered four pages of closely written notes for Dr Mayer to check. When not working on his equations he found time to write a press statement, which was issued on Friday 15 September, concerning allegations that had been circulating for some time that he was either a member of the Communist Party or was sympathetic to its causes. He had made such statements before and would be forced to do so again in America, particularly during the McCarthy witch hunts against suspected communists in the early 1950s. The occasion for the present denial was a pamphlet entitled *The Communist Solar System*, which some friends had sent him while he was in Norfolk. Published by the British Labour Party with a foreword by Herbert Morrison, it sought to uncover various organisations, including ostensibly pacifist ones, that were, it claimed, fronts for the Communist Party. Two of them, the Anti-War Movement and Workers' International Relief, were ones to which Einstein admitted he had been tricked into giving his support to but which he now realised were in reality nothing more than propaganda fronts for the Soviet Union. He deplored "any power … which enslaves the individual by terror and force, whether it arises under a Fascist or a Communist flag". It is not hard to see the hand of Locker-Lampson, veteran anti-Red campaigner, in this statement at this time.

The second week

Monday 18 September

The weekend just gone would prove to be the last really summery one of the year. Though there had been a little rain on Sunday the temperature had rarely fallen below 75° Fahrenheit during the day. Monday signalled a subtle shift in the season towards autumn, with lower average daytime temperatures and more cloud and rain. Einstein's four pages of maths for Mayer to check were posted. Going through his notebook after the letter had gone, Einstein realised he had made a mistake in one crucial calculation and quickly sent off another couple of pages with a further solution to the problem.

Monday was possibly the day when Einstein received the first of the three known visitors to the camp from outside the locality. His name was Walter Adams and his visit concerned a matter close to Einstein's heart: the rescue of his fellow Jewish academics being forced from their posts in Germany. Einstein knew his worldwide celebrity meant it was unlikely he would ever be without a home and an academic post should he be forced to leave Germany permanently. An invitation to join the Institute of Advanced Study in Princeton had already been accepted, and while his own safety and that of his immediate family and closest assistants seemed assured, he was acutely conscious of the peril in which other Jewish scholars in Germany now found themselves. Universities, schools, hospitals and the civil service were being systematically cleared of Jews. Thousands of Jewish professionals—doctors, teachers, scientists, technicians, engineers, lawyers, artists and intellectuals—were fleeing Germany without being able to take any of their savings or property with them and with no job or home to go to. It was at this time that several bodies were set up to offer financial and other forms of assistance to Jewish refugee scholars.

Walter Adams was to have a long and distinguished academic career, culminating in his appointment as Director of the London School of Economics in 1967 and he was knighted in 1970. In 1933 he was 27 and had just done two big things: resigned from his post as a history lecturer at University College London and got married. The resignation had followed his appointment as Secretary of the Academic Assistance Council (AAC). The fact he was not Jewish himself was deemed important by his employers. The AAC had followed the advice of the Royal Society not to appoint people of Jewish origin so as to avoid the accusation they were just a front for Jewish 'agitators' or only supported Jewish refugee academics.[21] Many years later the British Zionist Norman Bentwich wrote of Adams's appointment: "The Council was happy in the choice of its General Secretary … for six years, until almost the outbreak of the world war, he gave devoted service, and showed organising capacity of the highest order."[22] The AAC had been formed, like a number of similar bodies set up at this time, to help scholars who had been forced out of their posts because of anti-Semitic academic and civil service laws in Germany. Many years later Adams, looking back on this period in his life, observed that the exodus of Jewish scholars and professionals from Germany and Austria before the war did great harm to those countries, as they stupidly and with great brutality expelled many of their most highly skilled people, for whose education they had already paid. In contrast the countries and institutions who received these refugee scholars derived great benefit from the influx of these talented individuals, whose services they acquired at very little cost.[23]

Adams had hit upon the idea of a public meeting to draw attention to the situation of the refugee scholars and he was keen to secure a high-profile speaker. Einstein was the obvious choice. Presumably, he secured an interview with Einstein at Roughton via Locker-Lampson's office in Westminster. Adams and an unnamed companion, perhaps his new bride Tatiana Makaroff, drove from London to New Haven Court in Cromer, from where they were taken to the camp at Roughton. Adams's only published account of his visit appeared in Clark's biography of Einstein: "First we were confronted by one beautiful girl with a gun. Then there was a second one, also with a gun. Finally we saw Einstein who was walking round inside what seemed to be a little hedged compound."[24] Adams, not wanting to beat about the bush, literally or metaphorically, dispensed with the usual formalities and asked Einstein straight off if he would speak at a meeting in support of the AAC's work. Einstein agreed at once. According to Adams, as soon as Einstein had given his assent Locker-Lampson rushed off to make the arrangements. As there was no telephone at the camp Locker-Lampson presumably drove back to Cromer with Adams before going to use the phone at New Haven Court. Adams and Einstein seem to have envisaged a small meeting of a couple of hundred people at most. Locker-Lampson, however, with his usual flair for publicity and the grand gesture, immediately hired the Royal Albert Hall.

Tuesday 19 September

The enormity of the task ahead may only now have begun to sink in. Locker-Lampson had just two weeks to organise what would become the largest public demonstration yet held in Britain against Hitler's anti-Semitic policies. He calculated he needed to persuade five or six major public figures to speak in support of Einstein, as well as organise stewards, print flyers and posters, and sell enough tickets to make sure the 10,000-seat capacity auditorium looked full. Given the size of the task we might have expected Locker-Lampson to travel to London as soon as possible. In fact, he delayed leaving until late Tuesday evening, thirty or more hours after Walter Adams's visit. The reason was apparently that he had committed to speak at a public meeting in Roughton on the topic of international relations. On the face of it, it seems curious at a time like this he should choose to give a political speech in an obscure rural village that wasn't even in his constituency but there was method in his madness. Word may have reached him that two senior Conservative members of the National Government—Samuel Hoare and Neville Chamberlain—were staying in the area and so might reasonably be expected to hear about his speech on the local Tory grapevine or read about it in the papers. Reports presumably based on his own office's press release appeared in numerous provincial papers and in at least one national—the *Daily Mirror*. In it Locker-Lampson attacked the Labour Prime Minister, Ramsay MacDonald, current leader of the National Government, accusing him and his entire Cabinet, most of whom were Conservatives, of failing to provide leadership, especially over the crisis on the Continent:

> The Prime Minister was an extinct volcano. Indeed, had he ever erupted? He should cease his vain perambulations of foreign lands in search of audiences. If he cannot lead he should drop out. He could then become Lord of Lossiemouth [MacDonald's birthplace] and solve one, at least, of our most pressing problems.[25]

Sir Samuel Hoare, Secretary of State for India, was staying at his Norfolk home, Sidestrand Hall, only a couple of miles away from Roughton. The Hall's visitors' book shows between Tuesday 19 and Friday 22 September his house guests included the current Chancellor of the Exchequer, Neville Chamberlain, and his wife Anne, sister of Locker-Lampson's old friend, the notorious hoaxer Horace de Vere Cole. Locker-Lampson had initially been well regarded by Chamberlain, although he was always more of an acolyte of his older half-brother Austen. Neville Chamberlain had been impressed by his fluency and ease as a public speaker. However, he came to believe he could not be trusted and was an "arch intriguer". His association with his wife's disreputable brother would not have aided his cause either. While Ramsay MacDonald and Neville Chamberlain were two of the chief architects of the prevailing British foreign policy of appeasement, Sir Samuel Hoare, a future foreign secretary, was slightly more of a hawk, though not to the extent that satisfied either Churchill or Locker-Lampson. In the 1920s as Secretary of State for the Air in Lloyd George's Coalition Government, he had done much to secure the future of the fledgling RAF, a cause close to Locker-Lampson's heart as a former (non-flying) RNAS officer.

Wednesday 20 September to Friday 22 September

The weather had begun to turn more autumnal with a fresh breeze, occasional spots of rain and the rumble of thunder. The daytime temperature, however, remained mostly in the high 60s Fahrenheit, so still pleasantly warm enough to sit out of the shade. Locker-Lampson wasn't expected back from London before the weekend, and the running of the camp was left to Barbara and Margery.

Wednesday was a quiet day. Einstein was left undisturbed and when not reading or working on his calculations, he entertained himself by playing the piano wedged inside one of the huts or with playing his violin on the Heath. In 1994 Pamela Pycroft recalled as a young girl of about 10 or 12 she had been sent to the camp by her parents, Ernest and Hilda Harrison of Pond Farm, who did odd jobs for the Commander, such as driving him to and from Norwich station. His guest had asked to hear some quiet music while he worked: "I was sent up there and played records outside another hut while he just sat about writing away. I did not know what a renowned professor he was, I was too young."[26]

On Thursday, news of Einstein was back in the *EDP* in the form of a report under the headline 'Einstein and Hitler'. Einstein, it said, had refuted a Nazi official, a certain Dr Thost, who had publicly stated he was in no danger from the authorities in Germany, contradicting himself immediately by saying he would face punishment for spreading false propaganda about Germany while he was abroad. Einstein is quoted as having responded "Hitler has perhaps forgotten that my position is founded on hard and honest work, while his rests on the folly and gullibility of his fellow citizens". Hans Wilhelm Thost was a German journalist with a doctorate in political science who had joined the Nazi Party in the 1920s when it was small and comparatively powerless. In 1930 he had been sent to Britain by the Party's official newspaper, *Der Völkischer Beobachter*, as its London representative. At this period the paper was edited by Alfred Rosenberg, with whom Locker-Lampson would dine on lobsters at the Savoy two years later.[27] Thost managed to persuade Arnold Leese's Imperial Fascist League to accept a donation from the Nazi Party when it agreed to feature the swastika on its party flag and to churn out even more anti-Semitic propaganda. In 1935 Thost was expelled from Britain by the Foreign Office as a suspected spy; MI5 had been keeping a close eye on him since he had arrived. A fluent English speaker, Thost went on to work as an interpreter for the SD (*Sicherheitsdienst*), Nazi Germany's internal state security service, during the Second World War. After the war he gave testimony to the Occupying authorities about the torture and murder of Allied prisoners of war at Mauthausen concentration camp. Rosenberg, who in 1939 called for Einstein and other leading Jews to be exiled to a "wild island with a deadly climate" was tried for war crimes at Nuremberg and executed in 1946.[28]

Meanwhile, Locker-Lampson in London was busy making arrangements for the Royal Albert Hall meeting. On Thursday 21 September a notice was placed in the personal column of *The Times*: "Professor Einstein will Discuss 'Science and Civilization'" on 3 October. Tickets, which were available from Locker-Lampson's Westminster office in St Stephen's House, were priced at 1s (5p), 2/6d (12 and a half pence), 5s (25p), 7/6d (37 and a half pence) and upwards. In a very short time he had lined up an impressive platform of speakers to support Einstein, including the physicist Lord Rutherford, who agreed to chair the meeting, and Locker-Lampson's old political mentor, Sir Austen Chamberlain. The notice was repeated in *The Times* on Friday but now, significantly, it said tickets were also available from the usual agencies, suggesting Locker-Lampson's Westminster office had been overwhelmed by requests. News of the meeting also appeared in the *EDP* on Friday, reporting that Einstein was for the first time going to speak in public on a non-scientific subject: "Fair play for the oppressed". Where the reporter had gathered this information from isn't stated, although the phrase "Fair play" suggests Locker-Lampson was behind it. Interestingly, it also contradicted the title given to Einstein's planned speech in *The Times* advert—"Science and civilization". Possibly, Locker-Lampson had issued a statement to the *EDP* before leaving for London on Tuesday and had subsequently been persuaded to play down the suggestion his speech would be political and directly hostile to Hitler and Germany. Not all the press was supportive. An editorial in the fascist-supporting *Daily Mail* urged the cancellation of Einstein's planned appearance at the Albert Hall, asserting it would only antagonise the German Government, which it believed was a strong bulwark against the spread of communism. Einstein was accused of being a pacifist with communist sympathies and as such not the right person to plead for Germany's Jews; Sir Austen Chamberlain was accused of associating with "Reds"; and Locker-Lampson was characterised as a shameless and ridiculous self-promoter. Photographs of him defending Einstein in Roughton were held up for derision.[29]

As if all this wasn't enough to occupy him, Locker-Lampson also found time to write to Professor Yahuda, enclosing a clipping from the *Sunday Times*, presumably about Einstein's flight to England, and to interview two people who wished to visit Einstein. One was the sculptor Jacob Epstein, who had been corresponding with him about arranging a series of sittings for a portrait bust he wished to make. The other was Dimitri Marianoff, the Russian journalist husband of Einstein's younger step-daughter, Margot. Marianoff, who had been commissioned to write a popular account of Relativity theory was seeking an interview. Meanwhile, Einstein in Roughton spent this time writing letters: one to Elsa, telling her he had sent Mayer two lots of mathematical notes; another to a former colleague in Berlin, Wolf Muller, complaining how a "devilish" storm of correspondence was raining down on him but if he really must see him in person he could find him at Locker-Lampson's camp, which was located about 3 miles (5 km) from Cromer, telling him he would be there until 10 October, which is puzzling as his ship was due to sail to New York on the 7th. On Sunday Einstein wrote to Professor David Cohen of the University of Amsterdam, mentioning his stepson Rudolf Kayser, who had fled to the Netherlands after he and Ilse had done all they could to rescue Einstein's papers from the Nazis in Berlin. Here he was working on a collection of Einstein's non-scientific essays, that would be published in Amsterdam in 1934. Cohen was an academic historian and Zionist who had recently set up the Committee for Special Jewish Affairs in the Netherlands to assist refugees fleeing Germany. He was later to survive Theresienstadt concentration camp and write a history of Jewish refugees in the Netherlands. Ilse's movements at this time are not clear. She either stayed with Kayser in Amsterdam for a short time before moving to France or may have travelled directly from Berlin to Paris where she stayed with Margot and Marianoff. After Einstein fled to England Margot and Ilse moved to Le Coq-sur-Mer to be with their mother. Ilse's health was failing and she was to die of cancer in Paris in 1934, after which Kayser emigrated to the United States where he became a professor of literature.

Notes

1 *Peterborough Standard, 8 August 1930.*

2 *The Bystander, 12 November 1930.*

3 *Daily Herald, 12 November 1926.*

4 *Stibbons, The Baker Brothers, p.213.*

5 *Battersea, Reminiscences, p.362.*

6 *Thanks are due to Eddie Anderson who interviewed Oliver Locker-Lampson's niece, Mrs Jane Madden née Delmar Morgan, in the 1980s.*

7 *From a taped interview of Philip Colman made by the author on 4 September 1997; transcribed by Paul Robinson.*

8 *Western Mail, 20 September 1933.*

9 *Eastern Daily Press, 11 September 1933.*

10 *Ibid., 22 March 1979.*

11 *News Chronicle, 12 September 1933.*

12 *Nathan and Norden, Einstein on Peace, pp.235–6.*

13 *Eastern Daily Press, 15 September 1933.*

14 *Clark, Einstein, p.441.*

15 *Mitchell, 'Fascism in East Anglia', ch.3.*

16 *Albert Einstein Archives, The Hebrew University of Jerusalem; AEA: 18-180.*

17 *Reported in Eastern Daily Press, 17 November 2001; letter sold by Christie's in London, 16 November 2001; facsimile accessed online, website now closed.*

18 *Norfolk Chronicle, 15 September 1933.*

19 *Evening Star (Washington, DC), 11 September 1933.*

20 *Eastern Daily Press, 13 September 1933.*

21 *Medawar and Pyke, Hitler's Gift, p.62.*

22 *Bentwich, The Rescue and Achievement of Refugee Scholars, p.12.*

23 *Adams, 'The refugee scholars of the 1930s'.*

24 *Ibid.14, p.471.*

25 *News Chronicle*, 22 September 1933.

26 *Eastern Daily Press*, 21 January 1994.

27 Winterbotham, *The Nazi Connection*, pp.34–5.

28 Cecil, *The Myth of the Master Race*, p.226.

29 *Daily Mail*, 26 September 1933.

Death and Other Visitors

THE three weeks Einstein spent in Norfolk were not entirely confined to the Roughton camp. It is likely he was occasionally driven over to New Haven Court where a room had been reserved for him. He is said to have admired Cromer church and he may also have been taken on other excursions such as to Cromer lighthouse, inspiring the famous lighthouse keeper idea he would outline in his Albert Hall speech in October. He is also known to have visited Sidestrand Hall, the home of Sir Samuel Hoare on the north Norfolk coast. He may also have visited London on one occasion and spent the night there before returning to Norfolk.

The third week

Saturday 23 to Friday 29 September

During Einstein's last full week in Roughton the weather continued to be warmer than average for late September, with daytime temperatures hovering around the mid-60s Fahrenheit, while hazy mornings and low, late afternoon sunshine provided the authentic English autumnal atmosphere of mists and mellow fruitfulness. This was the week when Einstein's 'splendid isolation' drew to a close, as the syren song of events pulled him inexorably back into the fretful world outside his private realm of mathematical thought.

The Russian stepson-in-law

The exact date of Dimitri Marianoff's visit is not known but as Locker-Lampson could not have been back at his Westminster office before Wednesday 20 September, where, according to Marianoff, arrangements for his visit were made, it cannot have been earlier than the 21st and no later than the 25th, the day before Jacob Epstein was scheduled to start work on a sculpted clay bust of Einstein at the camp. Marianoff and Epstein make no mention of each other's presence in their accounts of their visits to the camp and it is unlikely Locker-Lampson would have scheduled two such visits on the same day.

Marianoff, a Russian Jewish journalist, had first come into the Einsteins' lives in Berlin in 1926. Marianoff at that time was employed by the Soviet Chamber of Commerce in Berlin in some unspecified public relations capacity, possibly merely as a gatherer of titbits of intelligence about Berlin's cultural and intellectual elite, though it has been suggested he was in reality an agent of OGPU, the Soviet Union's secret police, tasked with gaining access to Einstein's inner circle.[1]

Whatever the truth, his entry into the Einsteins' closely guarded family life began bizarrely. In his biography of Einstein, Marianoff admits he was so determined to meet him he took private dancing lessons at an apartment in the same Berlin housing block as Einstein, hoping to bump into him; a faintly ludicrous scenario as he readily admitted, given the 37-year-old's somewhat portly appearance, whose dancing was, in his own estimate, "as clumsy as a bear … sweating like a pugilist".[2] For several weeks this strategy got him nowhere, then, either by luck or perhaps the machinations of OGPU, he met a Russian Jewish émigré, Isaac Steinberg, in the bar of Berlin's Theater des Westens following a performance by the Moscow Jewish Theatre. Steinberg told Marianoff he had attended that evening's performance with Einstein, who had expressed an interest in learning more about Russian Jewish theatre. According to Marianoff, Steinberg had been a minister in Kerensky's Provisional Government in Petrograd in 1917. In reality he had been the People's Commissar for Justice for the Socialist Revolutionary Party during its short-lived coalition with Lenin's Bolsheviks in 1917 and 1918. It seems unlikely Marianoff would not have known this and one can only conclude he bent the facts to suit his American publisher's wish to avoid any communist associations in his biography of Einstein.

As Marianoff had just been retained by the director of the Berlin Jewish Theatre as its public relations officer, a meeting with Einstein at his home was arranged—a rare privilege. Here he made a favourable impression on the younger of Einstein's step-daughters, the almost pathologically shy Margot whom Marianoff described in particularly mawkish terms as having "that shyness pussy cats have who rarely leave their mother's side".[3] Seizing this opportunity he cynically began courting her in order to gain further access to the inner family circle. The subterfuge worked only too well, as she fell in love and they soon became engaged. After a fairly long engagement they married in 1930. Thereafter, as a member of the family, often living in the same apartment with Albert, Elsa and Margot, he had a level of access denied to all other would-be Einstein biographers, including even Einstein's other stepson-in-law Rudolf Kayser, who published one of the earliest book-length biographies under a pseudonym. Marianoff doesn't seem to have been particularly liked by Einstein although Elsa was more kindly disposed towards him.

Einstein had little time for journalists, especially those who appeared to be solely interested in his personal life rather than his ideas. However, as the purpose of Marianoff's visit to Norfolk was to interview him about his scientific theories it was presumably deemed acceptable. Marianoff had been commissioned to write a popular account of Relativity theory for the French newspaper *L'Intransigeant*. According to Marianoff he approached Louis Louis-Dreyfus, an immensely wealthy French grain importer, parliamentarian and owner of the newspaper, with a proposal to raise funds for Jewish refugees. In Paris that September Marianoff had set up a Jewish refugee organisation, *Le Renouveau* (Renewal), the aim of which was to buy land in southern France where thirty German Jewish refugee families could settle and farm. A Jew himself, Louis-Dreyfus was also an ultra-French nationalist and refused to give any direct financial assistance to Germans, even German Jewish refugees. He suggested instead Marianoff write a series of articles on famous personalities, starting with his father-in-law, and then donate his fee to whichever organisation he wished. To start with he particularly wanted an explanation of Relativity theory his readers could understand. A tall task but Marianoff accepted at once.

Marianoff's biography of Einstein is a true curiosity. The book is virtually unknown in Britain. Published by Doubleday, Doran & Co. in New York in 1944, then the largest publisher in the English-speaking world, it was specifically aimed at an American readership at a time when, following D-Day, justifying the nation's sacrifice in the war to defeat Hitler was very much on the American public's mind. As Marianoff's English was deemed inadequate for the task, professional writer Palma Wayne was brought in to Americanise the text and give some semblance of coherence to his somewhat rambling recollections. Previously only known under her own name for a biography of the scandal-ridden life of the celebrity heiress Gloria Vanderbilt, she was essentially a ghost writer of celebrities' autobiographies and it shows; one reviewer aptly described the book as "dreamy-eyed nonsense", while Helen Dukas dismissed it as completely unreliable.[4] It is full of purple patches, inaccuracies, anachronisms and numerous unfortunate turns of phrase, including the immortal line: "He has but one ruling passion of the soul—to defecate it of its suffering and its evils."

According to Marianoff, after having been granted permission by Einstein, presumably over the phone from New Haven Court, he was instructed to come over from Paris and make contact with Locker-Lampson at his Westminster office. "Sir Oliver", as Marianoff insisted on calling him, was, he believed, connected with the "British Intelligence Department", though "exactly in what capacity, I was too excited to learn, as the secrecy with which Einstein's whereabouts was maintained sounded like a page out of Edgar Wallace."[5] England, he was told, was "a patchwork of German spies" eager to discover Einstein's whereabouts. He left for the interview armed only with a set of travel instructions and a map. Just over three hours after leaving Liverpool Street Station, Marianoff stepped off the train at Gunton Station as instructed. Presumably, Locker-Lampson felt he would attract less attention there than at Cromer Station. Gunton in those days was a rather grand affair for a minor country halt, with a large, Tudor-style waiting room built in 1876 for the convenience of Lord Suffield, owner of Gunton Hall and chairman of the East Norfolk Railway. From here Marianoff was faced with a longish walk—there were no taxis or buses and no car was sent to meet him—of about 3 miles (5 km) to the Roughton camp. He emerged from the station to be confronted by a vast expanse of flat, featureless fields with barely a dwelling in sight. Paths seemed to go off in every direction and the map he had been given told him nothing. Some inner instinct told him to follow the centre path, and after a mile or two he came upon a long stretch of meadowland where he spotted a young woman mounted on a horse with a rifle balanced across the saddle—presumably Barbara or Margery. After checking he was the person expected she directed him to follow "a circuitous path on the right", which eventually brought him to the camp, which suggests he was probably found on the Thorpe Market Road and directed into Eastoe's loke from there. Marianoff next described the scene that met him after he had scrambled through the gap in the hedge:

> Here was another beautiful girl in khaki, also with a rifle but not on horseback. She was standing before a closed gate which led to a property entirely surrounded by a wire fencing. I told her my mission. She answered that I was expected, and opened the gate, and there, in a small log hut overlooking the English coast, was Einstein.[6]

Marianoff quickly perceived that for Einstein the drama of his situation contained a large element of comedy: "The beauty of my bodyguards would disarm a conspirator sooner than their rifles." Nevertheless, the camp gave him the quiet and isolation he needed for his work. Perhaps there was a hint here Marianoff should come to the point as soon possible and leave him in peace. But before he could do so lunch was served, providing Marianoff with another opportunity to study Einstein's bodyguards, who clearly fascinated him:

Barbara Goodall, Einstein's 'attendant angel'. Watercolour by unknown artist.

> The two English beauties were private secretaries of Locker-Lampson, with a long line of family dead in their ancestral churchyards. Their faces were like the flags of England flying, something quite lovely and fine, with race in them. The four of us were served luncheon from another small log hut where Einstein's meals were prepared. With all their beauty, his young bodyguards classified their situation as one of great responsibility and, with that on their minds, soon left us.[7]

If by "the four of us" he meant himself, Einstein, Barbara and Margery, it would seem Locker-Lampson was not present and so presumably still in London making arrangements for the Albert Hall meeting. After lunch Marianoff and Einstein took a stroll on the Heath and while Einstein smoked his pipe, Marianoff finally plucked up the courage to ask him to explain Relativity in easy-to-understand terms. The moment was a comic one, with Marianoff nervously fearing Einstein's reaction and Einstein making the most of his embarrassment. "Einstein paused, took a puff from his pipe, and then said in a more or less jocular vein: 'When shall we begin?'" Contrary to expectation the task seems to have pleased him. Marianoff said he had never seen him in a happier mood, which considering he was a witness at his wedding to Margot is telling. Einstein perhaps felt relieved they could dispense with family small talk. He had delivered so many popular explanations of Relativity all he needed to do was to recite one from memory. They returned to the log cabin and Einstein began to dictate. Once during the session having noticed a look of utter bewilderment on Marianoff's face, he stopped and patiently went over what he had said, trying to use more "digestible food", as he called it. As society funded scientists' work, Einstein reasoned, people were entitled to be able to read about their work in a form they could understand. Marianoff ended his account of the visit with a word picture of Einstein on the "barren" heath:

Dmitri and Margot's wedding day, Berlin, 1930. Left to right: Einstein, Rudolf Kayser, Margot, Marianoff.

> I left him that day at the door of a small house [presumably Eastoe's cottage]. The North Sea had begun to blow a gale, and his hair flared about his head more than ever like a nimbus. There was not a house or an inhabitant in sight. He stood there with all his greatness, a helpless figure in the barren rugged land, a prisoner of the world.[8]

Marianoff and Margot emigrated to America in 1935 where their marriage began to fall apart. Marianoff claimed he could no longer support a wife, while Margot, fully occupied in nursing her sick and dying mother, seems to have had little time for him anymore. They divorced in 1937. Friends of the family were relieved, having concluded he was essentially "a bit of a con-man".[9]

The industrialist

In his curious not to say bizarre biography of Einstein Marianoff mentions one visit during this period for which there is no other source. In the chapter "Hear, O Israel", which is mainly about the Royal Albert Hall meeting in October, he wrote:

> A few nights after I had seen Albert on the Norfolk heath, he came to London to keep an appointment to dine at the home of the Jewish industrialist Henry Mond, the 2nd Baron Melchett, in Lowndes Square. Lord Melchett's house was an example of a distinguished English establishment. Immemorial custom was here observed to the last detail.[10]

At the time of writing his biography Marianoff was remembering events that had happened a decade earlier, so it is possible he was recalling an occasion that took place after Einstein had left Roughton in October. If so, his mention of a "few nights after" was somewhat off the mark. Nevertheless, a good train service between Cromer and London via Norwich, including a Sunday service, makes it easily possible for Einstein to have visited London during the weekend of 23 and 24 September and been back well in time for his first morning of sittings with Epstein on Tuesday 26 September. Indeed, a handwritten letter from Einstein to Elsa dated Cromer 24 September 1933 confirms he was in Norfolk that Sunday.[11]

Henry Ludwig Mond, the 2nd Baron Melchett, was heir to a great family fortune begun by his grandfather and consolidated by his father, Sir Alfred Mond, who had helped create Imperial Chemical Industries (ICI) in 1926. Sir Alfred had been a leading supporter of Zionism until his death in 1930 and was chairman of the Jewish Agency in the UK, a position his son inherited. Brought up within the Church of England, Mond had reverted to Judaism, the faith of his grandfather, early in 1933 in direct response to the persecution of Jews in Germany. His conversion had been facilitated by Rabbi Perlzweig, whom Einstein would meet just before he sailed for America in October.[12] Elected as a Liberal MP in 1923, he lost his seat in 1924 and in 1926 along with his father left the Liberal Party and was elected as a Conservative in 1929. At the time of their change of political party, an angry Lloyd George had compared Henry Mond's father to Judas with the anti-Semitic remark that "like other notorious members of his race he has gone back to his own place".

The venue for the dinner where Marianoff said "Immemorial custom" was observed—Lowndes Square—was actually the London home of Lord Melchett's late father, so he may have got this wrong. Melchett's own London home was Mulberry House in Smith Square. In 1930 it had become the focus of controversy when an Art Deco-style bronze relief entitled 'Scandal' was installed above the drawing-room fireplace. Charles Sargeant Jagger's sculpture, now in the Victoria & Albert Museum, depicts a nude couple standing in an erotic embrace surrounded by caricatured figures who appear to be sneering and raising their arms in shock and outrage. The composition is said to symbolise London Society's scandalised reaction to the *ménage à trois* relationship between Henry Mond, Gwen Wilson, a young South African art student whom he married in 1920, and the novelist Gilbert Cannan. It isn't known what Einstein and Mond discussed or indeed if they did actually meet at this time but the situation in Germany and how to help Jewish academics are likely, as is Marianoff's *Le Renouveau* project, of which both men were honorary presidents at this time.

The sculptor

There is a story, possibly apocryphal, that on being asked what he did for a living, Einstein answered "photographer's model". Einstein's captivating personality and iconic appearance attracted the attention of artists almost as much as photographers. After he had become world famous in 1919, sitting for his portrait was an activity he became familiar with, though it was not something he enjoyed, especially if it interfered too much with his work.

In May while at Le Coq-sur-Mer Einstein had sat for the Flemish painter Alfons Blomme, who drew a larger than life-sized naturalistic portrait in pencil and conté crayon, depicting him sun-tanned and relaxed, wearing an old sweater over his shirtless torso. They had become acquainted through a chance encounter. Out sketching in the countryside around Le Coq one day Blomme noticed a young woman drawing a goat, which looked to him more like a skyscraper. Offering to correct her sketch, he introduced himself, showing her his card as Director of the Academy of Ostend. She immediately implored him to give her lessons, which he refused until, to his immense surprise, she said her name and he realised who she was: Einstein's step-daughter. A stream of hopeful artists had been trying unsuccessfully to get permission to paint Einstein since he arrived and here an opportunity of meeting him had fallen right into his lap. Regular visits by Margot, Einstein and Mayer, who was entrusted with a key to Blomme's studio at the Villa Memlinc near the sand dunes, soon followed; Einstein often bringing that morning's post with him, much of it hate mail from Germany that he chucked straight into the bin.[13]

Another Belgian artist, the veteran Surrealist painter James Ensor, also met Einstein at Le Coq-sur-Mer that summer. By 1933, however, this once wild, Bohemian artist was now very much the elder statesman of the Belgian art scene and had been made a baron by King Albert. Outwardly, Ensor and Einstein seem to have done no more than smoke cigars, sip coffee and admire the waitresses when they met one sunny afternoon in early August at the *Au Coeur Volant* cafe in Le Coq-sur-Mer. However, the presence at their outside table of the French Minister for National Education, Anatole de Monzie, and his private secretary suggests this was no casual encounter. Ostensibly, de Monzie was there to give Ensor the news he was to be awarded the *Legion d'honneur*. Hoping to kill two birds with one stone, he also brought Einstein the offer of a chair in physics at the Collège de France in Paris. Einstein's presence at the café had apparently been somewhat reluctantly arranged by Baron Ensor at King Albert's suggestion as the Belgian Government wished to get Einstein safely out of the country as soon as possible. Just over a month later Einstein's friend, and later biographer, Antonina Vallentin, delivered the same offer from de Monzie, which he again declined.[14] Ensor, somewhat piqued perhaps at being made a stalking horse, ended up having an argument with Einstein, whom he accused of not understanding colour. Matters were not helped when Einstein, who barely knew who Ensor was, asked him what he painted and he replied "Nothing". The professorship at the Collège de France would also become nothing when the institution, perhaps saving face, decided it could not after all finance a new chair or change a vacant chair in literature to a science one.[15]

During his final week in the relaxed atmosphere at the Roughton camp, Einstein agreed to a sitting for the controversial Modernist sculptor Jacob Epstein. Epstein and Einstein had been linked in the popular imagination long before they met, partly because of the closeness of their names, their shared Jewish heritage and the public's perception of their 'difficulty'. It was to be the only time they met, although their names along with the American writer, Gertrude Stein, had already been linked in a famous limerick, whose authorship has never been definitively established:

There's a wonderful family called Stein,
There's Gert and there's Ep and there's Ein,
Gert's poems are bunk,
Ep's sculptures are junk,
And nobody understands Ein.

Epstein, a US citizen by birth, had permanently settled in Britain in 1905. He is unarguably the greatest artist to have portrayed Einstein from life and fortunately he wrote a brief but invaluable description of their encounter. First published in 1940, it contains a chapter on portrait commissions he undertook in the 1920s and 1930s. Sitters and their family and friends seem rarely to have been completely satisfied with the results: "The successful portrait sculptor", he wrote, "needs a front of brass, the hide of a rhinoceros, and all the guile of a courtier".[16] He was irked by the fact most of his portrait commissions were by necessity of old men, for they or their friends were the ones most likely to have achieved sufficient fame and wealth to commission a portrait bust. He hated that they tended to nod off after sitting for a few minutes, leaving him to ponder the top of their bald heads. This was not the problem with George Bernard Shaw, however, who, entirely without prompting and much to Epstein's horror, stripped off all his clothes at the first sitting and then proceeded to bore him intensely with his theories on modern art. Epstein's encounter with Einstein seems to have been one of his happier sittings. He found him "a very gentle, soulful kind of man".[17] More importantly, he didn't nod off, didn't insist on being sculpted in the nude and didn't trouble Epstein with his opinions on art.

Whether anyone formally commissioned Epstein to sculpt Einstein's bust in the sense of paying him for his work is not clear. One of his biographers states he received a letter from Locker-Lampson saying someone wanted a portrait bust of Einstein, which must be done at his secret hideaway near Cromer before he left for America.[18] Although Epstein's only livelihood at this time was through portrait commissions, it is likely he would have jumped at the chance of sculpting Einstein even without payment, not simply because he made an interesting subject but also because he felt the "great ones", as he called them, should be painted or sculpted and a special fund should be set up to enable this to happen. Epstein was also shrewd enough to realise bronze casts of an Einstein bust would not be difficult to sell and so it proved, with casts of this bust becoming one of his most sought-after works.

Although Epstein mentions in his autobiography corresponding with Locker-Lampson about "working from Einstein", it is not known whether they had met, though it seems probable given their mutual acquaintances. Locker-Lampson, for example, knew Augustus John quite well socially. It may also be worth noting Epstein's name had briefly been associated with another member of the Locker-Lampson family eight years earlier. In 1925 Oliver's elder brother Godfrey was Under-Secretary of State at the Home Office with official responsibility for public art. At this time controversy raged in the British right-wing press over a publicly funded memorial in the Bird Sanctuary in Hyde Park to the novelist and naturalist W. H. Hudson. The central part of the memorial featured a nude depiction of Rima the Jungle Girl, a kind of female Tarzan from Hudson's novel *Green Mansions: A Romance of the Tropical Forest.* For several weeks Godfrey came under pressure both in parliament and in the press to remove the sculpture on the grounds it was an affront to public decency. The *Daily Mail* described it as the 'Hyde Park Atrocity', while in the House of Commons the Conservative MP Basil Peto persistently harried Godfrey at each and every opportunity, urging the Government to remove this "Bolshevist art" and send it to the Soviet Union, while another Tory MP, Cuthbert James, joked that as Epstein's name was "foreign" he had probably misunderstood his commission to make a sculpture for the Bird House as an order for a scarecrow. Bored to the point of exasperation by such philistinism, Godfrey replied: "the more it is advertised by questions in the House the less it will be a sanctuary for the birds". The precise cause for this moral outrage was never stated and it is difficult to see today what all the fuss was about though it may have been something to do with the figure's robust naked torso and prominent nipples. Godfrey decided, in the best tradition of British officialdom, that the best course of action was to prevaricate until it had all blown over, which it duly did, and then forget about it.[19]

Whether Epstein remembered Oliver's brother's role in the Jungle Girl controversy is not known. If he did he may have confused the brothers, which was common. They did, however, have something else in common: both had been victims of the notorious practical joker Horace de Vere Cole. While Locker-Lampson's friendship with Cole had only cooled somewhat after the embarrassing gold watch incident in 1911, Epstein's relationship with Cole had always been antagonistic. Cole, who thought of himself as an aesthete, seems to have taken against Epstein's Modernist approach to sculpture from the start, and there was undoubtedly also a streak of anti-Semitism in the campaign of persecution he mounted against the artist over several years. This reached a crescendo in 1916 when the US-born Epstein was granted an exemption from war service by the British Government in order to continue his important cultural work. Cole on hearing this whipped up a public outcry, which eventually resulted in Epstein's exemption being revoked and his being conscripted into the British Army in 1918. One of the leading voices in the campaign against Epstein's military exemption was the sculptor Sir George Frampton, who was later given the commission to carve the London memorial to the Norfolk nurse Edith Cavell executed by the Germans in 1915. The strain of his two-year battle with Cole and the British establishment eventually precipitated Epstein's nervous breakdown.

Epstein had been based in London for many years and rarely travelled. Although he enjoyed the countryside, he usually only ventured out as far as Epping Forest for a week's break. Normally, his sitters came to his studio at Hyde Park Gate. This was not possible for Einstein, so Epstein travelled to Norfolk and combined the week of sittings with a holiday, working on the bust for two hours each morning and then returning to his hotel in Cromer for lunch before pottering around north Norfolk in the afternoon. During August Epstein had been confined indoors on jury service during a spell of very hot weather, with the additional strain of being foreman of the jury. When Locker-Lampson's invitation arrived in September he was back in his studio working on a bust of the actor John Gielgud, a commission which Gielgud felt sure bored him. No doubt Epstein looked forward to getting out into the fresh air and working on a head that interested him.

Epstein was the only one of Einstein's visitors whose presence was noted in the local press. On Wednesday, the second day of the sittings, a reporter from the *Norfolk Chronicle* spotted him in his trademark green beret outside his hotel (presumably the Royal Cromer) in the morning, struggling into a heavy, double-breasted overcoat before getting into a waiting car. At first, Epstein was reluctant to admit he was in Cromer for any other reason than a holiday but the reporter, possibly the same one who had interviewed Locker-Lampson at the Roughton camp two weeks earlier, had clearly been tipped off about the celebrated visitor and Epstein finally admitted he was here to make a bust of Einstein at the secret camp. When the weather was fine, he told the reporter, they sat outside; when it was wet they worked inside one of the cabins, where the clay sculpture was kept on a wooden stand. As to the future of the bust, what it was being made for or who had commissioned it, Epstein refused to be drawn: "It was too early to discuss that, and there were no plans." His working overalls in his hands, he was then driven away, probably by Locker-Lampson's hotel manager and occasional chauffeur, Tom Wilson.[20]

Epstein's first impression of Einstein was favourable: "Einstein appeared dressed very comfortably in a pullover with his wild hair floating in the wind. His glance contained a mixture of the humane, the humorous, and the profound. This was a combination which delighted me. He resembled the ageing Rembrandt."[21] Although Epstein described the camp as "a secluded and wild spot very near the sea", it was actually 3 miles (5 km) from the coast, which was not even visible on misty mornings. His description, however, fits the image of a romantic encampment he wished to convey. He goes on to describe Einstein playing his violin in the open air, which made him look "altogether like a wandering gypsy". On wet mornings—there was a light drizzle each day now until Einstein left Norfolk—Epstein worked inside the log cabin, which he found so cramped he could hardly turn around. Einstein in a letter to Mayer said he was sleeping in a hut about 10 feet square (just under 1 square metre). Things were not helped by the presence of a piano and the clouds of smoke from Einstein's constantly smouldering pipe, so thick at times Epstein claimed not to be able to see his subject. In order to increase his elbow room he asked Einstein's "attendant angels" if they could remove the door, which rather to his surprise they did, asking him if he wanted the roof off too, which he said he would have liked if it had been possible. At the second sitting on Wednesday he asked Einstein not to smoke during the sittings. It is little wonder he wanted more space, given this description of his physical activity when sculpting:

> Epstein at work was a being transformed ... the man himself, his movement, his stooping and bending, his leaping back, poised, then rushing forward, his trick of passing clay from one hand to the other over the top of his head while he scrutinised his work from all angles, was the equivalent of a dance.[22]

After the third morning's work Einstein's initially frosty attendant angels—'They seemed to resent a little my intrusion into the retreat of their Professor'—thawed and offered him a bottle of beer. Epstein mentions several "girl attendants", which suggests more than two. One was almost certainly Barbara Goodall but it is not clear who the others were; Margery Howard had left Roughton at the weekend to return to her family's home in Surrey because her father had been taken ill; possibly one or more of Locker-Lampson's young, unmarried nieces—Jane Delmar-Morgan, Ruth Fisher-Rowe and Stella and Betty Locker-Lampson.[23]

It was Epstein's practice to talk to his sitters about their lives and interests while he worked in order to put them at their ease so he could observe their natural expressions. Their conversation seems to have turned to Einstein's vilification at the hands of his erstwhile colleagues. Despite recent painful experiences, he was still able to joke at their stupidity. He told Epstein how a hundred professors, had joined together to condemn his theories: "Were I wrong, one professor would have been quite enough." He was probably referring to *Hundert Autoren gegen Einstein* (*A Hundred Authors Against Einstein*), published in Leipzig in 1931. It evidently still rankled with Einstein two years later.

The sittings came to an end on Saturday 30 September. On Sunday Epstein left Cromer by train. Presumably he either took the heavy clay model with him or had it packed up and sent on as freight. A portrait bust usually took him ten to fifteen sessions to complete—he had had just five.[24] A biographer of Epstein has described the bust as a flashback to *Sunflower*, a sculpture where the flower represented the being of some ancient god. Einstein was a reverse image: "a vision of a god-like creature as a sunflower".[25] This bronze bust was first exhibited in London at Tooth's Gallery in December 1933. One day it was found lying on the floor, slightly damaged. How it got there no one knows but an act of anti-Semitic vandalism was suspected. One of the three original casts is today owned by the Tate, having been acquired for the nation by the Chantry Bequest in 1934. In 2013 it came to Norfolk for the first time since its clay original had been created there, forming part of an exhibition at the University of East Anglia's Sainsbury's Centre.[26]

The statesman

The visitors' book at Sidestrand Hall, Sir Samuel Hoare's home in north Norfolk, records that during September 1933 he entertained at least sixteen guests. Among these were Neville and Anne Chamberlain on the 19th and Albert Einstein on the 27th, presumably in the afternoon or

Postcard of Sidestrand Hall, Norfolk.

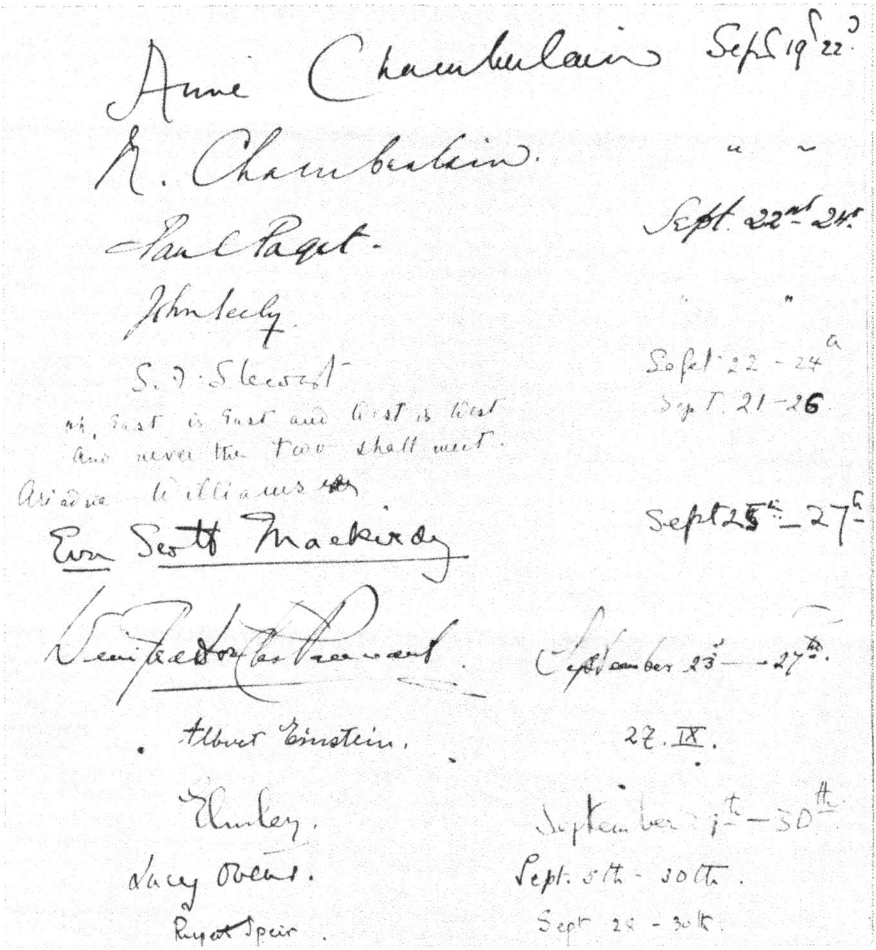

Eistein's signature (fourth from the bottom) in the Sidestrand Hall visitors' book, September 1933.

evening after his second morning of sittings with Epstein.[27] Interestingly, Locker-Lampson's name is not there. He and Hoare were by this time on far from friendly terms. Their early life and political career had closely paralleled each other. Both had been born in 1880 into the upper stratum of English society and educated at expensive public schools and elite universities, Harrow and Oxford in Hoare's case. Both had entered parliament in 1910 as Conservative Unionists, where they showed promise as future high-flyers. Both had also spent time on the Eastern Front in the First World War and had witnessed the Russian Revolution first hand. However, whereas Locker-Lampson's post-war political career had never really got off the ground, Hoare's steadily progressed through minor ministerial posts to a seat in the Cabinet. From Quaker stock—he was distantly related to the prison reformer, Elizabeth Fry—Hoare was a thick-set man who habitually wore the frock coat and wing collar of an Edwardian gentleman. He had a capacity for undertaking endless amounts of tedious committee work and a high level of tact and diplomacy, which the protean, jack-in-the-box Locker-Lampson totally lacked.

In 1933 Hoare was Secretary of State for India in Ramsey MacDonald's National Government and heavily engaged as a witness by the Joint Select Committee charged with reforming the Indian constitution; the beginning of a process which would lead, fourteen years later, to the setting-up of the independent states of India and Pakistan. In the 1930s on the subject of India, Locker-Lampson was a supporter of the stance taken by Winston Churchill, which vigorously opposed any change to the status quo of White British rule. Hoare, however, saw the necessity for constitutional reform, including Indian Home Rule if the British Empire was not to collapse under its own weight. Hoare's biographer writes of this period: "From July to October [1933] he spent 19 committee sessions as a witness and dealt with over 10,000 questions. It was a remarkable tour de force, but an incredibly time-consuming one, devastating all his other work."[28] On 27 July *The Times* announced Hoare hoped to leave London for his Norfolk home at the end of the following week. Sidestrand Hall, now a school, was a Georgian mansion on the north Norfolk coast. In his informal history of his family, Hoare described it as a rather uncomfortable place. It had been bought by his father in the 1890s because of its superior shooting compared with the family's old home in Cromer. Although the house was regarded as too small, additions were tacked on with no thought to form or proportion, and with rooms that mostly faced the North Sea—good for views but disastrously cold and draughty for most of the year.[29] In recent years coastal erosion has brought the sea perilously closer.

In his account of his political career during the 1930s, Hoare briefly mentions meeting Einstein. Remembering another famous Jewish refugee of that time he wrote:

> It is at least comforting to remember that in these months we gave a home to Freud in his old age, and that Einstein, who had once paid me a visit in Norfolk, was so much impressed by the possibilities for meditation and research in Great Britain that he suggested that some of the younger refugees should be permitted to live in British lightships, where they would be undisturbed in their study of basic problems.[30]

Hoare's reference to "these months" is either a rhetorical turn of phrase or a mistake of memory, as Freud did not move to London until June 1938, almost five years after he had met Einstein. As Home Secretary in 1938 it was he who had finally made the ailing Freud's move to Britain possible. It was a complex matter as Freud insisted on a large number of people coming with him, including his family, servants, doctors and even some of his pupils, as well as their families.

Bizarrely, Hoare, who had initially been reluctant to let them all come, had been persuaded to issue them with visas by Freud's Welsh biographer, Ernest Jones, who happened to belong to the same ice skating club as Hoare. It is interesting he only mentions lightships as places of refuge for young scholars, whereas in his Albert Hall speech Einstein mentioned lighthouses too. Perhaps the light on the old Trinity House light-vessel, *Haisbro*, which may have been visible from Sidestrand Hall on the evening of Einstein's visit, stayed in his memory.

From 1937 to the outbreak of the Second World War Hoare made great efforts to get thousands of ordinary Jewish refugees admitted to Britain. His first public mention of meeting Einstein in Norfolk was during a speech he made in February 1939 at University College London to the Society for the Protection of Science and Learning on how refugees can enrich a country. He recalled that Einstein had shown no bitterness at those who had forced his exile, only sorrow at the ignorance that seemed to be destroying so much intellectual life.[31] It is estimated 50,000 Jewish refugees came out of Germany and Austria, and 6,000 from Czechoslovakia before the war. All this was against considerable hostility from fellow politicians, right-wing and left-wing newspapers, trade union officials and professional interest groups, including physicians, who saw their livelihood threatened by an influx of Jewish practitioners. Although he later professed sadness he could not have done more, his work was praised by leaders of the Jewish community after the war.[32] It is tempting to conjecture that it may have been his meeting with Einstein at his home on the north Norfolk coast in September 1933 that provided the initial spark to his determination to help many thousands of Einstein's fellow Jews escape the death camps, despite the prejudices and fears expressed by much of British public opinion.

Despite this humanitarian side of his character, he was seen by some as an arch appeaser of fascism. By the spring crisis of 1940, as Neville Chamberlain's premiership fell apart, he was even seen by some as a potential British Quisling should Germany invade and conquer the United Kingdom.[33] Mistrusted by Churchill, in 1940 he was packed off to Spain to become British Ambassador. Locker-Lampson came to thoroughly loathe what he saw as Hoare's hypocrisy in helping Jewish refugees on the one hand and advocating closer ties with Hitler's regime on the other, in the tragically mistaken belief Nazi ideology could be tempered and made in time more tolerant and democratic, leading to what he called a "Golden Age of cooperation", which is somewhat ironic as this was precisely the same approach Locker-Lampson had espoused in the early 1930s.[34]

Death and the scientist

During Einstein's final week in Roughton news of the death of one of his oldest and dearest friends, Paul Ehrenfest, was announced in the British press.

Einstein with Paul Ehrenfest and his eldest son, Paul, in happier times. Leiden, 1920.

Perhaps due to Einstein's presence in Norfolk, the *Eastern Daily Press* on Tuesday 26 September carried a brief Reuter's report of his death in circumstances that looked like suicide. Ehrenfest was hardly a household name in Britain, let alone Norfolk, and it would have been surprising to see his death reported in a provincial paper otherwise. This was the first day of Einstein's week of sittings with Epstein but there is nothing in Epstein's account of his time at the camp to suggest Einstein learned the terrible news while he was there. He seemed to be in uniform good humour throughout the week. It is possible he did not learn the news until he reached London the following week. A letter from Elsa that mentioned it, written at Le Coq-sur-Mer on 30 September, may not have reached him before he left Norfolk.[35]

Einstein had known the brilliant, ebullient and charismatic Austrian Jewish physicist since 1912 when they had met in Prague, though they had corresponded for a few years prior to this. Only a year younger than Einstein, Ehrenfest shared Einstein's unorthodox approach to physics and a hatred of the petty strictures of academic life, as well as a sense of fun and a love of music-making. In 1912 Ehrenfest was appointed Professor of Theoretical Physics at Leiden University in Holland. Einstein was a regular visitor to his home, enjoying the loving family atmosphere created by Ehrenfest and his Russian wife Tatyana, who was a mathematician, and their children, Paul, Tatyana, Galinka and the youngest,

Vassily, known in the family as Wassik.

In November 1923 following Hitler's failed Munich Beer Hall Putsch Einstein sought refuge at the Ehrenfests' home in Leiden for six weeks having receiving death threats from shadowy far-right elements like the Black *Reichswehr*. The parallel between his situation then and now, ten years later, can hardly have eluded Einstein; however, by 1933 the Ehrenfests were no longer able to offer him the same welcoming hospitality he had enjoyed so much in the 1920s. Ehrenfest's mental health had deteriorated, his marriage with Tatyana was in difficulty and Wassik was now a patient at an institution for children with learning difficulties. Ehrenfest's mercurial personality included a dark side: a tendency to brooding and self-doubt. As the years passed he suffered from deeper and longer bouts of depression during which he convinced himself he was a failure as a physicist and as a man. Believing overwork was not helping and fearing there was a real danger he might attempt suicide, Einstein suggested to Leiden University it appoint a second professor of physics to ease the burdens on his friend. He also tried to find him a less demanding position in the United States while continuing to reassure him his theoretical work was still of the first calibre but his help, ultimately, would be of no avail.

The precise circumstances surrounding Ehrenfest's suicide have never been definitively established. In an unposted letter found among his papers dated 14 August 1933 and addressed to a number of his closest friends and colleagues, including Einstein and Niels Bohr, Ehrenfest wrote that life had become intolerable for him. He felt he no longer had the mental stamina to keep up with new developments in physics and believed he should either give up his position at Leiden and go back to the Soviet Union where he had once taught or if that wasn't possible, kill Wassik and then himself. Wassik, now aged 15, had Down's Syndrome and in 1933 had become a patient at The Professor Watering Institute for Afflicted Children in Amsterdam. Whether the law passed in Germany in July 1933 that allowed the compulsory sterilisation of 'imbeciles' had influenced Ehrenfest's terrible resolve to commit suicide and take his youngest son's life will never be known but is hardly likely to have eased his anxiety.

On Monday 25 September Ehrenfest travelled alone from Leiden to Amsterdam, where he met one of his former students. In the afternoon he took a cab to the Institute to visit his son. In some accounts he sat calmly in the reception area while Wassik was brought out to meet him. He then stood up and shot Wassik through the head, then shot himself through the head, dying instantly. In other versions the shooting took place in Wassik's room. In yet others he took Wassik for a walk in the nearby Vondelpark and shot him there, then killed himself. In still other accounts he took Wassik out on a small lake in the park in a hired rowing boat and shot him there. Most accounts agree Wassik was not killed outright but blinded, as the bullet passed through one eye. He is said to have taken two hours to die. Ehrenfest is reported to have died instantly. On the same day in Roughton, Jacob Epstein arrived and Margery left to be with her sick father.

Saturday 30 September to Sunday 1 October

During Einstein's last days at Roughton the weather became noticeably cooler and wetter. On Friday there had been a thick fog over the north Norfolk coast and the Cromer lifeboat was launched to help a steam drifter in trouble on the shifting Haisbro' Sands. Five years later the struggle between the forces of democracy and fascism would be played out dramatically right here off the Norfolk coast when the *Cantabria*, a cargo ship sailing under the flag of the Spanish Republic, was shelled and sunk by a Francoist gunboat within sight of Cromer. Coxswain Blogg and the volunteer crew of the *H. F. Bailey* took off the captain, his wife and children, and the remaining crew, the rest having already taken to the lifeboats.[36]

On Saturday Epstein conducted his last morning of sittings at the camp. Photographs exist of Einstein and Epstein together outside one of the huts, one showing the clay bust supported by an armature under the chin on a tripod stand between them. Epstein is wearing overalls, over which he wore an old, dark suit coat, his beret pulled down snugly to his ears. Einstein is wearing his usual grey baggy flannels and the same pale-coloured check pullover worn without a shirt seen in photos taken earlier in the summer in Belgium and England. Although Einstein was only five months older than Epstein, his great mane of white hair makes him look much the older of the two.

Einstein and Jacob Epstein at the Roughton Camp.

That final Saturday at the camp was Yom Kippur, the Jewish Day of Atonement. Though Einstein was not a practising Jew he and Epstein would have been acutely aware of the day's importance in the lives of very many Jews who at that very moment were suffering persecution and death in Germany. Though at least one news report said Epstein travelled with Einstein and Locker-Lampson on

Signed souvenir photo, which Locker-Lampson gave to those who had helped guard Einstein at Roughton.

the Monday, most reports say he left Cromer on Sunday on an afternoon train. Einstein's Norfolk adventure was drawing to a close. At the Roughton camp, Einstein, Locker-Lampson and Barbara Goodall, his sole remaining 'guardian angel', readied themselves for an early start on Monday.

Notes

1 *Grundmann, The Einstein Dossiers, pp.347–8.*

2 *Marianoff and Wayne, Einstein, p.4.*

3 *Ibid.2, p. 6.*

4 *Knight, The New Masses.*

5 *Ibid.2, p.160.*

6 *Ibid.2, p.161.*

7 *Ibid.*

8 *Ibid.2, p.163.*

9 *Brian, Einstein, p.267.*

10 *Ibid.2, p.164.*

11 *Albert Einstein Archive, The Hebrew University of Jerusalem, AEA: 143-263.*

12 *Perlzweig, 'The Reminiscences of Dr Maurice L. Perlzweig'.*

13 *'Interview with Alfons Blomme', in West-Vlaanderen (magazine), Vol. 7 (1958); accessed online: www.dbnl.org/tekst/_vla016195801_01/_vla016195801_01_0071.php*

14 Vallentin, Einstein, pp.163–4.
15 Madaule, 'A Modest Genius'.
16 Babson, The Epsteins, p.60.
17 Gardiner, Epstein, p.333.
18 Ibid., p.257.
19 Ibid., pp.166–7.
20 "Epstein Meets Einstein", Norfolk Chronicle, 29 September 1933.
21 Epstein, Let There Be Sculpture, p.78.
22 Sheridan, Nuda Veritas, p.124.
23 Dominion Sunday Times (Auckland, New Zealand), 27 July 1975.
24 Silber, The Sculptures of Jacob Epstein, p.39.
25 Ibid.17, p.333.
26 Blackburn, 'Einstein and Epstein'.
27 The author is grateful to Eddie Anderson for this information.
28 Cross, Sir Samuel Hoare, p.167.
29 Hoare, The Unbroken Thread, p.291.
30 Hoare, Nine Troubled Years, p.240.
31 Eastern Daily Press, 8 February 1939.
32 Ibid.28, pp.284–5.
33 Dilks, The Diaries of Sir Alexander Cadogan, pp.282–8.
34 Spier, Focus, p.145.
35 Ibid.11, AEA: 121-840.
36 Jolly, Henry Blogg of Cromer, ch.11, passim.

Lighthouse Keepers

The final week

Monday 2 October

UNDER a dull, overcast sky and a light drizzle, Einstein waited at Cromer High Station for the London train. While news of Einstein's departure first appeared in the *Eastern Daily Press* the following day, it was a lone reporter from the weekly *Norfolk Chronicle*, who was on hand to add colour to the reportage:

> Looking remarkably well—in fact having completely lost that hunted-by-the-Nazis look as a result of his Norfolk holiday—Professor Einstein left Cromer on Monday morning to return to London. He travelled up in the 9.17 train in a third class compartment and was accompanied by his friend and host, Commander Locker-Lampson, M.P., who has sheltered him from his persecutors during his stay in Norfolk. He was wearing his broad-brimmed hat and carrying his violin in a case. Beyond the railway people and the Commander's staff very few people saw the great man leave Cromer and as the train steamed out of the station he waved to those on the platform.[1]

This sketch, titled 'Farewell, Einstein', was buried deep in the inside pages, incongruously wedged between reports on milk prices and a pedigree pig sale. Einstein's Norfolk adventure had evidently slipped far down the local news agenda from the lead story it had been three weeks earlier. Just before the train pulled out Locker-Lampson told the reporter: "The professor had enjoyed every minute of his stay in Norfolk and had prepared an excellent speech to deliver at the Albert Hall. He hoped to return next year and sail on the Broads. The Nazis had stolen his boat and he wanted another." His mention of the Norfolk Broads is weirdly reminiscent of the story of his father sailing on Wroxham Broad with Tennyson in 1886 when Oliver was 5 years old and may very well have been present. Einstein's compact, well-made yacht *Tümmler* (German for porpoise) had been confiscated by the Nazi-controlled police at Caputh that June on the basis it was not in fact a small yacht but a highly valuable motor speed boat in disguise, which Einstein and his co-conspirators intended smuggling out of the country into the hands of Germany's enemies. Sailing was Einstein's favourite leisure pastime and his 'thick-timbered boat', as he called it, had been his pride and joy since he first acquired it in 1929, a 50th birthday gift from some wealthy admirers. Moored at its own landing stage at the bottom of his garden, he loved to slip away and sail on the Havel Lakes single-handed. His inability to swim and disinclination to wear a life jacket caused his wife and friends considerable anxiety. Though he would continue to enjoy sailing in America, he would never return to sail on the Norfolk Broads or the Havel Lakes, nor did he ever see *Tümmler* again. Despite making postal enquiries of the authorities in Caputh after the Second World War, its whereabouts could not be traced.

The Great Eastern train took Einstein through parts of Norfolk he would have been unfamiliar with, stopping every ten or twenty minutes at Gunton, North Walsham, Worstead, Wroxham, Salhouse and Whitlingham stations before changing trains at Norwich; arriving at Liverpool Street Station at around 2 p.m. where a photographer was on hand to capture his arrival accompanied by Locker-Lampson and Barbara Goodall. A small reception committee had gathered to greet him, including the Jewish property tycoon, Claude Moss Leigh, managing director of the Metropolitan Housing Corporation, which was said to be the largest private landlord of working-class housing in London. From the station, Locker-Lampson seems to have taken Einstein by car to his house in North Street in Westminster. However, while reports in the US press explicitly say he was driven to Locker-Lampson's house, as far as the British public knew his whereabouts were a matter of secrecy. Indeed, some British papers reported he was definitely not staying with Locker-Lampson nor at the London homes of two of the speakers at the following day's Royal Albert Hall meeting—Sir Austen Chamberlain and Lord Rutherford—and only "high officials" at Scotland Yard knew his whereabouts. For some of Einstein's friends, anxious to get him away from England with the minimum of fuss, such reports bore all the hallmarks of Locker-Lampson's publicity machine stoking up the drama of the situation with stories of secret hideaways, assassins lurking round every corner and an around-the-clock armed guard of plain-clothes detectives. The Labour-supporting *Daily Herald*, for example, no great fan of his, satirised the security arrangements as further examples of the "popgun parades" he had perpetrated in Norfolk.[2] Notwithstanding the hype, the recent example of Lessing's assassination showed the danger could not be underestimated. Later that evening Einstein attended a meeting of the allocations committee of the Central British Fund for German Jewry.[3] Claude Leigh, who had met Einstein at the station, was a major donor and he and Einstein were at some point that day photographed leaving a hotel together. The committee, chaired by an old acquaintance of Einstein's, the former Home

Einstein arriving at Liverpool Street Station, London, 2 October 1933. Left to right: unknown, Barbara Goodall, Locker-Lampson, Einstein, Claude Leigh.

Secretary, Sir Herbert Samuel, had been set up in March to provide stipends that would allow British universities, industrial laboratories and hospitals to employ displaced Jewish scholars, doctors and scientists from Germany without taking jobs from British people. By the end of 1933 it had raised a quarter of a million pounds. From 1938 until the outbreak of war it was also involved in helping to organise the *Kindertransport*, which saved thousands of Jewish children from the gas chambers. In 1933, however, it was riven by internal disputes between pro- and anti-Zionists, with the pro-Zionists advocating that funds should be sent to Palestine to help set up a Homeland for Jewish refugees and the unaligned and anti-Zionists arguing funds should be spent on settling refugees into sustainable economic positions in Britain.

Tuesday 3 October

A plethora of refugee committees and councils were at work by this date, raising funds and finding employment for Jewish students, teachers and other professionals such as doctors, lawyers and publishers who had been denied the right to follow their studies or practise their profession in Germany. Those helping Locker-Lampson organise the Albert Hall meeting had grouped themselves under the umbrella name of the German Refugee Assistance Fund and included the International Students Service, the Refugee Professionals Committee, the Society of Friends German Emergency Committee and the Academic Assistance Council (AAC), whose secretary, Walter Adams, had visited Einstein in Roughton in September. On 3 October *The Times* published a long letter by Walter Adams on the work he had been doing on behalf of the AAC. During the previous four weeks he had toured Europe seeking information on what was being done by a number of country's relief committees and gathering statistics on refugees who had already fled Germany. He had visited academic assistance committees in Belgium, Czechoslovakia, France, the Netherlands, Sweden and Switzerland, and had gathered data that suggested more than 50,000 German Jewish refugees were already in Czechoslovakia, France and Poland alone. Strangely, he made no mention of his recent meeting with Einstein, the world's most famous refugee at the time, nor of the Albert Hall meeting that evening. He may have been annoyed his initial idea for a small meeting to promote the AAC with Einstein as the guest speaker had effectively been hijacked by Locker-Lampson and turned into a massive rally, which had alarmed some of the AAC's supporters such as the Royal Society. Walter Adams was not the only one who may have been apprehensive about Einstein's participation in so public an event. Abraham Flexner, Einstein's employer at Princeton University's Institute of Advanced Study, having only just got wind of the Albert Hall meeting, telegraphed Einstein forbidding him to attend, fearful for his personal safety and concerned any adverse publicity would damage the reputation and funding of the Institute. Locker-Lampson is alleged to have intercepted the telegram and kept it from Einstein until shortly before he sailed to the United States on 7 October.[4]

This was to be Einstein's first and only visit to the Royal Albert Hall, the gigantic concert hall built in Kensington in 1871 as part of Victorian London's 'Albertopolis'. Locker-Lampson, however, was something of a regular performer there. Following the General Strike in 1926 he had conducted annual mass rallies there of his anti-Soviet Union 'Rout the Reds' and 'Hands Off the Empire' campaigns, stewarded by members of the British Fascisti and later by his own Blue Shirts. It was reported 10,000 seated tickets had been sold. Several hundred more tickets were sold on the night to people who stood in the aisles. The papers also reported that between 1,000 and 2,000 students from the University of London had been recruited as stewards, which was probably an exaggerated figure very likely to have been conjured up by Locker-Lampson. In reality there were probably no more than a few hundred, some organised by the American anti-fascist Dr S. M. Marcus.[5] In September Dr Marcus had offered to provide Einstein with a bodyguard of a hundred students. This was the same man who in 1932, following the placing of a wreath with a swastika on the Cenotaph by Alfred Rosenberg, had placed there a single lily with a card denouncing Hitler as a murderous dictator. The Metropolitan Police provided scores of uniformed constables, including mounted police officers, who guarded the entrances, patrolled the surrounding streets and mingled among the audience inside the Hall. In addition, it was rumoured "in every dark corner stood a plain clothes man, his hip pocket bulging with his truncheon".[6] Although the *Daily Mail* had that morning urged its readers to boycott the meeting and groups of Mosley's Black Shirts stood by the entrances handing out leaflets, long queues began to form two hours before the meeting began. An hour after it had officially started some ticket holders were still waiting to get inside. In some accounts Einstein arrived in a taxi with Locker-Lampson three minutes before the first speech was due to be delivered. Other accounts say he was driven there in the middle of a convoy of three cars. He entered via the artists' entrance "broadly smiling", surrounded, it was later reported, by a phalanx of a hundred detectives.

The meeting was to be filmed, so powerful lights had been set up in the auditorium focused on the raised platform behind which the non-speaking VIP guests were taking their seats, among them the acid-tongued Lady Margot Asquith, wife of the former Liberal Prime Minister, who was disturbed by the glare and asked to be moved. She would later confess in her autobiography: "I can't understand Mr Einstein's theory, but I am sure I agree with it."[7] The meeting or at least Einstein's contribution to it, was recorded by the BBC; its archives show it paid him 10 guineas for a wireless broadcast talk on this date. Also among the non-speaking VIP guests was Rufus Isaacs (Lord Reading), who had been Attorney General before the First World War, when he had been harried by Locker-Lampson over his alleged involvement in the Marconi scandal. In 1923 readers of the *Jewish Tribune* had voted Reading and Einstein among the twelve greatest Jews in the world.[8] The souvenir programme of the rally sold after the meeting featured a photograph of Lord Reading greeting Einstein at the Albert Hall, a smiling Locker-Lampson beside them, past differences presumably put aside for the night.

The first speaker was Lord Rutherford, who also chaired the meeting. The eminent New Zealand-born physicist was the first of no less than three Nobel Laureates to speak that night, along with Einstein and Sir Austen Chamberlain. As president of the AAC, Rutherford spoke of the growing refugee problem in Europe without specifically mentioning its cause. Although it was clear to everyone assembled the crisis had been caused by racial policies being adopted by the new government in Germany, he stressed the help his organisation and others were providing was not confined to refugees from any one country or of any one race or religion, which was somewhat disingenuous as in fact almost 99 per cent of the refugees it helped were Germans of Jewish origin. The prevailing foreign policy tendency later known as Appeasement may have been evident here. Rutherford and the AAC were anxious at this stage to do nothing that would provide the Nazis with a propaganda weapon by appearing to be anti-German and pro-Jewish rather than simply humanitarian. The AAC's supporters in the Royal Society, while willing to provide them with free office space in London, refused to publicly endorse their work and let Rutherford know he had to be careful when appointing his chief operating officers that none were Jewish. A couple of days before the Albert Hall meeting, one of the AAC's secretaries, the non-Jewish Walter Adams, wrote to Rutherford to advise him Sir Austen Chamberlain was also anxious there should be no speeches hostile to Germany and preferred the word Germany should not be spoken by any of the speakers.[9] It is ironic, therefore, that Chamberlain's short speech at the rally contained eight mentions of Germany, including specific mentions of its government, its press and the National Socialist Party. Rutherford and some of the other speakers, including Chamberlain and the economist Sir William Beveridge, were acutely aware mass immigration into Britain was politically unpopular, especially while the country was trying to recover from the Depression and unemployment levels were still high.

The second speaker was the notoriously eccentric Lord Bishop of Exeter, William Gasgoyne-Cecil. Apart from a fondness for sprinkling his pastoral letters with puzzling metaphors drawn from Darwinism and Relativity theory, it is difficult to understand why he was asked to speak. "Amiable, earnest and unconventional to the verge of eccentricity" was the verdict of *The Tablet* on his appointment as a bishop in 1916, which had been a great surprise to everyone, including apparently himself.[10] One of his earliest clerical appointments was as a humble curate in Great Yarmouth, however, for the twenty-eight years before his elevation to a bishopric he had lived out a harmless and unexceptional existence as the rector of Hatfield near his family's ancestral estate in Hertfordshire, where the local police called him 'Burglar Bill' because of his habit of absent-mindedly riding off from parish calls on someone else's bicycle. Another nickname was 'Love in a Mist' because of his gentle nature, which he showed to all creatures, including two rats that lived in the wainscoting of his cottage—he refused to live in the Bishop's Palace—which he hand-fed with crumpets in front of his guests.[11] In his short speech at the Albert Hall he reminded the audience of the parable of the Good Samaritan and the teachings of Christ to help the stranger, the hungry and the miserable.

The third speaker was the scientist Sir James Jeans, a renowned astrophysicist. He and Rutherford had first met Einstein at the First Solvay Congress in Brussels in 1911. In 1920 he had recommended Einstein to Rutherford for a new chair of mathematical physics at Cambridge. His speech, the last before Einstein's, reiterated the appeal of Rutherford for funds to help refugee academics and students start new careers in Britain and further afield. He urged the audience to listen to Einstein with respect, as: "Such men as he do not labour for private gain, neither for themselves, nor for their family, nor for their tribe, nor for their country." During these speeches Einstein sat beside Locker-Lampson, his hands folded in his lap, his demeanour imperturbable and other worldly as he gazed towards the high domed roof of the auditorium. By contrast, photographs show Locker-Lampson was active throughout the evening: making and passing notes, whispering instructions behind his hand to an assistant and showing papers to Einstein.

When Einstein finally rose to speak there was a thunderous round of applause and cheering, which ricocheted around the Hall like machine-gun fire and could be plainly heard in Kensington Road despite the noise of passing traffic. Einstein rarely spoke in public in English, but he did so on this occasion in his soft south German accent. The version published in the souvenir brochure begins: "I am glad that you have given me the opportunity of expressing to you my deep sense of gratitude as a man, a good European and as a Jew."[12] However, the BBC's sound recording reveals that what he actually said was "I am glad that you have me given …", the word order he would have used if speaking in German. He had in fact hand-written the speech in German and was translating from it as he spoke. The manuscript copy survives, composed presumably in Roughton, as Locker-Lampson had told the reporter on Cromer Station on Monday.[13] This shows two paragraphs were omitted concerning the dangers to neighbouring countries

From the souvenir programme of the Royal Albert Hall rally, 3 October 1933.

COMMANDER LOCKER-LAMPSON SPEAKING.
MARQUESS OF READING GREETING PROFESSOR EINSTEIN
"YOU ARE FOURTH ON THE PROGRAMME."
FAR FROM THE
EINSTEIN AT CO
C
8

THE BISHOP OF EXETER, SIR AUSTEN CHAMBERLAIN, SIR WILLIAM BEVERIDGE, PROFESSOR EINSTEIN and SIR JAMES JEANS

(*Right*) THE PROFESSOR PREPARES HIS SPEECH

(*Left*) DELIVERING THE ADDRESS

ROWD. PROFESSOR LOCKER - LAMPSON'S OMER.

"EPSTEIN AND EINSTEIN"—IN CLAY

9

Photo: Planet News Ltd., London

posed by Germany's clandestine rearmament programme and aggressive foreign policy, possibly at the request of Lord Rutherford, chair of the meeting.

After calling for the preservation of tolerance and liberty, without which such great creative geniuses as Shakespeare, Goethe, Newton, Faraday, Pasteur and Lister would not have been able to flourish, he called for the international community to show unity in confronting aggressive states, thereby making war impossible. He then moved on to the need for scientists to have freedom to think: "When I was living in solitude in the country, I noticed that the monotony of a quiet life stimulates the creative mind." Might not such occupations as lighthouse or lightship keeper be ideal for young scientists, he reasoned? The image was a startling one. It does not appear in the German manuscript and so was possibly only added shortly before the meeting or improvised at the podium, perhaps to make up for the two paragraphs about German rearmament he may have been asked to omit. His recollection of his time in Roughton had perhaps reminded him of Cromer lighthouse, the flashing beam of which may have been visible at the camp at night and which he may very well have visited as it was easily accessible on foot along the cliff top path, as it still is. His lighthouse idea, however, was not a new one. On a visit to Jerusalem in 1923, while walking on the Mount of Olives with Norman Bentwich, the British Attorney General of the Palestine Mandate, Einstein had spoken wistfully of his recent long sea voyage from Japan, which had provided him with the ideal conditions for thinking: a regular routine, quiet and no distractions. Perhaps unaware of the hardships and stress of a lighthouse keeper's life, he told Bentwich lighthouses might provide similar conditions conducive to deep mathematical thought.[14]

Postcard of Cromer lighthouse.

The symbolic power of the lighthouse as a place of refuge for the embattled or exiled intellectual would have an enduring influence. Written in 1939, on the eve of war in Europe, the American playwright Robert Ardrey's philosophical melodrama *Thunder Rock* is largely set in a lighthouse. Produced on Broadway with little initial success, it was subsequently put on in London's West End shortly after the outbreak of war, when it received enthusiastic reviews and played to packed houses. The play tells the story of an idealistic journalist who is convinced civilisation is under imminent threat from the rise of fascistic regimes in Europe and the Far East. Unable to get anyone in a position of authority or influence to take him seriously and faced by a largely indifferent public, he despairs of mankind and retreats to an isolated lighthouse by Lake Michigan to await world war and the collapse of civilisation. Here his imagination is haunted by the lives of a group of immigrants who were drowned in the lake during a storm in 1849 as they fled intolerance, superstition and oppression in Europe. Through their lives and struggles he comes to realise civilisation depends on the courage and endurance of individuals to keep it alive and progressing. He determines therefore to return to the world and continue the struggle. Churchill recognised the play's propaganda value, and the British Government put money into its continued theatrical production. A live radio performance was broadcast by the BBC in 1940, while a film version produced and directed by the Boulting Brothers and starring Michael Redgrave as the journalist was released in 1942. The play became immensely popular during the war and was even performed by German internees at Hutchinson Camp on the Isle of Man.[15] While Ardrey claimed the idea for the play came to him virtually complete during a dreamlike trance, the parallels with Einstein's lighthouse idea are intriguing. In the film version, David Charleston, the journalist played by Redgrave, meets a pacifist diplomat at the League of Nations in Geneva in 1931 whose pipe, moustache and soft south German accent are clearly modelled on Einstein's persona. Touring Britain giving talks to half-empty halls on the growing threat of fascism and the dangers of appeasement, Charleston stands before a banner bearing the slogan 'Britain Awake!' The closeness of this to Locker-Lampson's 'England Awake!' campaign in 1934 about the dangers of German rearmament is striking.

The speaker who had the unenviable task of following Einstein was Locker-Lampson himself. His speech proved to be the most florid and combative of the whole evening. There was no chance he would hold back from directly criticising Nazi Germany's persecution of the Jews: "Germany has not expelled her blackguards and her cut-throats: she has expelled the most civilized of her citizens. Never in the world has there been this pogrom of the intellect." By contrast, England and the British Empire were a beacon of freedom in the world, where "men behave better to women, women are kinder to animals, children are decent even to dogs under the Union Jack". Concluding, he urged all exiled

German Jewish scholars to learn to speak and write English, to have no fear and build a new homeland, a new "Oxford University of the Orient and a Cambridge of the East" in Palestine, and punning on the literal meaning of Einstein's name in German: "the stone the builders rejected, the outlaw Einstein, shall become the headstone of the corner of your temple. So, chosen people, be of good cheer."

Locker-Lampson's speech was followed by the longest of the evening, given by the honorary secretary of the AAC, Sir William Beveridge, an economist and social reformer whose 1942 report on social insurance would lay the foundations of the post-war welfare state. His over cautious, somewhat cheese-paring advice, however, seems to have struck the only flat note of the evening. He urged all Jews in Germany who had not yet been denied employment to remain so as not to damage the chances of those who had already come of finding employment. Britain, he argued, with its high unemployment levels could not accommodate all of Germany's Jews without causing social unrest. However, the case with ejected academic refugees was different. If funds could be found to provide them with bursaries, they would not displace British scholars but add to the fund of knowledge and experience in the universities.

Next came Sir Austen Chamberlain, who had stipulated before the rally "politics are strictly forbidden to the speakers" but who now made a political point himself, directly attributing the refugee crisis to the actions of the

Sir Austen Chamberlain (seated right)—the second Nobel Laureate to visit the Roughton Camp—with Locker-Lampson, Lady Chamberlain and Barbara Goodall (standing second left), 1934.

German Government. Dr Maude Royden, a woman's suffragist and pacifist who campaigned for the ordination of women in the Anglican Church, and Viscount Buckmaster, a distinguished lawyer and Liberal politician, were the final two speakers. The meeting concluded with an appeal for money from the meeting's Secretary, Charles Cooley, the man who had organised many of Locker-Lampson's 'Rout the Reds' and Blue Shirt rallies. The audience was urged to fill in the slips attached to their programmes and pledge at least £1. Dr Royden had been the only speaker to point out that for some of those present, many of them students, £1 was a lot of money and they should rack their brains for other ways of helping, such as providing hospitality or gifts in kind to refugees. The meeting is reported to have raised £2,000, equivalent to around £100,000 today. After the meeting and before he left the building, Einstein gave a short statement to the press:

> I could not believe that it was possible that such spontaneous affection could be extended to one who is a wanderer on the face of the earth. The kindness of your people has touched my heart so deeply that I cannot find words to express in English what I feel. I shall leave England for America at the end of the week, but no matter how long I live I shall never forget the kindness which I have received from the people of England.[16]

Einstein then left by a side entrance, accompanied by Locker-Lampson and three women, one of whom was presumably Barbara Goodall. Margery Howard, Einstein's other 'attendant angel', as Jacob Epstein had described her, does not seem to have attended the meeting, presumably because she was still attending her ill father. She did see him one more time, though, when he visited her family home in Mitcham in Surrey to pay his respects shortly before he sailed for America.[17]

Wednesday 4 to Friday 6 October

The day after the rally most of the British newspapers covered the story and in the following days their political cartoonists seem to have found Einstein's image irresistible, though in two notable instances their satire was directed not towards the situation in Germany but against the National Government's inability to deal decisively with the question of Indian Home Rule. Sidney Strube in the *Daily Express* depicted Einstein as "Professor Stan Baldstein", a reference to Stanley Baldwin, the de facto Prime Minister given Ramsay MacDonald's deteriorating health, sat atop a lighthouse reading by the light of a candle, oblivious to the stormy seas that threaten to wreck a passing ship named *India Policy*.[18] On the same theme, Leonard Raven-Hill in *Punch* depicted Winston Churchill, Stafford Cripps and Lord Beaverbrook in rowing boats named respectively *India The British Raj*, *Proletariat Autocracy* and *Imperial Isolation* in "The Race for the Eddystein Lighthouse".[19] Both cartoons included quotes about lighthouses from Einstein's speech in case the reader didn't get the allusion. Will Dyson in the left-wing *Daily Herald* seems to have been alone in directing the satire in his cartoon towards pro-Nazi British sympathisers, depicting a typical bowler-hatted Englishman with a cricket bat tucked under his arm berating Einstein for complaining that the Nazis had stolen his trousers as Hitler stands by trying to look innocent while holding the purloined trousers and some spoons, the ground strewn with Einstein's books, violin, home and honours as well as the grave of his friends.[20]

That Wednesday, after the tumultuous events at the Albert Hall, Professor Lindemann drove from Oxford to London, where he telephoned Locker-Lampson to arrange a meeting with Einstein the following day. Lindemann was desperate to secure an agreement with him that he would return to England in 1934 to lecture at Oxford University, as he had verbally promised, hoping thereby to persuade him to settle in England permanently. For some reason they did not meet. Years later when it became clear Einstein was never likely to leave America, Lindemann is said to have spread a rumour around Oxford that Locker-Lampson had deliberately withheld his message and had frightened Einstein from Europe with all his talk of lurking assassins.[21] That he read Einstein's mail and probably valeted his phone calls too is revealed in a letter from Yahuda to Einstein written on 10 October when Einstein was crossing the Atlantic.[22] On 5 October or possibly the evening of 4 October, Locker-Lampson said his final farewell to Einstein as he left London to attend the Conservative Party's Annual Conference in Birmingham, where he was programmed to give a speech on 'subversive propaganda'.

A day or two after the Albert Hall meeting, Einstein had what would prove to be his last formal meeting before he left for America. At his meeting with the Central British Fund of German Jewry on Monday he had agreed to meet one of its members, Rabbi Dr Maurice L. Perlzweig, privately before he sailed. Perlzweig was the current chairman of the World Union of Jewish Student (WUJS), which was founded in 1924 with Einstein as its Honorary President. Fortunately, Perlzweig left a fascinating account of the meeting in a taped interview he made in New York in 1982, only three years before his death at the age of 89. Recalling events almost fifty years earlier, Rabbi Perlzweig thought his meeting with Einstein in London had been in 1936 rather than 1933. His attention had been drawn to a problem affecting Jewish students in Poland, where anti-Semitic academic staff were forcing them to sit in segregated seats at the rear of lecture halls. It had been suggested to him he take advantage of Einstein's visit to London to ask him to write a letter of protest. Curiously, despite Einstein's role in the founding of the WUJS, Perlzweig seemed to have little idea at the time of just how famous Einstein was or of his present circumstances. He was surprised therefore to find him under police guard:

> [Einstein] gave me an address in the West End of London which he said was secret. He had been sworn to secrecy by the British police, who was afraid that he would be murdered, and I remember very vividly one morning in that year when I made my way through various channels and obstacles in order at last to see him. He was very closely guarded. … I remember being shown into a big room in which there was a piano, and on the piano was a violin case, and the room otherwise rather sparsely furnished. And then all of a sudden, without warning in walked Albert Einstein, and he looked and was dressed exactly as the caricature picture, that is to say he had no socks on—he had shoes, but no socks. His other garment was a pullover. He didn't wear a jacket or anything like that. He did have a tie, I with astonishment noticed.[23]

On being told about the Polish students, Einstein immediately agreed, once he had approved it, to put his name to whatever Perlzweig drafted. The statement had little to do specifically with Polish Jewish students. Emphasising that intellectual study for Jews was a sacred activity and not merely a means to an end, he warned that Jewish refugees may need to find employment below their abilities and outside the professions they had trained for. In a way it was a practical response to Beveridge's warning in his Albert Hall speech that not every refugee could be found a job commensurate with his or her professional skill. This done they sat down and had a long discussion on the future of Jews in Europe. Perlzweig believed five million Jews would need to be moved out of Europe for their safety. Einstein believed the figure was nearer seven million as it was necessary to take into account Jews in the Soviet Union, whom he believed would eventually come under the same pressures to leave their homes as those in Germany. After the meeting Perlzweig went home in a kind of daze: "I was completely overcome by the personality of this man, who seemed to me to be as near to a saint as anything I've ever met."

Saturday 7 October

Various versions of Einstein's final departure from Britain exist. Rather like the atomic particle in Heisenberg's Uncertainty Principle, it seems to have been impossible for anyone to accurately report his position and momentum at the same time. According to Barbara Goodall, who in Locker-Lampson's absence was now the last member of the Roughton guard on duty, she drove him to Southampton on Saturday. It was perhaps during this journey they stopped off in Mitcham in Surrey to say goodbye to his other "attendant angel", Margery Howard, although Margery's own recollection was Barbara only drove him as far as Victoria Station. *The Times* reported he travelled from London to Southampton on the boat train.[24] Curiously, Marianoff in his biography claimed he travelled over to France with Einstein four days after the Albert Hall meeting and while he returned to Paris, Einstein travelled on to Belgium to collect Elsa. This would have been on the same Saturday he sailed to America. In his biography he extemporised at length about the Channel crossing, which according to Marianoff was very rough. While everyone else was alarmed or seasick, the great man stood imperturbably on the deck at night contemplating the majesty of the universe.[25] This was total fiction. The English Channel was calm that Saturday and British immigration records show Einstein boarded the Red Star liner *Westernland* in Southampton on Saturday 7 October.

Already on board were Elsa Einstein, Dr Walther Mayer and Helen Dukas, who had embarked at Antwerp the previous day. Years later, Barbara recalled that as Einstein waited on the dock side for the tender that would convey him to the liner he looked lost and sad. His last words to her recalled his arrival at Victoria Station a month ago, when he had misplaced a parcel of books: "I feel just like a parcel. You met me, looked after me and now you're posting me off."[26] The *Westernland* sailed on the evening tide. As the liner steamed out of Southampton Water in the gathering dusk, Einstein, had he wished, might have seen a sight familiar to generations of passengers: the beam of the bright-red Trinity House lightship, *LV78*, anchored off Calshot Spit. The Dutch-owned *Westernland* would later play another significant part in the struggle against Nazism. Following the invasion of the Netherlands in 1940, its crew sailed it to England where for a few months it became the headquarters of the Netherlands Government in exile. It was later converted by the Admiralty into a troopship. Einstein, meanwhile, the advocate of lighthouses and lightships as places of scholarly refuge, had 3,500 miles to travel before he could settle down to think and work in his own beacon of civilization in Princeton, New Jersey.

Notes

1 *Norfolk Chronicle, 6 October 1933.*

2 *Daily Herald, 3 October 1933.*

3 *Jewish Chronicle, 13 October 1933; cited in Gottlieb, Men of Vision, note 44, pp.219–20.*

4 *Fölsing, Albert Einstein, p.681.*

5 *Chicago Daily Tribune, 12 September 1933.*

6 *Daily Express, 6 October 1933.*

7 *Asquith, Myself When Young, p.122.*

8 *New Outlook, vol. 135 (1923), p.200.*

9 *Clark, Einstein, p.472.*

10 *The Tablet, 28 October 1916, p.6.*

11 *Beeson, The Bishops, pp.12–15.*

12 *Details of the speeches are from a copy of the souvenir programme sold after the Royal Albert Hall meeting, used by courtesy of the Locker-Lampson family.*

13 *Albert Einstein Archive, The University of Jerusalem, AEA: 28-253.*

14 *Ibid.9, p.375.*

15 *Clarke, 'German Refugee Theatre in British Internment'.*

16 *Eastern Daily Press, 4 October 1933.*

17 *Dominion Sunday Times (Auckland, New Zealand), 27 July 1975.*

18 *Daily Express, 6 October 1933.*

19 *Punch, 11 October 1933.*

20 *Daily Herald, 4 October 1933.*

21 *Ibid.9, p.475.*

22 *Ibid.13, AEA: 121-856.*

23 *Perlzweig, 'The Reminiscences of Dr Maurice L. Perlzweig'.*

24 *The Times, 9 October 1933.*

25 *Marianoff and Wayne, Einstein, pp.171–2.*

26 *From interview with Mrs Barbara Mulholland, 'Tracing Oliver Locker-Lampson's life', Crawley Advertiser, 8 October 1971; the author is grateful to Steve Locker-Lampson for this cutting.*

A Righteous Gentile

TEN days after leaving Southampton, the *Westernland* docked in Manhattan. It was raining and Einstein was nowhere to be found. The crossing had been rough but otherwise uneventful and Einstein had utilised the time catching up with correspondence. In one letter—to a geologist at the Académie des Sciences—he mentioned the Roughton camp, apologising for not having sent him a signed photograph as there had been no way of making one there. Interestingly, he looked forward to meeting him in Paris the following spring, suggesting a prolonged, uninterrupted stay in the USA was not yet his intention.[1]

Whether Einstein made any acquaintances during the voyage isn't known but he was a sociable fellow when it suited him so it is interesting to speculate. The passenger list included at least one fellow 'alien' with whom he might have found something in common to talk about as he strolled the deck puffing on his pipe. Irish-Canadian inventor William F. Mahoney, had patented numerous gadgets, including in 1926 a refrigerated soft drinks dispenser.[2] Einstein was of course an expert on patents and by a bizarre coincidence had also patented a new type of refrigerator in 1926. Disturbed by a report of a Berlin family who died in their sleep poisoned by a toxic gas leak from a domestic refrigerator, he had developed with his friend and fellow physicist, Leo Szilard, plans for a 'silent' fridge that used non-toxic gases. Szilard was a brilliant former student of Einstein's at the University of Berlin. A Hungarian Jew, in 1933 he fled to London with his life savings hidden in his shoes. As Einstein settled in at Roughton that September, Szilard became preoccupied by a report in *The Times* that Lord Rutherford had described a theory that it might be possible to harness atomic energy as "moonshine". It was a theory close to his heart. Walking through Bloomsbury on 10 September pondering the problem of splitting the atom, he paused beside a column of traffic lights. As he watched the red Stop light being succeeded by the green Go light he had a revelation of how a nuclear chain reaction could be produced; a tiny moment in time that would lead to the terrible dilemma Einstein would face a decade later in the USA of whether or not to support the development of the Atom Bomb. Synchronicity, Carl Jung believed, owed a big debt to Relativity or was it the other way round?

At the rain-swept 23rd Street Pier the Mayor of New York waited to hand Einstein the keys to the city before conducting him on a parade accompanied by a marching band but he had slipped the net, a motor launch having conveyed him without fanfare from the ship to the Battery on the southern tip of Manhattan Island, where a waiting car took him, Elsa and their travelling companions, Helen Dukas and Walther Mayer, via the Holland Tunnel to a suite of rooms at the Peacock Hotel in Princeton, New Jersey. It had been a fortunate escape. Up for re-election and keen to impress New York's Jewish voters, the gaffe-prone Mayor O'Brien, known to the press as the 'winded bull in the china shop', had once introduced Einstein at a function in his honour as 'the scientist of scientists, Albert Weinstein'. His escape had been masterminded by the director of the Institute of Advanced Study, Abraham Flexner, who was anxious to keep Einstein out of the news. Flexner's need to control Einstein's movements, public statements and all access to him, which included turning down without his knowledge a personal invitation to visit the White House from President Roosevelt, would eventually become troublesome. Einstein had already had a taste of this in England with Locker-Lampson's interception of his mail and unauthorised statements about his wish to become a British citizen and interest in taking up a professorship in Palestine but seems to have accepted it there, perhaps because his life and those of his family and friends were in danger. Now it was different or so he hoped.

Einstein's first act on arriving in Princeton was to change into more comfortable clothing, his second to buy an ice cream. After months of being closely guarded he could finally move about in public as he pleased. He found himself on American soil for the second time that year and although he didn't know it yet would never again leave, apart from a brief trip to British-controlled Bermuda in 1935 to apply for permanent residence in the United States, which had to be done outside US territory—a stepping stone towards full naturalisation in 1940. Like his brain, most of which ended up in a glass jar in Kansas at the grey end of the rainbow, Einstein's life in America until his death in 1955 has been exhaustively analysed and dissected.[3] It was during these years his image became fixed in the popular imagination as the wild-haired sage of Princeton, the professor who received more fan mail than any movie star, the genius who pondered the nature of the universe while helping a schoolchild with her sums and, rather less happily, as the 'father' of the Atom Bomb and a suspected fellow traveller of the Communist Party.

Although he was no longer able to exert a direct personal influence Locker-Lampson continued to try to remotely control Einstein's direction of travel: away from permanent settlement in America towards a swift return to Britain and naturalisation as a British subject. His work to bolster British power and influence in the Mandate of Palestine was one strand of a long-held political agenda going back to the Balfour Declaration of 1917. To this end he continued to seek a commitment from Einstein to support the academic life of the Hebrew

University in Jerusalem by his actual presence rather than just his moral support. In a letter dated 9 January 1934 he thanked Einstein for a letter that seems to have been lost enclosing copies of Nazi propaganda being circulated among the Arab population in Palestine.[4] While inciting mass Jewish emigration by its anti-Semitic policies, the Nazis supported by Mussolini were fomenting unrest among Palestinian Arabs disturbed by rising Jewish immigration. Einstein had frequently argued against the creation of a Jewish state if it marginalised the civil rights of the Arabs. Two years later a full-scale Arab uprising would break out, taking considerable British military effort to repress with much brutality and loss of life.

Recalling how he had provided him with sanctuary in England under the painful circumstances of the previous year, Locker-Lampson promised to find Einstein a quiet place where he could live and work undisturbed while he acted as a "*Stosskissen*" (shock absorber) against the bombardment of "pushy" letter writers.[5] According to one of Einstein's biographers, this letter was probably written at Lindemann's behest, still hoping to persuade Einstein to take up a professorship at Oxford. Given Lindemann is said to have believed Locker-Lampson had frightened Einstein away from Britain this seems unlikely. Moreover, Einstein had already written to Lindemann in November 1933, offering to return his fee for lecturing at Oxford the following summer so it could be given to another scholar.[6] On 5 February 1934 Einstein replied, apologising for the delay in replying. It is possible this was a reply to another lost letter as he makes no mention of his *Stosskissen* offer, launching instead into an idea he had heard recently that Germany's displaced Jews be allowed to emigrate to Cyprus, then a British Crown Colony, where they might act as allies of the British against Greek Cypriots fighting for union with Greece.[7] Many German Jewish refugees saw Cyprus as a stepping stone to Palestine but the British authorities seeking to curb immigration required that they had personal capital of at least $20,000—equivalent of almost half a million dollars today.

On 17 August Locker-Lampson wrote from Cromer, this time with a plan to finance a physics laboratory at the Hebrew University in Jerusalem at a cost of "perhaps £100,000" (equivalent to more than £5 million today) if Einstein agreed to take up its chair of mathematics. He would only have to attend one month a year and a home in England would be provided for the remainder of the year. Moreover, it would mean his publications would not have Oxford University as its imprimatur.[8] It is not clear who if anyone was behind this plan. Clearly not Lindemann, the champion of Oxford's bid to secure Einstein. Locker-Lampson claimed it was his own idea and he had not spoken to Weizmann or Yahuda about it. The memorandum of a discussion between Locker-Lampson and Sir Philip Hartog, a member of the Hebrew University's Board of Governors, in London dated 10 October 1934, suggests he had represented himself as Einstein's envoy, entrusted with securing him a home in Europe and a chair at the university. The amount being offered was now stated to be "nearer £200,000". He was not offering his own money, he said, but was unable to reveal the name of the donor.[9] Hertzog agreed to put the offer to Einstein, though he felt uncomfortable not knowing the source of the funding. Nothing in the surviving correspondence suggests Locker-Lampson had any authority from Einstein to seek this outcome. Ten days later Einstein replied, drawing a line under further discussion. He would not accept any post at the Hebrew University under its present management, in which he had no confidence, and besides he was happy where he was.[10] As he had written to Yahuda the previous year when Locker-Lampson had been going about asserting in public he was actively seeking British citizenship: "God protect me from the good intention of my friends."[11]

Until a year before the outbreak of the Second World War Locker-Lampson and Einstein continued to correspond, even sending each other little gifts—a pipe from Einstein, perhaps one of his own as a souvenir as Locker-Lampson did not smoke; a mysterious "cherished keepsake to past times" from Locker-Lampson.[12] While he would never be able to bring him back to England to sail on the Norfolk Broads as he had once hoped, Einstein's magnetic influence on Locker-Lampson's political compass would prove to be profound and long-lasting. Although he had already begun to distance himself from the fascistic politics he had enthusiastically espoused in the 1920s and early 1930s, it was his friendship with Einstein that gave him the jolt that set him off on a radically different political trajectory. During the remaining twelve years of his active political career, he directed much of his intellectual and emotional energies to anti-fascist causes. These had three objectives: undermining home-grown fascism in Britain, turning the tide of public opinion against the British Government's policy of appeasement of the fascist dictators and helping Jewish victims of the Nazis and the Soviet Union escape to safety.

Garish Regimentals

Public disquiet at the violence that frequently accompanied political meetings steadily increased in the 1930s—a time of prolonged and severe economic depression. In February 1934 Locker-Lampson tried unsuccessfully to introduce a Bill in parliament banning the possession of rubber truncheons and knuckle-dusters, which were being used by Mosley's Black Shirts and their opponents in street fighting. In May he tried to gain parliamentary support for a Bill to ban the wearing of paramilitary uniforms by members of political groups, stating in the House of Commons: "The most serious clashes recently between the authorities and public people have been owing to the presence at meetings and in the streets of ominous dusky figures in garish regimentals."[13] While his chief target was the British Union of Fascists (BUF), he also argued that the mere presence of Mosley's black-shirted supporters only encouraged left-wing groups to make counter-demonstrations, leading to violent clashes.

Speaking against the Bill, the Conservative Privy Councillor the Earl Winterton could not resist reminding the House that not so long ago Locker-Lampson had himself been the leader of his own "blue shirt organisation", and while such laws might be needed on the Continent, "Bill Smith of England is a very different man from Gustav Schmidt of Germany" and did not need to be told what colour shirt he might wear, adding:

> With a chivalry which we all admire, he has constituted himself the special protector of many very distinguished German Jew émigrés. We all remember the picture that appeared of him last year, obviously feeling very strongly about the matter, with a gamekeeper in the background and a slightly embarrassed look on his face, armed with a shot gun.[14]

The gamekeeper was clearly Herbert Eastoe, who would no doubt have been astounded and not a little embarrassed to have learned he had been referred to in parliament. The motion to introduce the Bill was defeated, losing an early opportunity to curb the spread of home-grown fascism, which, as Locker-Lampson knew only too well, gained much of its attraction to disaffected young men and women by the dark glamour of its "garish regimentals".

The blue tunic that Locker-Lampson's relatively short-lived Blue Shirt movement adopted became the most fashionable of all the colours adopted by far-right groups, with examples in Belgium, Canada, China, France, Ireland, Portugal, Romania and Spain. Without any obvious object of hate other than communism and socialism, his own movement proved to be an expensive flop. It is highly doubtful the 100,000-strong membership he claimed ever existed or that his considerable personal financial outlay on publicity, hiring meeting halls and manufacturing uniforms, records and 'loyalist emblems' such as ties, badges, brooches and cuff links, was ever recouped through sales. Locker-Lampson's younger son, Stephen, remembered as a boy skimming Blue Shirt badges across the Square Pond at Rowfant. Eventually, most democratic countries across Europe enacted so-called 'blouse laws' to proscribe what one wit described as "indoctrinary haberdashery" and P. G. Wodehouse satirised in his Jeeves and Wooster stories in the form of the 'Black Shorts'.[15] Denmark

Blue Shirt cuff-links bearing the Locker-Lampson's family motto 'Fear God. Fear Naught'.

had been the first, followed in order by Sweden, Norway, Austria, Switzerland, Czechoslovakia, Finland, the Netherlands and Belgium but it would not be until 1936, when public opinion and the press turned against the breakdown in law and order, that the British Government finally acted. In his memoirs Winterton admitted that while he had opposed Locker-Lampson's Bill in 1934 when there had been no support for it in the press, the rising level of violence surrounding fascist and anti-fascist demonstrations such as at the Battle of Cable Street persuaded him to support the Government's very similar Public Order Bill in November 1936.[16] In the House of Commons and the press Locker-Lampson earned no credit for his far-sightedness and somewhat surprisingly took no part in the debate other than voting for the Bill, possibly as he had recently and somewhat embarrassingly fallen foul of Admiralty regulations on civilians wearing naval uniform after he had appeared at a public meeting against anti-Semitism in Cardiff wearing his old naval officer's tunic.

Barbara Goodall performing at the 'All Blue Gala', July 1931., *see p. 70.*

Locker-Lampson seems to have taken a personal dislike to the British fascist leader Oswald Mosley even before he deserted the Conservative Party and joined the Independent Labour Party in 1924. Although his older brother Godfrey had been a friend of Oswald and Cynthia Mosley socially and a political ally of Mosley in the early 1920s their personalities were probably too alike for them to see each other as anything other than rivals. During the General Election of May 1929 they had harangued each other at a political rally in the Rag Market in Birmingham. Both were fighting for Birmingham seats: Mosley for Labour in Smethwick, Locker-Lampson for the Conservatives in Handsworth. Locker-Lampson sarcastically addressed Mosley as comrade "because of his Communistic leanings", Mosley countered by appealing ironically to those of his supporters booing him to make allowances as Locker-Lampson clearly had an anti-Red obsession: "when anything goes wrong, from influenza to the Albion being beaten, he attributes it to Moscow".[17]

Locker-Lampson's animosity towards Mosley rumbled on for years. In 1931 when Mosley left the Labour Party and set up the New Party he called him "the perfumed popinjay of the London drawing-room". *Time* magazine in the United States, reporting on a Blue Shirt rally at this time, called Locker-Lampson "Sir Oswald's only rival for the title 'Britain's Hitler'", which may have initiated his unfortunate meeting with the Nazi theorist Alfred Rosenberg.[18] After Mosley set up the BUF in 1933 Locker-Lampson called him a "Continental dancing master" who "masquerades like Mussolini with his dirty shirts". In 1934, he issued a pamphlet under his own name entitled *The Blackshirt Outlook* with "Read Carefully" printed on the front. Its inner pages were printed entirely in black. In 1938 the BUF newspaper *Action* lampooned the "double-barrelled" Locker-Lampson as "Two-gun", ridiculing his efforts to protect "a certain notorious German-Jew ... striding up and down before this fugitive's window … a rifle at slope and a look of grim determination on those classical features".[19] In 1941 he asked the Home Secretary whether Mosley, interned as a German sympathiser, should be tried as a spy and later in the war called for him to added to the list of war criminal and if convicted, executed. He also asked the same question about Mosley's former lieutenant William Joyce, popularly known as 'Lord Haw-Haw' because of the braying tone of his propaganda radio broadcasts from Berlin during the war. In 1940 Joyce had ridiculed Locker-Lampson as a "libidinous little nincompoop" who had mounted guard with his shotgun over "the Jew Einstein … lest any wicked Nazi should attempt to harm him".[20] Captured by the Allies in Germany in 1945, Joyce was found guilty of treason and hanged in 1946.

Another fascist Locker-Lampson sought to undermine during the 1930s was Arnold Leese, an oddball fanatic who never achieved the same level of support as Mosley. Leese, a former army veterinary officer and expert on the diseases of camels, was virulently anti-Semitic. He called for the total expulsion, compulsory sterilisation or extermination of Britain's Jewish population. In 1933 he rejected a merger of his Imperial Fascist League (IFL) with the newly formed BUF, calling them "kosher fascists" because of Mosley's lack of interest at that time in stirring up anti-Semitic unrest. Mosley in turn described the IFL as "one of those little crank societies. They are mad about the Jews". In 1935 Locker-Lampson vigorously lobbied the Home Office to ban publication of the latest issue of the anti-Semitic German newspaper *Der Stürmer* because it contained an anonymous article, 'Jewish ritual murder', thought to have been written by Leese. The Home Secretary, Sir John Simon, declined to act as there was no evidence the journal was generally available in Britain. The following year, Leese published an English version of his spurious history of the 'Blood Libel' in the Imperial Fascist League's own party newspaper.[21] Locker-Lampson immediately called on the Government to prosecute Leese for libelling the King's subjects and outraging public decency. This time it acted, resulting in

Leese and his printer receiving sentences of six months' imprisonment. During his trial and afterwards he continued to attack Locker-Lampson's staunchly pro-Semitic stance, predictably attributing it to his alleged financial backing by "his childhood friends" the Rothschilds.

England Awake!

In March 1934 Locker-Lampson suddenly began to take an interest in gliding. Over the next 12 months he asked a string of questions in parliament: on the number of gliding clubs in the country, the small number of glider pilot certificates held by British flyers compared with German, the possibility of government subsidy to set up a national gliding week on the South Downs and even the threat to gliders posed by owners of grouse moors. In November 1934, unsurprisingly, he became joint vice-president of the newly formed Norfolk Gliding Club based at the disused lighthouse in Winterton owned by the Club's other vice-president, Viscount Elmley, Liberal MP for East Norfolk. The fact the club did not possess a glider until September 1935 somewhat hampered its activities and it closed in 1938.[22]

Locker-Lampson was playing his own uniquely eccentric part in the 'Air Panic' of 1934–5, in which politicians and the press stoked up public anxiety that Britain and her Locarno Treaty ally France had fallen behind in the aviation arms race with Germany, Italy and the Soviet Union.[23] Intelligence on German rearmament had been brought to him in the summer of 1934 by a friend of Einstein's, the prominent German pacifist Otto Lehmann-Russbüldt, who had fled to Holland in March 1933 without a passport following the Nazi's clampdown on its opponents in the aftermath of the Reichstag fire.[24] Faced with a resurgent militaristic nationalism in Europe, Locker-Lampson wanted the Government to kick-start the creation of a corps of citizen aviators ready and willing to roster the RAF when called upon. He also called for a government loan so British business could build the infrastructure—the aerodromes and bomb and aircraft factories—necessary to mobilise and equip a long-range bomber air force. On 28 June 1934 the inaugural, and as it turned out sole, meeting of the 'Hands off Britain' Air Defence League (ADL) was held at Kingsway Hall in Holborn. He had used the 'Hands Off' slogan ('Hands Off Britain', 'Hands Off Our Empire') at his anti-communist meetings in the 1920s and early 1930s. Although the object of his ire were now fascists as well as communists, those most receptive to his rhetoric were little different from those who had attended his 'Rout the Reds' rallies a few years earlier—politically dissatisfied, socially conservative and jingoistic. Significantly, the ADL's Secretary was Charles Cooley, who had organised Locker-Lampson's Blue Shirt rallies, as well as the Royal Albert Hall meeting at which Einstein had spoken in October 1933.

The ADL's 'Hands off Britain' meeting opened with a medley of patriotic songs sung by Scottish soprano Flora Woodman and Australian baritone Harold Williams. Woodman had been a soloist at the Norfolk & Norwich Triennial Music Festival and Williams was the voice of the Blue Shirts on the 78 rpm recording of 'March On' issued with a spoken introduction by Locker-Lampson. After an introduction by his old naval and parliamentary comrade, Admiral Sir Murray Sueter MP, Locker-Lampson gave the keynote speech. How unfair it was, he said, to be called a war-monger when his only interest was the security of his country. He hated bloodshed but hated tyranny more. Germany was a slave state ruled by a despot who threatened to "spring at the throat of humanity" like a tiger. The development of long-range bombing technology meant: "the age of frontiers and fortresses and dividing seas and trenches was gone. That form of defence was as dead as a Dodo." The National Government led by Ramsay MacDonald had, he said, been hijacked by pacifists in the Labour Party and it was no good looking to them to increase the Air Estimates (the RAF's annual budget). A leaflet produced by Locker-Lampson's Westminster office at this time, *England Awake!* focussed on the threat to homeland security by long-range bomber aircraft from Germany. It is unlikely Locker-Lampson would have been unaware of the title's echoing of the Nazi slogan *'Deutschland Erwache!'* (Germany Awake!), which made the ADL seem like the last throw to his failed Blue Shirt movement. While the Kingsway Hall meeting was a sell-out, the aims of the ADL did not gain traction among the wider public and it was wound up shortly afterwards. In the press Locker-Lampson was ridiculed as a Colonel Blimp-like character peddling "hysterical propaganda".[25] Thereafter, he decided to hitch his rearmament and anti-appeasement wagon to Winston Churchill via a secretive organisation known as Focus.

The origins of Focus or to give it its full title Focus for the Defence of Freedom and Peace are obscure. It grew gradually and almost imperceptibly out of a loose coalition of various groups and individuals from across the political spectrum opposed to the Government's prevailing policy of appeasement, including the broadly left-wing Anti-Nazi Council and Churchill's Conservative-orientated 'Arms and the Covenant' movement, which supported his call for rearmament. Locker-Lampson's role in Focus remained hidden until described in a book published after his death by one of its chief motivators, a London-based German Jewish businessman, Eugen Spier.[26] In 1935 Spier was contacted by A. H. Richards, organising secretary of the Anti-Nazi Council, and invited to a private luncheon at the Savoy Hotel to meet others sympathetic to his anti-appeasement stance, including Churchill. From this meeting came the idea of a pressure group dedicated to raising awareness among the general public and politicians of the dangers of not confronting totalitarian regimes head on—aware that many were uninformed, complaisant or fearful of 'war-mongers'.

From the start Focus members, drawn from across the political spectrum, were adamant its existence should not be publicised. Churchill, anxious not to be seen leading an anti-government cabal, ordered that no word of their private meetings be leaked to the press. Membership was to be informal, there were to be no rules or constitution, no minutes were to be taken at its meetings and Churchill was to be referred to among its members by the code name 'Oscar'. Discussion of its financing, even within the group, was regarded as taboo. In April 1938, following one of their lunches, Harold Nicolson wrote: "On to the Focus. This is a mysterious organisation. I do not understand who pays. We lunch excellently in the Pinafore Room at the Savoy. Who pays?"[27] The Pinafore Room had been the setting for an earlier cross-party political dining society, the Other Club, set up by Churchill and F. E. Smith (later ennobled as Lord Birkenhead) in 1911. Locker-Lampson was an early member. This first Focus lunch set the tone and milieu for the rest of its existence—a slightly preposterous series of upper-class tableaux, mirror image of the pro-appeasement Cliveden set at which the great and the good met in agreeable country house surroundings to listen to after-dinner speeches praising Hitler and to others such the Anglo-German Group and the more overtly anti-Semitic The Link, which included several Conservative MPs.[28] More than a year later, in October 1936 as parliament was due to reassemble, the first formal Focus luncheon was held at the Savoy Hotel. Churchill dominated proceedings, speaking on the advisability of Britain remaining neutral in the Spanish Civil War and the need for rearmament. It was agreed he would head a deputation to the Prime Minister Stanley Baldwin. Later, outside the meeting in a private conversation with Spier, Locker-Lampson expressed doubts Baldwin would actually listen to Churchill and suggested Sir Austen Chamberlain make the approach instead, brokered by himself as a close associate, politically and socially, of both men. His reputation as the 'arch intriguer' was clearly still warranted.

On 3 December 1936 Focus held its first and the largest of its two public meetings at the Royal Albert Hall. Called Movement for the Defence of Freedom and Peace, it was ostensibly organised by the pacifist and politically left-of-centre League of Nations Union. Churchill was the principal speaker but it was felt his speech was lacklustre, concentrating mainly on attacking the far-right and far-left in British politics and calling for a centrist alliance. Locker-Lampson attended but did not speak. His old mentor Sir Austen Chamberlain sent his support but did not attend. After the meeting Locker-Lampson played host at a party for Focus members where the conversation was almost entirely confined to the constitutional crisis surrounding the wish of Edward VIII to marry a divorced American, Mrs Wallis Simpson. Churchill had wanted to speak about the King at the meeting, linking the constitutional crisis with the need for collective security but had been persuaded not to. Locker-Lampson, piqued perhaps at not being allowed to speak himself, felt the meeting had gone on too long. The British press, taken up with the abdication crisis, scarcely mentioned it. A follow-up meeting at the Free Trade Hall, Manchester, was largely ignored by the press. Ten days later King Edward abdicated.

Following the Manchester meeting a programme of further Focus activities was drawn up. Number three on the list was publication of eleven anti-appeasement, pro-rearmament and anti-Nazi pamphlets. Locker-Lampson volunteered to manage their publication. In October he had written to Einstein, asking if he had any articles he could contribute to a brochure he was preparing to alert the British public to the danger of Nazism, offering him a fee of £100. Einstein did not reply until the following January, excusing himself for the delay due to his large workload, ill health and the long painful illness of Elsa, who had died on 20 December of heart and kidney problems. He praised the sample publication Locker-Lampson had sent on the dangers to England from the German air force. Regrettably, however, he had to decline his request as he felt his name attached to such a publication—presumably remembering *The Brown Book of the Hitler Terror* debacle—would only cause the Nazis to redouble their persecutions of his fellow Jews. The sample pamphlet sounds very much like the one he had produced for his 'England Awake!' ADL rally, which may account for Einstein's convoluted metaphor that he was pleased England was at last waking up from the slumber into which the "Sleeping Beauty", Prime Minister Ramsay MacDonald, had put it, though his "Red soul" regretted it was taking the Conservatives to do the awakening. MacDonald resigned in 1935 in declining health and died in 1937. Moderate expansion in the strengths of the British Army, Royal Navy and RAF under his successor as Prime Minister, Stanley Baldwin, gave some hope to Focus that if and when war came Britain would be slightly better prepared. Meanwhile, Baldwin's Government and that of his successor, Neville Chamberlain, continued disastrously to appease the dictators as they marched over Spain, Abyssinia, the Rhinelands, Manchuria, Austria and Czechoslovakia.

Locker-Lampson had been an MP now continuously for nearly twenty-eight years. His loyal support for Churchill and Focus and its ultimately unsuccessful campaign to reverse the prevailing policy of appeasement had effectively ended any hope he may still have harboured to advance beyond the back benches or receive some sort of honour for his long public service. Spier in his account of Focus singled out Locker-Lampson as the one member whose activities on its behalf "might well have been ruinous for him". Its cost had not just been political but financial too, as he seems to have personally taken on much of the cost of its publishing and lavish entertaining.[29]

A Righteous Gentile

Oliver Locker-Lampson would prove to be a useful contact for Einstein back in the Old World. Being a fluent German speaker was a great advantage. It meant he was able to do useful work on his behalf helping friends and relations get out of Germany: telephoning and writing to officials, calling in favours from high-level contacts at home and abroad, and placing money where it was needed to help grease the machinery of bureaucracy.

In January 1934 Locker-Lampson wrote to Einstein about his efforts to help a Jewish family, the Juliusburgers, escape from Germany. Dr Otto Juliusburger, a psychoanalyst, had been Einstein's personal physician in Berlin and had treated him through a nervous collapse in 1917. As a Jew, his medical practice by the mid-1930s had been severely curtailed. Under the Nazis Jewish physicians were forbidden to attend Aryan patients and he was suffering financial hardship. Locker-Lampson offered to send him a cheque for £50 (worth around £3,500 today) and "somewhat more" later. His daughter then visited him in London and advised him not to send money "in the usual way" for fear the Nazis would intercept it. [30] In 1937, with Einstein's help, his son and daughter were finally able to emigrate to America. Dr Juliusburger and his wife Elise miraculously managed to survive in Germany until July 1941, when they were also permitted to leave for the USA.[31]

In 1934 Locker-Lampson helped the Austrian Jewish sculptor and engraver Artur Immanuel Loewental find refuge in England. In 1930 Einstein had sat for a plaque and a bust by Loewental commissioned by the Weimar Republic. He later recalled this encounter in terms curiously reminiscent of Jacob Epstein's about his sittings with Einstein in Roughton: "There clad in baggy flannel trousers, wearing a grey woollen jersey, his hair dishevelled, Einstein sat relaxed in an arm chair, deep in thought, oblivious to everything and everyone in the room."[32] Following the elevation of Hitler to the Reich Chancellorship in January 1933 Loewental and his wife sought refuge in Britain, arriving virtually penniless but at least with his engraving tools and enough materials to carry on his livelihood. His biographer wondered why he was able to leave with even this much, even returning in 1939 to collect further possessions, speculating that his association with the powerful Krupp family may have helped.[33] Locker-Lampson's role, however,

Artur Loewental sculpting Einstein, 1930.

seems to have been overlooked. In 1936 Loewental wrote to "Sir Oliver Locker-Lampson" to congratulate him on the birth of his son Jonathan, recalling how he had come to him two years ago for help in acquiring a permanent right to stay in the United Kingdom, which the Home Office had now granted.[34]

Following his involvement with Einstein, Locker-Lampson was alert to the publicity opportunities that campaigns to help other high-profile victims of fascism might afford the cause of anti-appeasement. The arrival in London of the exiled emperor of Abyssinia, Haile Selassie, in June 1936 following the conquest of his country by Italy was just such an opportunity. As with Hitler, Locker-Lampson's views on Mussolini had undergone a dramatic reversal in recent years. Although he was now frequently rude about him, calling him the "Castor Oil King" after stories his black-shirted *Squadristi* forced their victims to drink castor oil, his previous admiration had been staunch and long-lasting. In 1927 he had auctioned an autographed photograph of *Il Duce* from his own collection for £11 (equal to around £450 today) at an Elizabethan-themed fete at Blickling Hall in north Norfolk and in 1932 he had sent Mussolini, in admiration for his work to "clear out the Reds" from Italy, a set of gold and enamel Blue Shirt badges and cufflinks and a recording of the Blue Shirt song 'March On' "to drown out the singing of 'The Red Flag'". By 1936 his attitude had changed and he went with other members of the British Friends of Ethiopia to meet the recently exiled emperor at the Ethiopian Legation in Kensington.

While the press and general public were largely sympathetic to the plight of Haile Selassie's subjects, members of Baldwin's National Government pointedly avoided meeting him to such an extent that the political cartoonist David Low, a friend of Locker-Lampson's, drew a cartoon for the *Evening Standard* captioned: "Rat alley. Detour to Westminster. Special traffic arrangements have been made to permit shamefaced statesmen to dodge passing the Imperial lodgings." Hoping to recreate the same level of public interest Epstein's bust of Einstein had created and to help raise money for victims of chemical warfare in Ethiopia, Locker-Lampson commissioned Epstein to make a bust of Haile Selassie. In his autobiography Epstein noted that though he enjoyed the experience of meeting the emperor's "African Court", his bust did not bear the hoped-for fruit, noting somewhat sourly in his autobiography: "The Commander fondly believed that I might do a work which in reproduction would be popular and raise funds for the heroic struggle. As it turned out my bust had no popularity, and was a matter of great expense to myself."[35]

Throughout the 1930s the British Mandate of Palestine remained high on the list of Locker-Lampson's political obsessions. On 12 April 1938 he introduced a Private Member's Bill: "That leave be given to bring in a Bill to extend Palestinian nationality." Its aim was to provide Jews in the Third Reich a measure of diplomatic protection from persecution by granting them Palestinian passports; a variation on an idea Lehmann-Russbüldt had brought to him in 1934 to establish a right to diplomatic asylum in Britain for politically endangered persons and Jews in Germany.[36] In 1933 Locker-Lampson had tried and failed to introduce a similar Bill. Einstein had then been the *cause célèbre* he had built public support around. The personal focus of his proposed Bill this time was Sigmund Freud under house arrest in Vienna, awaiting permission from the Nazi-controlled Austrian authorities to travel to Britain. Freud and Einstein had met once or twice and respected each other as humanitarians, though Einstein did not believe psychoanalysis was a real science. In 1933 they had published an exchange of letters on the subject 'Why War?'[37] Introducing his Bill, Locker-Lampson satirised Hitler's "chilly personal correctitude"—vegetarian, non-smoking, abstaining from alcohol and apparently uninterested in the opposite sex—implying presumably that his military and political aggressiveness were in compensation for his suppressed libido. Voting on the Bill was evenly split 144/144 and had to be decided by the House of Common's Speaker who, following parliamentary tradition, voted 'aye'. News reports of the dramatic scene in the House describe Locker-Lampson as initially "a trifle bewildered" by the result. It was only the second dead-heat in a parliamentary division since 1910 and Locker-Lampson was one of only ten MPs who was present on both occasions, the others included Churchill and his old adversary, the Earl Winterton. Although the Speaker's casting vote gave the Bill leave to proceed to a second reading, in reality it had no chance of success. The Foreign Office had advised the Government that determination of nationality in the Mandate of Palestine was legally in the control of the military commander there not the British Government and in any case without government support Locker-Lampson's Bill only had a 600-to-1 chance of winning the ballot for the tabling of Private Members' Bills that autumn. Even if it did get selected the Leader of the House would probably not allow enough parliamentary time for it to be debated.[38] The extent to which he was swimming against the tide within his own party may be gauged by the fact only seven other National Government Conservatives voted for it and it had had to rely on the support of the Labour Party, his erstwhile political foe. On 4 May 1938 Prime Minister Neville Chamberlain, the man who had once called Locker-Lampson "the arch intriguer", effectively buried any chance of his Bill becoming law when he refused to allow him time to debate a related motion: "This House protests against the expropriation in Germany of non-Aryan nationals, and urges joint action with the United States to preserve the primitive rights of helpless minorities."[39]

Freud and his family were finally able to travel to London in early June 1938. On 26 August Locker-Lampson wrote to him, mentioning he had looked after Professor Einstein and asking if he could come and see him and find out if he could help him. On 6 September he wrote again, thanking Freud for his handwritten reply. He was distressed to learn he was about to undergo an operation and wished it soon over, leaving him feeling much better. Freud, however, felt Locker-Lampson had exaggerated the direness of his personal situation in his speech in the House of Commons in April, which Locker-Lampson acknowledged but justified in the cause of better getting the plight of his fellow Jews before the public.[40] Freud's friend and biographer Ernest Jones had written to *The Times* two days after his speech seeking to play down what he saw as its "alarmist" elements even though the facts spoke for themselves: Freud's apartment in Vienna had been invaded by armed Nazi thugs while he was in considerable distress with cancer of the jaw. Freud died in exile in London in September 1939. Four of his sisters, unable to escape the Holocaust, were murdered in concentration camps.

In September 1938 Einstein called on Locker-Lampson's services again to help a distant cousin, Rudolf Moos (they shared common ancestors on his mother's side of the family) and his wife Gertrude escape "the German Hell".[41] Moos had been a successful shoe retailer in Berlin before the First World War and had helped develop the Salamander, a popular brand of shoe, at his factory in Kornwestheim near Stuttgart. Despite having been decorated by the Grand Duchy of Baden with the War Merit Cross for supplying military footwear during the Great War, nothing short of an impoverished exile could save him now from a fate that pointed increasingly towards death in a concentration camp. Largely due to Moos's entrepreneurial efforts Salamander had become the largest shoe manufacturer in Germany by the 1920s and he had retired from the business a wealthy man in 1925. By 1938 the Nazis had stolen all his shares, property and savings. Much worse was to follow. Following Nazification of the company, prisoners at the Sachsenhausen concentration camp known as *Schuhläufer-Kommando* were forced to test the company's military boots on death marches on a circular track while burdened with heavy packs. Those who fell from exhaustion were shot. It is estimated ten to twenty prisoners were murdered on the track every day. Locker-Lampson was able to pull strings and place funds in the Moos family's name in accounts outside Germany and so ease their flight, first to Holland and then to England in August 1939, almost at the last moment before war was declared on 3 September. They settled with their daughter Hilde and son-in-law Gerhard Salinger—presumably not by coincidence—in a small house in Underwood Road in Locker-Lampson's parliamentary constituency of Handsworth.[42]

Another Jewish family Locker-Lampson may have helped was actually named Locker, a fairly common East European Jewish family name. Yad Vashem's Shoah database of victims of the Holocaust names more than 180 people named Locker, mainly from Poland and Romania. A family of three Polish Jewish refugees,

Gedalie Locker, a 51-year-old merchant, his wife Freyda and their 17-year-old daughter Herta, a hairdresser, had resettled in Walthamstow in 1939 and been declared exempt from alien internment by a tribunal in November. They may have been refugees from Soviet occupation not Nazi, as Gedalie's alien registration card records his place of origin as Kuty (in present-day Ukraine), which the Red Army occupied between 1939 and 1941 when Nazi forces captured it. In 1942 its entire Jewish population was rounded up and exterminated. In 1940 the Locker family emigrated to the United States, arriving in Boston on board the *Newfoundland* in July. The ship's manifest of alien passengers listed their nearest relative or friend in the United Kingdom as "Cmdr. Locker-Lampson of St Stephens, London. Friend".[43] Whether a coincidence or not, in March 1940 Locker-Lampson had met the leading Hungarian Zionist and future Israeli politician Berl Locker at a dinner at the Dorchester Hotel organised by the niece of the former British Prime Minister, Arthur Balfour—Blanche 'Baffy' Dugdale, who was known as 'Zionism's Joan of Arc'.[44]

The most complete account of Locker-Lampson's help for an ordinary Jewish refugee appeared in 1992. *Du Kannst Vor Nichts Davonlaufen* (*You Can't Run From Anything*) are the memoirs of Anna Lambert, who escaped to Britain from Austria just before the Second World War.[45] Born Anna Kohn, she grew up in Krems near the spa town of Baden bei Wien where she had a difficult childhood with an abusive father who drank heavily and frequently beat her mother and terrorised her and her brother Hans. Married to a non-Jewish Austrian, Franz Binishofer in 1929, she had one child, Kurt, and another on the way when the *Anschluss*—the virtual annexation of Austria by Germany after a rigged plebiscite—took effect in the spring of 1938. Long before this she had determined that should she have any children and the Nazis took over her country she would do all she could to save them from the misery she had suffered as a child. She therefore decided the family must escape. Her husband, however, believed the Nazi regime wouldn't last long and they should sit it out. The situation for Jews in Austria following the *Anschluss* was if anything worse than in Germany. Synagogues and Jewish-run businesses were ransacked and Jews assaulted on the streets with impunity. The foreign consulates were overwhelmed by Jews seeking to escape. It is estimated that within a month of the *Anschluss* more than 500 Austrian Jews committed suicide.[46] In desperation Anna searched her memory for anyone she could call on for help and "like a drowning woman to a straw" remembered an English gentleman she had met apparently by chance several years before in the Kurpark in Baden bei Wien, to whom she had expressed her anxieties about the rise of Nazism. He had told her: "If the war comes and you don't want to stay in Austria, come to me, I have a big house."[47] His name, she recalled, was 'Lord Locker-Lampson'—a variation on the usual 'Sir Oliver'. Visiting the British Quaker mission in Vienna, she wrote to him seeking his help. The Quakers agreed to post her letter using their return address so the Nazi authorities would not know she was trying to escape. Six weeks later she received a reply. Locker-Lampson told her he would bring her to England and she was to stay with the Quakers while her papers were sorted out. While waiting she endued a horrible ordeal in hospital after giving birth to her second child, Manfred. Here she witnessed two Jewish women who had just given birth being dragged by their hair from the maternity ward by a doctor as their beds were required for the wives of Gestapo officers. When she complained to a nurse she was told she shouldn't cause trouble as that was just the way things were now. Men in brown uniforms then took the women away and they and their babies were never seen again. As the wife of a man classified as Aryan she had not been formally registered by the hospital as Jewish and she had to stifle her horror when people gave the Nazi salute over her baby's cot, mistaking him for a new member of the master race.

In July 1939 after many tribulations and lucky escapes she finally sailed from Hamburg to Scotland with her two young sons but without her husband, who still refused to leave. Once in Scotland the Quakers placed her in a home for unmarried mothers in Edinburgh, where it came as a shock to her to realise few people spoke German. For several weeks she felt constantly lonely, homesick and afraid, especially when one of her sons contracted measles and she was accused of bringing in contagion and threatened with deportation. Eventually, a letter from Locker-Lampson reached her, inviting her to stay at his *Ferienanlage* (holiday camp) in Norfolk, where he usually spent the late summer and early autumn. Not knowing what to expect she decided to leave her children with some Anglo-German nuns, the Pallottine Missionary Sisters, at their convent in Rochdale.

It is clear from her description that the *Ferienanlage* was the Roughton camp. Locker-Lampson had married his secretary Barbara Goodall at Blarney church in County Cork, Ireland, in December 1935 and by the summer of 1939 when Anna met them in Norfolk they had two sons—Jonathan and Stephen. At the Roughton camp Anna was billeted in one of the huts, which she had to share with the children's elderly nurse, possibly the same hut Einstein had slept in six years earlier. The camp seems to have grown since then. A cabin twice as large as hers had been decorated and fitted out as a nursery for the boys, while Barbara slept in another hut nearby. Locker-Lampson slept in a separate hut next to his *Bibliothekshütte* or library hut. The camp, she recalled was quite large and shielded from prying eyes, and there was also a cabin with a kitchen and an adjoining room for the cook to sleep in—just as during Einstein's stay. An employee and his wife who lived in a small nearby brick cottage, presumably Herbert and Ellen Eastoe, also helped with the domestic work at the camp. As there was still no mains water supply, Herbert maintained the camp's latrine, while Mrs Eastoe did any other jobs required. Every so often they would visit New Haven Court where Anna was registered in 1939 as an enemy alien working as a domestic servant and so exempt from internment. The Home Office under Sir Samuel Hoare, alarmed at the rising number of Jewish refugees from Austria following the *Anschluss*, introduced a visa entry system. One of the few loop holes that remained before the war was to apply for a domestic servant visa, which is presumably what Locker-Lampson had arranged for Anna.

That summer, the last before the outbreak of the Second World War, they had a royal visitor. Princess Marie Louise of Schleswig-Holstein was another of Locker-Lampson's many royal acquaintances. A granddaughter of Queen Victoria, she was unofficially a member of the British Royal Family and had lived most of her life in England following the annulment of her marriage to Prince Aribert of Anhalt, who was rumoured to have been found in bed with a male servant. Her letters to Locker-Lampson, eight years her junior, written during the First World War, speak of an intense friendship.[48] One of his first acts on arriving in Russia in 1916 was to send her a Russian icon. A devout Roman Catholic, the princess made regular summer visits to the shrine of Our Lady of Walsingham in north Norfolk. Locker-Lampson and Barbara decided it would be nice to entertain her with a picnic on the beach at Cromer with the boys. Anna was invited too, mainly it seems because the princess was fond of national

Picnic on Cromer beach, 1939. Left to right: Oliver Locker-Lampson, Anna Kohn, Barbara L-L, Princess Marie Louise, Jonathan L-L, Stephen L-L, unknown woman, children's nurse

costumes, so she dutifully though reluctantly wore her Austrian dirndl skirt under her overcoat. As a reward she was allowed to travel in the back of the smaller of the two royal-crested limousines with the boys and their nurse, and was surprised to see local women curtsy as they passed.

After war was declared the Roughton camp was commandeered by the British Army and Oliver, Barbara and the boys moved to Rowfant in Sussex. Here Anna felt much more isolated. Locker-Lampson was away for much of the time attending to parliamentary and constituency business. While at Rowfant she was bullied by Rowfant's elderly caretaker and his wife, who ridiculed her because of her Austrian accent and lack of English, spreading rumours she was a spy and taunting her with First World War-era pamphlets detailing atrocities committed by German troops in Belgium. The caretaker insisted on drawing her bath himself to make sure she didn't 'steal' more bath water than was officially permitted under wartime rationing and always checked her room's black-out curtains were drawn before she went to bed, accusing her of signalling to enemy aircraft. All this she kept to herself, not wanting to trouble Barbara or Oliver with matters she considered trivial compared with what she had endured in Austria. During the winter of 1939, heavy snow left her feeling even more cut off. The railway line was closed so she couldn't travel to Rochdale to visit her boys. One evening Barbara told her she should marry again. A bachelor friend of the family, a middle-aged banker ten or fifteen years older than her who lived alone with his widowed mother was apparently in love with her and wished to marry her. She refused. As far as she knew the husband she had left behind in Austria was still alive. Barbara asked her: "Do you really think he'll wait for you?" After the war she discovered he had indeed taken up with another woman and wished to divorce her on grounds of separation.

After Rowfant House and its grounds were commandeered by the Canadian Army, the Locker-Lampsons moved to their London home. They wanted Anna to come with them but told her there would be no room for her sons. Not wishing to be separated from them any longer and disliking living in a big city she decided it was time to strike out on her own. Armed with a good reference and a very much better command of English than when she had arrived, she left to train to be a nurse, then moved with Kurt and Freddy to St Osyth in Essex. After the war she found that her brother Hans had also come to England but had now returned to Austria without either of them knowing the other had escaped the Holocaust. Following publication of her book in Vienna in 1992 Anna returned to celebrate its launch, visiting her former home and the Kurpark where she had first met "her saviour"—Oliver Locker-Lampson. She died in 1993 and a plaque to her memory was placed near her former home in Krems.

Locker-Lampson's efforts on behalf of Einstein and Freud are fairly well recorded by their biographers; his help for ordinary Jewish refugees like Anna Kohn is by its nature harder to uncover. It is clear from Einstein's letter to Locker-Lampson sent on 18 September 1938 that the assistance he had given the Juliusburger and Moos families was only the tip of the iceberg: "Your brave and untiring intervention for my tormented brothers fill me with deep gratitude ... it is a special joy to me to have this opportunity to clasp your hand".[49] Locker-Lampson's younger son Stephen recalled walking with his father through Jewish areas of the East End after the war, when people would come out of their homes and shops to shake his hand and thank him for his help. For Stephen Locker-Lampson, who knew almost nothing about his father's extraordinary life and career at that time, it was all rather baffling. Many years later, while editing his father's unfinished memoirs he wrote: "He also handed money to several rather scruffy looking men whom we used to pass in the street. I assume these were all Jewish refugees."[50] While his efforts were not on the heroic scale of an Oskar Schindler or a Major Frank Foley, who risked their lives to save Jews and have been recognised by Yad Vashem as Righteous Among The Nations, the extent of Oliver Locker-Lampson's humanitarian work on behalf of Jewish refugees has only very rarely been acknowledged. In 1955, following Einstein's death, an article appeared in the *Journal of the Association of Jewish Refugees* (*AJR*) on 'Einstein in Britain', which perhaps for the first time since the 1930s recalled his work to help Einstein and his efforts to introduce Jewish refugee legislation in parliament, lauding him as: "one of the noble lineage of Britain's staunch and faithful champions of the Jewish cause".[51] A correspondent in the following month's issue wrote: "Let the memory of this man remain as a blessing."[52]

In 2010 the veteran British foreign correspondent John Simpson published a collection of newspaper stories telling the story of the 20th century as it happened.[53] The one that caught many reviewers' attention was Locker-Lampson's claim that Hitler had studied the laws of cricket with British POWs in the First World War.[54] He was characterised by them as an absurd figure: a "Right wing zealot and fervent admirer of Hitler".[55] This persuaded Locker-Lampson's older son Jonathan to write to *The Times* defending his father's record as a "champion of the underdog" and highlighting his work to secure Einstein's escape to Britain.[56] A letter from a Mr Anthony Cohn also defended his record as a humanitarian. His grandfather had escaped with his family to England in 1939 only a week before the outbreak of war, having been sponsored by Locker-Lampson after hundreds of other individuals and organisations had rejected his pleas:

> My grandfather contacted him because he had a reputation in Germany for going out of his way to save Jews. My family owe him a tremendous debt of gratitude—without his acts of kindness my grandparents would have been murdered along with those relatives who were not lucky enough to leave.[57]

An article by Anthony Grenville, a leading historian of the Jewish diaspora and editor of the *AJR*, was then published describing the work of people who had supported Jewish refugees coming to Britain in the 1930s against public opinion, including Locker-Lampson, whom, he said, at first sight seemed "an improbable ally" because of his "staunchly right-wing" views.[58] This elicited a letter from Anthony Cohn's father, Norbert Cohn, thanking Grenville for mentioning Locker-Lampson in his article as his family owed him "an immense debt of gratitude". A profile in the *AJR* of Norbert Cohn, a retired optometrist, provided more background information on Locker-Lampson's role in the Cohn family's rescue. His father Karl Cohn had been a supplier to clothing manufacturers in Berlin before the Second World War. Following the destruction of their synagogue at Grunewald on *Kristallnacht* in November 1938, he began to look for a means of escape, principally how to acquire entry visas to Britain for himself, his mother, his wife and two sons, and a work permit for himself. Letters to the Chief Rabbi and Lord Rothschild went unanswered and after nine months of trying Locker-Lampson was the only person in Britain to respond, offering his personal guarantee for the Cohn family.[59] Interviewed in 1975, Norbet Cohen's mother Erna, said: "The really humanitarian aspect of Commander Locker-Lampson and his friends was that they didn't just help famous people to escape. We were nothing special."[60] Her sister and several other relatives died in the concentration camps. Many years later Norbert Cohn added this to his family's story:

> After Kristallnacht my father wrote to a number of prominent people in this country to ask them to act as a guarantor that we would not be a financial burden on the state. … Commander Locker-Lampson agreed to give the guarantee to the Home Office—the only one of those approached who had the human kindness to help. After lengthy correspondence with the Home Office, the visa with a working permit was granted in July 1939 and we finally arrived in London exactly one week before the outbreak of war. Truly a Righteous Gentile.[61]

Notes

1 *Letter to Alfred Lacroix, 14 October 1933; accessed online: https://artsandculture.google.com*

2 *Statue of Liberty Ellis Island Foundation—Passenger Search; accessed online: https://heritage.statueofliberty.org*

3 *For example, Regis, Who Got Einstein's Office? and Paterniti, Driving Mr Albert.*

4 *Albert Einstein Archives, The Hebrew University of Jerusalem; AEA: 50-808.*

5 *Ibid.*

6 *Clark, Einstein, p.486.*

7 *Ibid.4, AEA: 50-809.*

8 *Ibid.4, AEA: 37-206.*

9 *Ibid.4, AEA: 37-211.*

10 *Ibid.4, AEA: 37-207.*

11 Ibid.4; AEA: 39-560.6.

12 Ibid. 4; AEA: 50-808, 50-809.

13 Hansard, House of Commons Debates, 16 May 1934.

14 Ibid.

15 Quoted unattributed in Loewenstein, 'Militant Democracy and Fundamental Rights'.

16 Winterton, Orders of the Day, pp.195–6.

17 Skidelsky, Oswald Mosley, p.176.

18 Time, 6 July 1931.

19 Action, 9 July 1938, p.14.

20 Joyce, Dämmerung über England, p.79.

21 The Fascist, 4 July 1936.

22 Eastern Daily Press, 8 November 1934 and Mason, 'The Norfolk Gliding Club (1935)'.

23 Holman, 'The Air Panic of 1935'.

24 Furness, 'The Moral Imperative of Exile', p.71.

25 Norwell Smith, letter, The Spectator, 20 July 1934.

26 Spier, Focus.

27 De Groot, Liberal Crusader, p.119.

28 Middlemas, Diplomacy of Illusion, pp.98–102.

29 Ibid.26, p.96.

30 Ibid.4.

31 Einstein, Albert Einstein, pp.79–82.

32 Loewental, 'The miracle of Einstein, by his Lincoln friend', Lincolnshire Echo, 9 January 1950.

33 Turner, Artur Immanuel Loewental, p.24.

34 Letter from Artur Loewental to Oliver Locker-Lampson dated 20 November 1936; from a bookseller's inventory accessed online, no longer available.

35 Epstein, Let There Be Sculpture, p.84.

36 Ibid.24, pp.71 & 74–5.

37 Nathan and Norden, Einstein on Peace, pp.185–203.

38 Clark, Freud, p.508.

39 Ibid.13, 4 May 1938.

40 Library of Congress, Sigmund Freud Papers, Washington, DC; accessed online: https://www.loc.gov/collections/sigmund-freud-papers

41 Ibid.4, AEA: 53-721.

42 Moos, Journey of Hope and Despair.

43 Immigrant Ship Transcribers Guild; accessed online: www.immigrantships.net

44 Dugdale, Baffy, entry for 5 March 1940.

45 Lambert, Du Kannst Vor Nichts Davonlaufen.

46 Smith, Foley, pp.88–91.

47 Ibid.45, p. 51.

48 Oliver Locker-Lampson Papers, Norfolk Record Office, Norwich; doc. file: OLL 17, box 317 x 2.

49 *Ibid*.41.

50 From private correspondence between Steve Locker-Lampson and the author.

51 C. C. Aronsfield, *AJR [Association of Jewish Refugees] Journal*, June 1955, p.5.

52 E. Hearst, letter, *AJR Journal*, July 1955, p.8.

53 Simpson, *Unreliable Sources*.

54 Oliver Locker-Lampson, 'Adolf Hitler as I know him', *Daily Mirror*, 30 September 1930.

55 Ben Macintyre, review, *The Times*, 18 March 2010.

56 Jonathan Locker-Lampson, letter, *The Times*, 24 March 2010.

57 Anthony Cohn, letter, *The Times*, 25 March 2010.

58 Anthony Grenville, 'Friends of the "enemy aliens"', *AJR Journal*, May 2010, p.2.

59 Ronald Channing, 'Profile', *AJR Journal*, October 2003, p.11.

60 *Dominion Sunday Times* (Auckland, New Zealand), 27 July 1975.

61 Norbert Cohn, letter, *AJR Journal*, June 2010, p.6.

Time Travellers

WITH war looking increasingly inevitable after the fudged agreement with Hitler over Czechoslovakia in September 1938, Locker-Lampson concentrated more and more of his time and energy to raising public awareness of the plight of Jews in Germany and eastern Europe and helping them escape. He had already pledged that June £100 a year—one-sixth of his MP's salary—to Jewish refugee causes for the next five years.[1] The tide of public opinion, however, was not with him and letters and commentaries regularly appeared in the press critical of any support for refugees, whom it was feared would take British jobs. Undaunted, he and the veteran Labour MP, George Lansbury, sponsored the Polish Jewish Refugee Fund (PJRF), which enabled it to set up an office in Soho Square in London in the same building as a number of other Jewish refugee organisations.[2] It is indicative of how far he had travelled politically since his 'Rout the Reds' rallies of the 1920s to find him allied with a former leader of the Labour Party.

At the end of November Locker-Lampson was in Newcastle speaking to a Jewish group raising money for the PJRF, which was by now devoting its fund-raising to the *Kindertransport*, eventually enabling more than three hundred Jewish children and five hundred adults to escape to Britain. Rabbi Julius Kyanski, who met him there, wrote: "He is a true friend of Jewry, and a fine type of Englishman, somewhat like the outstanding character of a Gladstone—Christian and humane."[3] On 29 January 1939 Locker-Lampson spoke on the refugee crisis at a packed meeting in Norwich alongside the leading Jewish lawyer, Neville Laski, comparing Europe's dictators to "go-getting gangsters … who suffer, alas, from the digestions of dragons and from public consciences made of the best elastic." Hitler in particular was a "Misleader not a leader. A Nero—not a hero."[4] The meeting, held in a splendid Art Deco-style Odeon picture house, had been organised to raise money for the Earl Baldwin Fund for Refugees. It had been set up in December in response to the Government's insistence that refugee children could only be brought to Britain without state assistance. Financial guarantees were therefore necessary if they were to be supported. By the time the fund closed it had raised half a million pounds—equivalent to around £20 million today—to support the settlement of 10,000 mostly Jewish children in Britain.[5]

In his autobiography, RAF fighter pilot Group Captain Dennis 'Hurricane'

David mentions meeting his godfather Oliver Locker-Lampson for a "hilarious" lunch during the war at the House of Commons with the author, barrister and Conservative MP, A. P. Herbert. "They were both handsome men, and I couldn't help noting the glamorous young secretaries they brought with them!"[6] His description gives the impression of two men in late middle-age basking in their well-earned glory. In fact, the final five years of Locker-Lampson's long parliamentary career were his saddest. Colin Coote, who had described him as "unflappable" in his first election campaign in 1910 felt he had "rather faded out in the House; and, I fear, was unhappy towards the close of his life."[7] He had done all he could to warn Britain about the danger of appeasing the fascist dictators but war when it came in September 1939 left him more politically isolated and friendless than at any other time of his life. He was now too old to take any very active part in the armed services, though he does not seem to have realised this yet. In April 1940 he told the press he had volunteered for the Free Norwegian Ski Corps and was about to join them to repel the German invaders. Five months earlier he had informed the press he had volunteered to fight for the Finnish Army in the Winter War of 1939 against the Soviet Union. In 1941 he petitioned the War Office with demands he be parachuted into Yugoslavia, where he claimed to have fought during the First World War—he hadn't, the closest he had come was eastern Romania. In the end he had to settle for joining the Home Guard where he gamely sported his old naval uniform, while Barbara volunteered for the women's Mechanised Transport Corps, which drove ammunition trucks, petrol tankers and staff cars for senior officers.

The Locker-Lampsons in uniform. Oliver in his old naval tunic for service in the Home Guard, and Barbara in the women's Mechanised Transport Corps.

Given his staunch support for Churchill during his 'wilderness' years he may have expected to be brought into government or given another important role in the national war effort when Churchill became Prime Minister on 10 May 1940 but it was not to be. Under intense pressure from the Conservative Parliamentary Party whips and a threat of deselection by his Handsworth constituency's Conservative Association, he had voted for Neville Chamberlain's Munich Agreement in the House on 6 October 1938 rather than abstain, as Churchill and his small band of supporters had done. Churchill probably did not forget nor completely forgive him for having compromised his ideals and failed to support him at this crucial juncture. Additionally, there is evidence in comments about his sometimes bizarre behaviour from parliamentary colleagues and government officials to suggest his mental health was failing. A file of Prime Minister's Office correspondence of November 1940 tells how he repeatedly pestered the Conservative Party's chief whip, David Margesson, and Churchill's private secretary, Jock Colville, with requests for interviews with Churchill to show him sheaves of anti-Nazi cartoons—some by his old friend David Low—he wished to be used for propaganda. At an acrimonious meeting with the Conservative Party chairman, Sir Douglas Hacking, he is said to have displayed "strange behaviour" and appeared "unbalanced", and the Prime Minister's staff were ordered to prevent him meeting Churchill.[8] When he turned up uninvited at Chartwell, he had to be physically prevented from entering. In July 1943 he got into a fist fight in a corridor outside the House of Commons chamber with another Conservative MP, Captain Alec Cunningham-Reid, a former Royal Flying Corps fighter ace fifteen years his junior, running at him whirling his arms above his head. Locker-Lampson had accused him in the House of cowardice for not being in London during the Blitz. Both men were ordered by the Speaker to make public apologies for their behaviour. The following February, Conservative backbencher Sir Henry 'Chips' Channon noted in his diary that Locker-Lampson "sometimes seems demented", waving his Order Paper each time Churchill appeared in the House.[9]

Throughout these years Einstein remained his touchstone of hope for civilisation. For one of his anti-Nazi pamphlets—'To Herr Hitler: A Tonic Talk'—printed at his own expense, he penned a long satirical poem in rhyming couplets: "Down the false cults of racial rot and rant!/ Back to the gods of Goethe, Einstein, Kant!" [10], echoing Einstein's invocation of the principles of Kant and Goethe in the statement he made before leaving the United States in March 1933 on the necessity of living in a state "where political liberty, tolerance and equality of all citizens before the law prevails." Despite his increasingly eccentric behaviour he continued to play an active part in parliamentary debates, speaking on average twenty-seven times a year, often on issues concerned with Jewish refugees, such as the *Struma* disaster of February 1942 when a cargo ship with around 800 mostly Romanian Jewish refugees trying to flee to Palestine was torpedoed and sunk by a Soviet submarine in the Black Sea with great loss of life. He also repeatedly advocated the creation of a Jewish army in Palestine to defend the British Mandate and the Suez Canal. In May 1945 his Handsworth constituency's Conservative Association, which had grown weary of his eccentricities and out-spoken, contrarian line on many points of Tory dogma, finally deselected him. Things had been going sour in his constituency association since at least the 1935 General Election when the Tory Agent for Birmingham had complained to Neville Chamberlain that his speeches had caused "intense feelings of anxiety" locally by saying nothing about Conservative Party policy and concentrating instead almost entirely on attacking Hitler.[11] True to his combative character he vowed to carry on and stand for election as an "Iconoclastic Independent Unionist" but probably realising he would lose badly he withdrew his nomination on the eve of the election, saving face by stating he was taking up a new post overseas—presumably a fiction as no such job materialised. His last significant campaign in parliament was in June 1945 when he spoke against a Private Member's Bill being promoted by a notoriously anti-Semitic Scottish Unionist MP, Captain Archibald Ramsay, who sought to reintroduce into British law Edward I's Statute of Jewry, which had instituted draconian restrictions on Jews in 1275. His very last speech was on 14 June 1945, when he asked Prime Minister Churchill to send the nations' thanks to the US Armed Forces.

His MP's salary gone and with mounting debts, which led to him being sued in court by one of his creditors, he tried to earn a living by writing but failed to find a publisher interested in his stories or his memoirs, which he left largely unfinished at his death. He was reduced to promoting a football pools betting company with his by now largely forgotten public image and was clearly becoming desperate when in 1946, according to an anecdote by the politician and historian Roy Jenkins, he applied to his father, Arthur Jenkins, a junior minister in Atlee's Labour Government, to be given some sort of honour or pension, claiming the Conservative Party was prejudiced against him.[12] Interestingly, Arthur Jenkins' ministerial boss at this time was Ellen Wilkinson, the woman who had visited Einstein in Belgium in 1933. He was unsuccessful and it was about this time he began to include "refusing honours" as one of his hobbies in his biographical entry in *Who's Who*—he later removed it. In March 1946 New Haven Court was sold at auction and later that year his share of Rowfant was bought out by his niece, Betty Locker-Lampson. That May his brother Godfrey died and in 1950 his sister Dorothy also died, leaving him the last surviving member of the 'Rowfant Quartos'.

Locker-Lampson with his son Jonathan (Jack). The last known photo of the Einstein hut, Roughton, taken on the last summer before war, 1939.

After the war his marriage to Barbara became strained, they lived apart and his young sons Jonathan and Stephen rarely saw him. Ill health in 1951 and 1953 necessitated treatment in hospital.

In Princeton, Einstein, also in poor health, lived quietly at 112 Mercer Street with only his loyal secretary Helen Dukas remaining from the old days to keep him company. The use of the Atom Bomb at Hiroshima and Nagasaki greatly troubled him. Although he had not worked directly on the Bomb's development his theories of Relativity had helped open that terrible Pandora's box and he had reluctantly urged the Bomb's development to President Roosevelt in the knowledge sooner or later the Nazis would be able to make one too. In the early 1950s the Nuclear Age saw an all-pervasive mood of fear and suspicion sweep over America. In this febrile atmosphere demagogues such as Senator Joseph McCarthy helped whip up doubts about the loyalty of anyone with a liberal or left-of-centre political outlook. Suspicion even fell on Einstein, now in his seventies, who feared the prejudices and cowed acquiescence to the forces of intolerance he had witnessed in Europe before the war were now being played out in the United States. In 1951 he wrote to President Truman asking him to show clemency to Ethel and Julius Rosenberg, who had been found guilty of spying for the Soviet Union and condemned to death. When his letter was made public without his permission it caused an uproar in the public media. In May 1953 a New York schoolteacher, William Frauenglass, wrote to ask Einstein what he should do, having been called to answer questions by a Congressional committee investigating suspected communist influences in American high schools. Einstein advised him and anyone in his situation to refuse to appear. Again, his letter was made public without permission and once again he was pilloried in the US press as an ungrateful, unpatriotic refugee and communist stooge. In June the story appeared in the British press, which was generally more sympathetic to his stance. On reading this Locker-Lampson sent his last known message to Einstein on 14 June in a Western Union telegram: "Commander Locker-Lampson offers same humble hut as sanctuary in England."[13]

Locker-Lampson was now a sick man. One of the last people to see him was one of his former armoured car men, Robert Rule. Happening to be in Hyde Park, London, in October 1954, Rule asked a policeman for directions to Locker-Lampson's home in nearby Pimlico and called on the off chance of catching his old chief at home. After a considerable wait a stooped, shuffling figure wearing bedroom slippers and worn-out trousers with his old naval coat draped around him for a dressing gown answered the door. He was clearly unwell and almost unrecognisable until he spoke. Recalling the adventures they had had in Russia almost forty years earlier, his shoulders squared and his commanding voice briefly returned. After a few minutes he said he couldn't speak any longer as he still had much to do and they parted.[14] A few days later, on 7 October 1954, Oliver Locker-Lampson was admitted to St Mary Abbot's Hospital in Kensington. He died the following day. His funeral at Golders Green Crematorium was low key with just close family and four of his armoured car comrades acting as pall bearers. His younger son Stephen, then aged 16, who knew little about his father's extraordinary life, was astonished to see the wreathes had cards from Sir Winston and Lady Churchill, a White Russian general and a Norfolk gamekeeper called Herbert Eastoe.[15] Few of the newspaper obituaries mentioned his friendship with Einstein, which seems to have been almost completely forgotten. Six months later Einstein died in Princeton.

Notes

1 *Bradford Observer, 13 June 1938.*

2 *Craig-Norton, The Kindertransport, p.37.*

3 *The 'Dear Benny' letters of Rabbi Julius Kyanski; accessed online, no longer available.*

4 *Eastern Daily Press and Jewish Telegraphic Agency News, both 30 January 1939.*

5 *Richard Hawkins, 'The Lord Baldwin Fund for Refugees, 1938–39', conference paper, Copenhagen, 2013; accessed online, no longer available.*

6 *David, My Autobiography, p.6.*

7 *Coote, Editorial, p.76.*

8 *Churchill Archive, CHAR 20/6A/13-34.*

9 *James, 'Chips', p.387.*

10 *From the author's collection used by courtesy of the Locker-Lampson family.*

11 *Self, The Neville Chamberlain Diary Letters, p.162.*

12 *Jenkins, The Chancellors, p.150.*

13 *Albert Einstein Archives, The Hebrew University of Jerusalem; AEA: 60-345.*

14 *Perret and Lord, The Czar's British Squadron, pp.181–2.*

15 *Steve Locker-Lampson, Nothing to Offer But Blood, p.ix.*

"Still much to do." The last known photo of Oliver Locker-Lampson.

Bibliography

Adams, Walter, 'The refugee scholars of the 1930s', *Political Quarterly*, No. 39 (1968), pp.7–14

Adelson, Roger, *Mark Sykes. Portrait of an Amateur* (Jonathan Cape, London, 1975)

Asquith, Lady Margot, *Myself When Young* (Frederick Muller, London, 1938)

Babson, Jane F., *The Epsteins. A Family Album* (Taylor Hall Publishing, Chearsley, 1984)

Ball, Stuart, ed., *Parliament and Politics in the Age of Baldwin and MacDonald. The Headlam Diaries 1923–1935* (The Historians' Press, London, 1992)

Barnes, John, and David Nicholson, eds, *The Empire at Bay. The Leo Amery Diaries, 1929–1945* (Hutchinson, London, 1988)

Barratt, David, *History of Duff Morgan. In Celebration of 100 Years of Motoring* (privately published, Norwich, 2009); abridged version online: www.duffmorgan.com/citroen/about-us

Battersea, Constance de Rothschild Flower, Lady, *Reminiscences* (Macmillan, London, 1922)

Beeson, Trevor, *The Bishops* (SCM Press, London, 2002)

Bentwich, Norman, *The Rescue and Achievement of Refugee Scholars. The Story of Displaced Scholars and Scientists, 1933–1952* (Martinus Nijhoft, The Hague, 1953)

Bigham, Clive, *A Picture of Life, 1872–1940* (John Murray, London, 1941)

Birkenhead, Frederick, 2nd Earl of, *The Prof in Two Worlds. The Official Life of Professor F. A. Lindemann, Viscount Cherwell* (Collins, London, 1961)

Birrell, Augustine, *Frederick Locker-Lampson. A Character Sketch* (Constable, London, 1920)

Blackburn, Julia, 'Einstein and Epstein', in *Masterpieces. Art and East Anglia*, ed. Ian Collins (Sainsbury Centre for Visual Arts, University of East Anglia, Norwich, 2013), pp.222–3

Blackburn, Julia, *Threads. The Delicate Life of John Craske* (Jonathan Cape, London, 2015)

Boyle, Andrew, *Poor, Dear Brendan. The Quest for Brendan Bracken* (Hutchinson, London, 1974)

Brian, Denis, *Einstein. A Life* (John Wiley & Sons, New York, 1996)

Brock, Peter, *Twentieth-Century Pacifism* (Van Nostrand Reinhold, New York, 1970)

Browne, Sir Thomas, *Hydriotaphia. Urne-buriall; or, a Discourse of the Sepulchrall Urnes lately found in Norfolk* (1st published 1658)

Calaprice, Alice, ed., *The Quotable Einstein* (Princeton University Press, Princeton, 1996)

Campbell, John, *F. E. Smith. The First Earl of Birkenhead* (Jonathan Cape, London, 1983)

Cecil, Robert, *The Myth of the Master Race. Alfred Rosenberg and Nazi Ideology* (Batsford, London, 1972)

Chester, Rev. Greville J., 'Account of the discovery of ancient British remains near Cromer', *Norfolk Archaeology*, Vol. 5 (1859), pp.263–7

Chisholm, Anne, and Michael Davie, *Beaverbrook. A Life* (Hutchinson, London, 1992)

Clark, Ronald W., *Einstein. The Life and Times* (Sceptre edn, 1996; 1st published by Hodder and Stoughton, London, 1973)

Clark, Ronald W., *Freud. The Man and the Cause* (Grenada edn,1982; 1st published by Jonathan Cape and

Weidenfeld & Nicolson, London, 1980)

Clarke, Alan, 'German Refugee Theatre in British Internment', in *Theatre and War, 1933–45. Performance in Extremis*, ed. Michael Balfour (Berghahn Books, New York, Oxford, 2001), p.107.

Cohen, Lucy, *Lady de Rothschild and Her Daughters, 1821–1931* (J. Murray, London, 1935)

Collins, Jodie, 'Clear out the Reds! Anti-Communism and the Conservative Right. The Case of Oliver Locker-Lampson, 1926–1933' (MA dissertation, University of Leeds, 2016); accessed online: https://jodebloggs.files.wordpress.com/2016/10/clear_out_the_reds.pdf

Coote, Colin, *Editorial. The Memoirs of Colin R. Coote* (Eyre & Spottiswoode, London, 1965)

Craig-Norton, Jennifer, *The Kindertransport. Contesting Memory* (Indiana University Press, Bloomington, 2019)

Cromer Museum, *Oh The Mud! Brief History Guide No. 14* (Norfolk Museums & Archaeology Service, Cromer, 2008)

Cross, J. A., *Sir Samuel Hoare. A Political Biography* (Jonathan Cape, London, 1977)

David, Dennis, *My Autobiography* (Grub Street, London, 2000)

De Groot, Gerard, *Liberal Crusader. The Life of Archibald Sinclair* (C. Hurst & Co., London, 1993)

Defries, Harry, *Conservative Party Attitudes to Jews, 1900–1950* (Frank Cass, London, 2001)

Dent, Major Herbert, 'Reminiscences of a Cromer Doctor', unpublished manuscript (Cromer Library, Norfolk Library Service)

Dilks, David, ed., *The Diaries of Sir Alexander Cadogan* (G. P. Putnam's Sons, London, 1972)

Donaldson, Frances, *The Marconi Scandal* (Rupert Hart-Davis, London, 1962)

Dugdale, Blanche, *Baffy. The Diaries of Blanche Dugdale, 1936–1947*, ed. N. A. Rose (Vallentine, Mitchell, London, 1973)

Downer, Martyn, *The Sultan of Zanzibar. The bizarre world and spectacular hoaxes of Horace de Vere Cole* (Black Spring Press, London, 2010)

Ellmann, Richard, *Oscar Wilde* (Hamish Hamilton, London, 1987)

Einstein, Albert, *Historic recordings, 1930–1947*, CD (British Library, London, 2005)

Einstein, Albert, *Ideas and Opinions*, based on *Mein Weltbild*, trans. Sonja Bargmann (Alvin Redman, London, 1954)

Einstein, Albert, *Albert Einstein. The Human Side. New Glimpses from His Archives*, eds Helen Dukas and Banesh Hoffman (Princeton University Press, Princeton, 1979)

Einstein, Albert, *Letters to Solovine* (Carol Publishing, New York, 1993)

Ekwall, Eilert, *The Concise Oxford Dictionary of English Place-Names*, 4th edn (Oxford University Press, Oxford, 1960)

Epstein, Jacob, *Let There Be Sculpture. The Autobiography of Jacob Epstein* (Readers Union edn, 1942; 1st published by Michael Joseph, London, 1940)

Falls, Cyril, *The History of the 36th (Ulster) Division* (Constable, London, 1922)

Fölsing, Albrecht, *Albert Einstein. A Biography*, trans. Ewald Osers (Viking Penguin edn, 1997; 1st published by Suhrkamp Verlag., Frankfurt am Main, 1993)

Furness, N. A., 'The Moral Imperative of Exile: Otto Lehmann-Russbueldt's Mediation for Victims of Nazi Persecution', in *Between Two Languages. German-speaking Exiles in Great Britain, 1933–45*, eds William Abbey et al (Institute of Germanic Studies, Stuttgart, 1995), pp.71 & 74–5

Gardiner, Stephen, *Epstein. Artist Against the Establishment* (Michael Joseph, London, 1992)

Garnett, Henrietta, *Anny. A Life of Anne Thackeray Ritchie* (Chatto & Windus, London, 2004)

Gilbert, Martin, *Winston S. Churchill. Vol. V: Prophet of Truth, 1922–1939* (Minerva edn, 1990; 1st published by William Heinemann, London, 1978)

Gottlieb, Amy Zahl, *Men of Vision. Anglo-Jewry's Aid to Victims of the Nazi Regime, 1933–1945* (Weidenfeld and Nicolson, London, 1998)

Grundmann, Siegfried, *The Einstein Dossiers, Science and Politics. Einstein's Berlin Period* (Springer, Berlin, 2005)

Harrod, R. F., *The Prof. A Personal Memoir of Lord Cherwell* (Macmillan, London, 1959)

Hart-Davis, Duff, ed., *End of an Era. The Letters and Journals of Sir Alan Lascelles, 1887–1920* (Hamish Hamilton, London, 1986)

Hayes, Glenda, *St. Mary's. The First 300 Years. The History of St. Mary's (Endowed) Voluntary Aided Church of England Primary School* (Lancaster Press, Fakenham, no date)

Highfield, Roger, and Paul Carter, *The Private Lives of Albert Einstein* (Faber and Faber, London, 1993)

Hitchings, Glenys, with Del Styan, *Locker-Lampson. Einstein's protector* (Norfolk Museums & Archaeology Service, Cromer, 2010)

Hoare, Viscount Templewood, Sir Samuel, *The Unbroken Thread* (Collins, London, 1949)

Hoare, Viscount Templewood, Sir Samuel, *Nine Troubled Years* (Collins, London, 1954)

Hoffmann, Banesh, with Helen Dukas, *Albert Einstein. Creator and Rebel* (Paladin edn, 1975; 1st published by Hart-Davis, MacGibbon, London, 1973)

Holman, Brett, 'The Air Panic of 1935. British Press Opinion Between Disarmament and Rearmament', *Journal of Contemporary History*, Vol. 46, issue 2, April 2011, pp.288–307.

Hutchinson, Horace G., ed., *The Private Diaries of Rt Hon. Sir Algernon West* (John Murray, London, 1922)

Isaacson, Walter, *Einstein. His Life and Universe* (Pocket Books edn, 2008; 1st published by Simon & Schuster, London, 2007)

James, Montague Rhodes, 'The Haunted Doll's House', *The Empire Review*, Vol. 38, No. 265 (1923)

James, Montague Rhodes, *Letters to a Friend*, ed. G. McBryde (Edward Arnold, London, 1956)

James, Robert Rhodes, ed., *'Chips'. The Diaries of Sir Henry Channon* (Phoenix edn, 1996, first published by Weidenfeld & Nicolson, London, 1967)

James, William, *The Varieties of Religious Experience. A Study in Human Nature* (Longmans, Green & Co., London, 1902)

Jenkins, Roy, *The Chancellors* (Macmillan, London, 1998)

Jolly, Cyril, *Henry Blogg of Cromer. The Greatest of the Lifeboatmen* (Poppyland Publishing edn, Cromer, 2002; 1st published by Harrap, London, 1977)

Jones, Elizabeth, *Poppyland in Pictures* (Poppyland Publishing, Cromer, 1983)

Joyce, William, *Dämmerung über England [Twilight over England]* (Internationaler Verlag, Berlin, 1940)

Ketton-Cremer, R. W., *Norfolk Portraits* (Faber and Faber, London, 1944)

Knight, James, *The New Masses* (magazine), 12 September 1944, p.27

Lambert, Anna, *Du Kannst Vor Nichts Davonlaufen [You cannot run away from anything]* (Picus, Vienna, 1992)

Lessing, Theodor, "Zu 'Der Irrtum Einsteins'" ["On 'Einstein's error'"], *Der Forscher* [*The Researcher*] (1922)

Lessing, Theodor, *Haarmann. Geschichte eines Werwolfs* [*Haarmann. The Story of a Werewolf*] (1925), reprinted in an English trans. in *Monsters of Weimar* (Nemesis Books, London, 1993)

Locker-Lampson, Frederick, *My Confidences. An Autobiographical Sketch Addressed to My Descendants* (Smith, Elder, London, 1896)

Locker-Lampson, Godfrey, *The Rowfant Library. An Appendix to the Catalogue* (Chiswick Press, London, 1900)

Locker-Lampson, Godfrey, *The Country Gentleman and Other Essays* (Jonathan Cape, London, 1932)

Locker-Lampson, Hannah Jane, *What the Blackbird Said. A Story in Four Chirps* (G. Routledge & Sons, London, 1881)

Locker-Lampson, Steve, 'Memories of O.L-L', unpublished typescript in the author's collection

Locker-Lampson, Steve, ed., *Nothing to Offer But Blood*, the collected autobiographical writings of Oliver Locker-Lampson (privately published, Wellington, New Zealand, 1998)

Long, Neville, *Lights of East Anglia* (Terence Dalton, Lavenham, 1983)

Loewenstein, Karl, 'Militant Democracy and Fundamental Rights' (1937), reprinted in *Militant Democracy*, ed. Adrás Sajó (Eleven International Publishers, Utrecht, 2004), p.254

McDonald, Deborah, *The Prince, His Tutor and the Ripper* (McFarland, Jefferson, North Carolina, 2007)

Marianoff, Dmitri, with Palma Wayne, *Einstein. An Intimate Study of a Great Man* (Doubleday, Doran and Co., New York, 1944)

Madaule, Jacques, 'A Modest Genius', in *Einstein*, eds Louis de Broglie, Louis Armand et al (Peebles Press edn, New York, 1979; 1st published by Hachette, Paris, 1966), pp.26–7

Mason, Joseph, 'The Norfolk Gliding Club (1935)'; accessed online: https://joemasonspage.wordpress.com/2012/04/10/the-norfolk-gliding-club-1935

Medawar, Jean, and David Pyke, *Hitler's Gift. Scientists who fled Nazi Germany* (Richard Cohen Books, London, 2000)

Michelmore, Peter, *Einstein. Profile of the Man* (Frederick Muller, London, 1963)

Middlemas, Keith, *Diplomacy of Illusion. The British Government and Germany, 1937–39* (Weidenfeld and Nicolson, London, 1972)

Mills, A. D., *A Dictionary of English Place-Names*, 2nd edn (Oxford University Press, Oxford, 1998)

Mitchell, Andrew Martin, 'Fascism in East Anglia. The British Union of Fascists in Norfolk, Suffolk and Essex, 1933–1940' (Sheffield University PhD thesis, 1999); accessed online: http://etheses.whiterose.ac.uk/3071

Moos, Rudolf, *Journey of Hope and Despair. Memoirs*, Vol. 1 (Xlibris Corporation, Bloomington, Indiana, 2010)

Muller, Leonhard, 'Biography of Karl Ott'; accessed online: www.karlsruhe.de/b1/stadtgeschichte/blick_geschichte/blick68/ott.de

Napley, Sir David, *Rasputin in Hollywood* (Weidenfeld and Nicolson, London, 1990)

Nathan, Otto, and Heinz Norden, eds, *Einstein on Peace* (Methuen, London, 1963)

Overbye, Dennis, *Einstein in Love. A Scientific Romance* (Bloomsbury Publishing, London, 2001)

Paterniti, Michael, *Driving Mr Albert. A Trip Across America with Einstein's Brain* (Little, Brown, London,

2000)

Perlzweig, Maurice L., 'The Reminiscences of Dr Maurice L. Perlzweig' (Oral History Research Office, Columbia University, 1993); accessed online: www.columbia.edu/cu/libraries/inside/ccoh_assets/ccoh_4074305_transcript.pdf

Perrett, Bryan and Anthony Lord, *The Czar's British Squadron* (William Kimber, London, 1981)

Peterson, Margaret, *The Rowfant Story. A chronicle of times past & present* (Teodor Pupurins, Crawley, 1980)

Rawson, Geoffrey, ed., *Nelson's Letters* (J. M. Dent, London, 1960)

Regis, Ed, *Who Got Einstein's Office? Eccentricity and Genius at the Institute for Advanced Study* (Addison-Wesley Publishing, Reading, Mass., 1987)

Robinson, Andrew, *Einstein on the Run. How Britain Saved the World's Greatest Scientist* (Yale University Press, London, 2019)

Rowland, Peter, *Lloyd George* (Barrie and Jenkins, London, 1975)

Savin, Alfred, *History of Cromer* (Rounce and Wortley, Holt, 1937)

Schwing, Heinrich, *Alfred Apfel. Sein Schriftwerk. Autobiografien und Publikationen* [*Alfred Apfel. His Writings, Autobiographies and Publications*] (epubli, Berlin, 2014)

Self, Robert, ed., *The Austen Chamberlain Diary Letters. The Correspondence of Sir Austen Chamberlain with His Sisters Hilda and Ida, 1916–1937* (Cambridge University Press, Cambridge, 1995)

Self, Robert, ed., *The Neville Chamberlain Diary Letters. Vol. 4, The Downing Street Years, 1934–1940* (Ashgate, Aldershot, 2005)

Sharman, Victor T., *Nelson's Hero. The Story of his 'Sea-Daddy' Captain William Locker* (Pen & Sword Military, Barnsley, 2005)

Sheridan, Clare, *Nuda Veritas* (Thornton Butterworth, London, 1927)

Silber, Evelyn, *The Sculptures of Jacob Epstein* (Phaidon, Oxford, 1986)

Simpson, John, *Unreliable Sources* (Pan Macmillan, London, 2010)

Skidelsky, Robert, *Oswald Mosley* (Macmillan, London, 1975)

Smith, Michael, *Foley. The Spy Who Saved 10,000 Jews* (Politico's Publishing revised edn, 2004; 1st published by Hodder and Stoughton, 1999)

Spier, Eugen, *Focus. A Footnote to the History of the Thirties* (Oswald Wolff, London, 1963)

Stevens, Austin, *The Dispossessed* (Barrie & Jenkins, London, 1975)

Stibbons, Brenda, *The Baker Brothers. Diaries from the Eastern Front, 1914–1919. Oliver Locker-Lampson & the Cromer Men of the Russian Armoured Car Division* (Poppyland Publishing, Lowestoft, 2018)

Taylor, Ina, *The Art of Kate Greenaway. A Nostalgic Portrait of Childhood* (Webb and Bower, Exeter, 1991)

Tennyson, Charles, *Stars and Markets* (Chatto & Windus, London,1957)

Tennyson, Hallam, *Alfred Lord Tennyson. A Memoir by his Son*, Vol. 2 (Macmillan, London, 1897)

Turner, John T., *Artur Immanuel Loewental* (The Society for Lincolnshire History and Archaeology, Lincoln, 2014)

Vallentin, Antonina, *Einstein. A Biography* (Weidenfeld & Nicolson, London, 1954)

Vernon, Betty D., *Ellen Wilkinson* (Croom Helm, London, 1982)

Winterbotham, Frederick W., *Secret and Personal* (William Kimber, London, 1969)

Winterbotham, Frederick W., *The Nazi Connection* (Weidenfeld & Nicolson, London, 1978)

Winterton, Edward, Earl, *Orders of the Day* (Cassell, London,1953)

Woodward, E. L., ed., *Documents on British Foreign Policy, 1919–1939*, 2nd series, Vol. V, 1933 (HMSO, London, 1956)

Zucker, Wolf, 'Weidersehen mit England' ['We meet again, England'], in *Die Weltbühne* [*The World's Stage*], 27 February 1931; accessed online: https://archive.org/stream/DieWeltbhne27-21931/DieWeltbhne27-21931_djvu.txt

Index

A

B

C

D

E

F

G

M

N

S

T

U

Printed in Great Britain
by Amazon

39926409R00126